mayaNomics - Geoeconomics Series

mayaNomics

Geo-Economics

of the digitally Transformed World

AUTHOR: MAYA SURESH KANNAN

(www.mayakannan.com)

About the Author:

Maya Suresh Kannan (www.mayakannan.com) is a distinguished Geoeconomic Strategist, Innovator, Entrepreneur, Fund Manager, and Financial Adviser. He delivers top-tier advisory and consulting services to governments, public and private enterprises, leading brand organizations, investment firms, family offices, and various funds.

A proud father of three, Maya Kannan, embodies life balance through the principles of Karma Yoga, inspiring others to embrace this philosophy. A global traveler, he deeply appreciates diverse cultures, traditions, and values. His passion for history allows him to analyze world events through a comprehensive lens covering over 7,000 years.

With a solid foundation in electronics and telecommunications engineering, combined with advanced training in strategic management and law, Maya boasts over 25 years of invaluable experience. His expertise spans investment, business, technology, and economics. A goal-oriented and ambitious individual, he understands the multifaceted nature of success from a profound spiritual perspective.

A deep-tech pioneer, Maya built his first robot at 20. Through his groundbreaking invention, KarmaCapsuleNetwork (Reinforced CapsNet), he has created a forward-thinking framework that addresses the needs of a digitally transformed world marked by decentralization, distributed economics, and AI-powered digital assets. His research on neural networks led him to the ideas of recent Nobel Prize winner Geoffrey Hinton, inspiring him to base KarmaCapsuleNetwork on Hinton's CapsNet, thus the title Reinforced CapsNet. He went on to develop the mayaNomics framework using the KCN blueprint.

The white paper is available at:
https://github.com/karmaCapsuleNetwork/KCN1.0/blob/master/KarmaCapsuleNetworkV1.1.pdf

Maya is also a compelling author and speaker, sharing his insights across the globe on topics such as technology, business, investments, life strategy, geopolitics, Geoeconomics, and spiritualism. His strategies unfold through four transformative frameworks: mayaNomics, mayaNess, mayaLogical, and mayaNation. He is committed to liberating individuals, brands, institutions, and nations from stagnation, guiding them toward digitally accelerated paths of success.

Maya's innovative approach to life, career, finance, and business transformations, termed "Karma Yoga," has positively impacted countless people. Since the age of 21, he has practiced physical, mental, and spiritual yoga, blending these disciplines to unlock potential and apply the knowledge gained to uplift individuals, organizations, and societies.

Word of Gratitude

"I believe that no one can be a truly self-made success. I am always grateful to my parents, mentors, my family, friends, well-wishers and confidants who have helped me become the person I am today. I feel a strong responsibility to assist as many people as possible in achieving their own success during my lifetime and beyond."

-Maya Suresh Kannan

Author's Preface

In this book, I present a groundbreaking concept called mayaNomics, which outlines a comprehensive geoeconomic framework and principles articulated in clear terms. I will assertively clarify what geoeconomics entails and explore the urgent reasons why nations and organizations—often wielding immense power—struggle with geopolitical complexities due to the misapplication of geoeconomic strategies. Geoeconomics is frequently dismissed as merely a subcomponent of geopolitics, yet it is rapidly becoming the essential driver of geopolitical advantage. While geopolitics focuses on exercising power and dominance on the global stage, geoeconomics provides decision-makers with the critical tools needed to establish and maintain that hegemony. Entrepreneurs, national leaders, policymakers, and influencers must understand and engage with geoeconomics proactively. Unfortunately, many fail to do so, which is a significant oversight. In this book, I offer a concise and precise explanation of geoeconomics and its indispensable role in shaping contemporary geopolitics. Geoeconomics represents the strategic application of economic instruments to secure favorable geopolitical and geostrategic outcomes, maximizing trade benefits while optimizing the use of capital resources.

To fully grasp the significance of geoeconomics, it is essential to understand the dynamics of power within geopolitical contexts. According to Susan Strange, the four pillars of international power include: 1) Financial Power—leveraging finance and the creation of money to gain an edge over competing nations; 2) Production—dominating global markets through superior means of production; 3) Security—safeguarding national and regional security, often through military might; and 4) Knowledge.

Up until 2000, countries and large organizations primarily relied on the first three components to assert their dominance. However, with the advent of the information age, these powers have become replicable, prompting nations to embrace knowledge as the fourth pillar of power. In this book, I spotlight knowledge, which has emerged as a critical asset for nations aspiring to lead through innovation over the last two decades. The rapid advancements in artificial intelligence have elevated knowledge into a new realm—wisdom. This is where visionary thinkers like me come into play, combining deep technology with geoeconomics to pioneer innovative solutions. Recent developments in technologies such as ChatGPT, coupled with Google's struggles and Microsoft's natural integration of AI into its offerings, underscore the urgent need for transformation. Many established companies may falter in the AI landscape due to entrenched practices that hinder their ability to align with the innovative models necessary for effective geoeconomic strategies.

This scenario presents a powerful opportunity for emerging nations and organizations to transform the international landscape by decisively shifting from knowledge to wisdom. Throughout the past few centuries, a wealth of economic tools and theories has emerged from various intellectual traditions. However, the current challenge is to forge a cohesive set of geoeconomic tools that can deliver global benefits on a scale. Economics operates on a continuum, and given the rapid changes in the global landscape, these tools often prove effective only in specific contexts, such as particular regions or markets. Therefore, it is crucial to develop global geoeconomic instruments, and mayaNomics lays the groundwork for this innovation. These tools must strategically align with geopolitical objectives and aim to maximize trade benefits, ensuring that additional advantages organically follow in their wake.

I wish you all the best!

-Maya Suresh Kannan

Table Of Contents

Chapter 1. Introduction to Geoeconomics and mayaNomics

Dear Friend,

Greetings!

Before we dive into our topics, I'd like to start with an anecdote and a quick imaginary disclaimer from God.

God created Man (representing all genders and divisions of humans), and Man created money. Money led to the creation of wealth, and Man began to desire even more wealth. In their pursuit, Man generated more money, but money alone could not create additional wealth, leading Man to blame God.

God created Man, and Man created money, which in turn created misery. Misery led to sorrow, and consequently, Man blamed God.

In response, God said, "Hey, it's not my responsibility; I can only take accountability for what I created. You are responsible for your own creation—the 'Money.'"

As my mentor Zig Ziglar once said, "Money isn't everything in life, but it's as essential as oxygen—when you need it, you really need it."

So, if God is unable or unwilling to help, where can humans turn? They need to turn back to what God is accountable for: the human themselves and their brain and heart. So, the best course of action is for humans to both individually and collectively establish a framework for managing money—the Art, Science, and Mathematics of Money and Wealth. That is the essence of Economics.

As we navigate the contemporary landscape of globalization, it is evident that we are witnessing a transformative phase characterized by challenges to the principles of free trade. The decline of neoliberal frameworks and institutions has significantly impacted not only smaller economies but also larger ones, leading to a reshaping of the global economic environment in unprecedented ways.

In this evolving context, there is a notable increase in the use of economic instruments and strategies by nations and international players, aimed at fulfilling geopolitical and strategic goals. This trend illustrates a complex relationship between economic authority and political or security objectives, manifested through various mechanisms and approaches.

Countries and international actors are strategically employing a range of economic tools, such as trade agreements that influence market dynamics, investments that promote development, sanctions that impose limitations, and infrastructure projects that improve connectivity. These initiatives serve a dual purpose: they aim for economic advancement while aligning with broader strategic interests. As global interconnectedness intensifies, the importance of these cooperative mechanisms is underscored, revealing the intertwined relationship between economic dependence and political influence.

Furthermore, the ongoing digital transformation and the widespread integration of artificial intelligence across sectors are pushing us into largely uncharted territories in global political economic and civil society. Traditional economic theories, often based on static models, have historically overlooked the complexities of real-world scenarios. Consequently, these theories frequently yield conclusions that reinforce their initial assumptions, neglecting the various controls and contextual factors that significantly influence economic processes. A clear example of this limitation is the conventional demand and supply theory, which fails to adequately capture the dynamic nature of market conditions. This highlights the necessity for a re-examination of our economic understanding considering these intricate realities.

Economic theories as a branch of social science were developed over 1000 years. But when we look deeply into recent decades of international economics, such socio-economic theories proved irrelevant to a nation's success. These economic theories and principles, although they may work at the community and local market, fail to scale it to the national and international level as they fail to adjust and adhere to the dynamic market, social and political conditions globally. Some countries could master such new dynamics of global economics and thrive outperforming others. Countries like Germany, South Korea and Japan are perfect examples. The major reason behind their success is two tiered: 1. The Basic Economics of Production Excellence, Engineering, natural science and resources and 2. Socio-Political Dynamics. The moment economics reaches to national and international level, there are tensors of forces who started playing upon it, making it impossible to predict, measure or derive using the same methods, mathematical models and principles that worked at local scale. There seemed to be a big disconnect between Practice, theory and Philosophy. It seems that these PTP Cycle, while could iterate very well at certain local socio-political-economic conditions, fails to complete and sustain the completion. That's where the discipline of Geoeconomics is born.

Geoeconomics refers to the strategic employment of economic tools and policies to achieve favorable geopolitical and geostrategic outcomes. This approach is characterized by several key features that distinguish it from more confrontational tactics. Examples of such Tools are oil, gold, US Dollar, AI, Lithium, Semiconductor Chip, etc., Geoeconomics tends to prioritize non-confrontational methods and fosters alignment and coherence among nations, emphasizing collaboration over conflict. In this sense, geoeconomics is not merely about short-term responses to crises or immediate challenges; rather, it advocates comprehensive and transformative changes over time, reflecting a long-term vision in international relations.

Within the geoeconomic framework, the economic landscape is multifaceted and includes crucial industrial sectors, complex supply chains, and vibrant markets. These components are intricately interwoven, illustrating the profound and often reciprocal relationships between economic policies and the distribution of power on the global stage. Nations leverage their economic strengths, such as technological innovations, resource endowments, and market access, to exert influence and shape international dynamics in a manner that aligns with their broader strategic goals.

As countries navigate this interconnected economic environment, understanding the nuances of geoeconomics becomes essential. It underscores how nations can utilize their economic resources not just for immediate gain, but to pursue long-term objectives that enhance their position in the global hierarchy. This comprehensive approach acknowledges the interplay between economic actions and geopolitical strategies, paving the way for a more integrated understanding of how economic power can be mobilized to advance national interests in a complex and evolving world.

mayaNomics is an initiative designed to provide a comprehensive framework and principles for Geoeconomics in our digitally transformed world. It acknowledges the complex nature of this landscape and addresses the Triad of

Social Systems: 1. Human Evolution, 2. Collectivism, and 3. Individualism. Each of these element's functions independently, often leading to divisions and tensions among people as they choose sides. However, we are at a critical juncture in the history of human, social, civil, and economic evolution, where there is an urgent need for a framework that harmonizes all these elements. mayaNomics aims to address this need by grounding itself in fundamental principles of society, evolution, and economic transformation at both local and international levels.

While the foundational Social Systems continue to hold significance, and the tensions between them persist, mayaNomics strives to reach a point of convergence where they can be integrated with a common understanding and mutual acceptance among participants from all three systems. It presents a new dimension of economics that facilitates the collaboration of both individual and disjointed elements, allowing for unique modes of participation and engagement (such as trade and the exchange of goodwill) in a harmonious manner, supported by the characteristics of their interactions. To achieve this, mayaNomics introduces two significant adjustments to existing socio-economic frameworks:

1. Adding a fourth leg to the Triad, which consists of Machines and Artificial Intelligence; and

2. Transforming the basic characteristics of the elements within these economic systems from Vector to Tensor values.

Let's first consider AI. Historically, human evolution, along with societal and economic development, has been influenced by opinions, thoughts, biases, and greed present in human-created social systems. With AI and machines now playing a vital role in these systems, it becomes essential to adjust our methods of communication, bias management, vocabulary, perceptions, sentiments, and more. Secondly, we need to re-evaluate the characteristics of the fundamental elements of the social system. Each element within a system can and should be analyzed based on multiple characteristics. To clarify, let's use ice cream as an example. Personally, I believe that very few people in the world dislike ice cream. Additionally, I have a special connection to it; I was part of the 100th batch of "The Ice Cream Course" conducted by Pennsylvania State University. So, if you're in the mood for ice cream, feel free to grab some before continuing. I want to ensure your attention remains focused!

Done? Let's get back to business. Ice cream has three primary characteristics: flavor, color, and form. These traits are commonly perceived, felt, and enjoyed when it comes to ice cream. Let's refer to these as vector values (as having more than two characteristics forms a vector). However, ice cream possesses more than just these three traits; it also includes texture, aging, viscosity, composition, air content, crystallization, and more. Thus, we can identify at least nine different characteristics that define ice cream, which we will refer to as tensor characteristics. According to Aristotle's Nominalism, a thing does not have an ideal state but a nominal state, defined by the dynamic inputs from the environment in which it exists. These "things" can be measured based on nine characteristics: **Quantity, Quality, Place, Time, Action, Passion, Situation, Habit, and Relation**. My entire research focused on the Karma Capsule Network (reinforced CapsNet) AI was built on this principle and ultimately led to the development of the mayaNomics framework. Applying nominalism in triad social systems is crucial, given the complexity of the modern world. Simple vector character analysis may not suffice for properly perceiving or valuing things or for making cognitive economic decisions. Instead, we need to apply nominalism while considering various tensor characteristics and influences, such as quality, quantity, productivity, skills, expertise, individual integrity, collective integrity, causability, mutability, distributability, shareability, conceivability, integrability, and differentiability. Essentially, the mayaNomics framework introduces a third leg to society when combined with AI, creating a harmonious integration layer and a utopia where there can be a level playing field on a global economic scale for traders, investors, businesses, and governments. mayaNomics facilitates distributedness across multiple silos and facets of society while still integrating them both horizontally and vertically. This approach generates new value for any "thing" within and across a controlled system. The world is composed of control systems with inputs, outputs, controls, processes, feedback, and training mechanisms. Adopting a systemic approach to societal elements and these "things" provides significant value in our endeavors and transforms core values, intelligence, knowledge, and information into assets. As a Geoeconomic framework, mayaNomics incorporates social models, cultural models, economic models, political models, business models, technology models, trade models, legal models, and diplomacy models, all reinforced through an integrated approach that prioritizes outcomes rather than activities.

In summary, mayaNomics offers a holistic perspective that fosters a larger community of people winning together as an ecosystem, leading to the emergence of trillion-dollar companies and assets, particularly in new asset classes like digital ones. While many previous socio-economic theories focus on limited resources, as outlined by Kenneth Boulding in his theory of Ecodynamics, mayaNomics emphasizes the unlimited potential of a digitally transformed world. This approach prioritizes infinity as a goal, allowing us to operate beyond restrictions and hurdles. mayaNomics adopts an infinity-to-zero-to-infinity integral approach, which forms the cornerstone of mayaNomics that will be applicable across every industry.

Chapter 2. Times of Change, a Snapshot History of Society, Trade & Economics

We are shaped by the thoughts that have influenced us throughout history. As humans, both individually and collectively, we have experienced thousands of years of development through various periods marked by significant changes and cultural shifts. Therefore, it is essential to study the history of people, societies, trade, and economics during these transformative times. This chapter aims to provide a brief overview of such periods of change. To understand these changes, we must analyze the complete history of human society through four key aspects: 1) Social consciousness, 2) Social Hierarchical Arrangements, 3) Assets, 4) Money, 5) Trust Custodians and 6) Technological Innovation.

2.1 Times of Change of Social Consciousness

Social consciousness refers to the awareness that individuals and groups possess regarding prevalent social issues, injustices, and inequalities, as well as the sense of collective responsibility that urges them to address these challenges. This awareness is not static; it evolves and varies across different historical contexts and cultural landscapes. At its core, social consciousness plays a fundamental role in Geoeconomic development, influencing economic policies and societal norms. Over the ages, the world has oscillated between different forms of social governance and levels of awareness, yet the pursuit of social consciousness has consistently served as a catalyst for progress. In the 21st century, while we benefit from the freedoms afforded by democratic systems and republicanism, it is essential to remember that these freedoms came after more than 7,000 years of trials, corrections, and evolving social models.

Ancient and Classical Civilizations

In the early civilizations of Ancient Greece, Egypt, and Mesopotamia, social consciousness was predominantly the purview of the ruling class or religious elites. These societies were characterized by firmly established hierarchies, often neglecting the welfare of the lower classes. Conversely, there exists a largely overshadowed history of the Sangam Tamil Kingdoms, which thrived with a rich social consciousness that later influenced Roman governance structures. The Sangam Tamil Social System was notable for its emphasis on decentralization and power distribution, fostering robust local communities managed by minimal central authority.

Tamil Sanga Age Roman: This governance model flourished over a period of 4,000 years, from around 5,000 BC to 1,000 BC, establishing a foundation that would eventually contribute to the political frameworks of the Roman Republic, particularly during the era of increased trade between 1,000 BC and 300 BC. During this epoch, Greek philosophers such as Plato and Aristotle engaged deeply with concepts surrounding justice, governance, and the ideal state. Their discussions laid the groundwork for future notions of fairness and the role of government in enhancing societal well-being. However, it is important to note that these philosophical dialogues were often abstract and did not inherently challenge the existing social order, which continued to marginalize significant portions of the population.

China During the Second Sanga Age (2850 BC – 2070 BC)

This period in China before Xia dynasty. This was considered as divine, golden era of culture heroes and were worshipped as "Ancestorial Spirits". This period also termed as "Three Sovereigns and Five Emperors", the sovereigns being demigods. This period was termed the golden age with moral characters, knowledge and communication between humans and divine powers. The most interesting fact is that these qualities of the era and the sovereign and divine emperor are very much in alignment with the Ayyanars of Aaseevagam religion of Ancient Tamils which still is the major baseline for the Tamil Ethnic population in the southern part of the union of India, Sri Lanka, Singapore, Malaysia, Myanmar, Cambodia, Thailand, China, Reunion, Papua New Guinea, etc. although it's been smoke-screened by the modern day blanked words like Dravida, Hindu etc., May evidences point to Buddha being one of the Ayyanars. This golden era of China was destroyed and followed by monarchial era of Xia dynastic that ruled between 2070 BC to 1600 BC followed by Shan Dynasty of 1600 BC – 1045 BC, Zhou Dynasty of 1046 BC – 256 BC and Qin Dynasty of 900 BC – 207 BC. During this period of over 700 years, there were 18 kingdoms in China and was pretty much a military and oppressive rule. But Economic prosperity returned to China under Hans Empire which not only united the kingdoms into one empire but also created a positive social system.

Middle Ages

The Middle Ages were marked by the dominance of the feudal system, which solidified rigid social hierarchies. In this period, peasants occupied the lowest tier of the social structure, with limited opportunities for upward mobility. The church played a pivotal role in shaping societal attitudes towards morality, poverty, and duty. While Christian doctrines underlined the virtues of charity and the imperative of aiding the impoverished, systemic social hierarchies remained largely unchallenged. The pace of social change was sluggish, and individual agency in matters of societal reform was severely constrained.

The Renaissance and Early Modern Period (14th–18th Century)

The Renaissance ushered in a transformative era that reignited interest in human rights, individualism, and the application of rational thought. Intellectuals such as Machiavelli, Thomas More, and Erasmus began to critically examine existing social structures, governance frameworks, and the potential pathways for societal improvement. The 16th-century Reformation led to profound shifts in religious consciousness, challenging established authorities and advocating for greater personal agency in spiritual matters. During this period, a burgeoning middle class emerged, increasingly questioning the absolute power held by monarchs and the ecclesiastical authority of the church. This questioning laid a crucial foundation for future social movements that aimed to address inequalities and promote broader social reforms. The ideas born from this period would eventually fuel greater demands for political and social liberation, revolutionizing the relationship between individuals and the state. The interplay of these historical developments signifies the complex and evolving nature of social consciousness throughout history, highlighting its profound impact on the pursuit of justice and equity in society.

Enlightenment (17th–18th Century)

The Enlightenment was a transformative period characterized by the emergence of new philosophical and political ideas that emphasized reason, individualism, and skepticism of traditional authority. Influential thinkers such as John Locke, Jean-Jacques Rousseau, and Voltaire played critical roles in advocating social equality, democracy, and the fundamental rights of individuals.

John Locke introduced the concept of the social contract, which proposed that government should be based on the consent of the governed and that individuals have inherent rights to life, liberty, and property. Rousseau expanded on these ideas, emphasizing the importance of collective sovereignty and the common good, arguing that legitimate political authority arises from the people's will. Voltaire was a champion of freedom of speech and religious tolerance, often critiquing the dogmas and institutions of his time.

These Enlightenment ideas ignited a wave of political and social revolutions across the globe. The American Revolution (1775–1783) was heavily influenced by Enlightenment principles, leading to the establishment of a government grounded in the recognition of individual rights and democratic governance. Similarly, the French Revolution (1789–1799) was fueled by the desire for liberty, equality, and fraternity, ultimately resulting in the overthrow of monarchic rule and the declaration of rights for citizens. This era marked a significant leap in social consciousness, leading society to recognize the importance of collective responsibility for justice and fairness.

Industrial Revolution (18th–19th Century) - Social Struggles and Class Conflict

The Industrial Revolution, which began in the late 18th century and continued into the 19th century, brought radical changes to economies, societies, and cultures worldwide. As industrial capitalism flourished, it spurred unprecedented economic growth and technological advancements. However, this rapid progress came at a cost, as laborers faced harsh working conditions, long hours, and exploitation in factories and mines. The rise of a new urban working class highlighted the disparities between the wealthy elite and the impoverished laborers. In response, social consciousness grew, leading to various movements advocating for social change. Abolitionism emerged as a powerful movement to end slavery, driven by moral imperatives and human rights considerations. The labor rights movement sought to improve working conditions, secure fair wages, and establish workers' rights, eventually leading to the formation of labor unions. The fight for women's suffrage became a crucial aspect of social reform, as women organized and campaigned for their right to vote and participate fully in civic life.

The early roots of socialism and communism saw thinkers like Karl Marx emerging as critical voices against the capitalist system. Marx's theories exposed inherent inequalities and class struggles within capitalism, advocating for the rights of workers and envisioning a more equitable society where the means of production would be communally owned. As various social movements gained momentum, they responded to the inequalities entrenched in industrial society, championing causes such as the abolition of slavery and the fight for women's rights.

20th Century (Early and Mid) - Civil Rights and Global Movements

The early to mid-20th century witnessed the amplification of global social consciousness, as a multitude of movements emerged to challenge injustices and fight for equal rights. The labor movement grew stronger, advocating for better working conditions and fair wages, while the feminist movement began to gain traction, pushing for gender equality, reproductive rights, and access to education. Civil rights movements emerged in various countries, most notably in the United States, where activists campaigned against racial discrimination and segregation. The movement, led by figures such as Martin Luther King Jr., aimed to dismantle systemic racism and ensure equal rights for African Americans. Inspired by the principles of nonviolent protest and civil disobedience, King and others mobilized communities, organized protests, and fought for the passage of landmark legislation such as the Civil Rights Act of 1964 and the Voting Rights Act of 1965.

In the wake of the World Wars, particularly after the Holocaust, there was a profound global reckoning with human rights abuses and the consequences of totalitarian regimes. This led to the establishment of international organizations like the United Nations in 1945, which aimed to promote peace, security, and human rights worldwide. In 1948, the adoption of the Universal Declaration of Human Rights marked a significant milestone in the global commitment to social justice, declaring the fundamental rights and freedoms entitled to all individuals.

As decolonization efforts unfolded across Africa, Asia, and Latin America, colonized nations sought independence and self-determination, often mobilizing popular movements to resist colonial rule. These global struggles for justice and equality shaped a new world consciousness, emphasizing the interconnections between social justice and human rights, and paving the way for ongoing advocacy for equality and justice in various forms around the world.

Late 20th Century to Present (Post-World War II)

The aftermath of World War II ushered in a transformative era characterized by extensive decolonization across Asia, Africa, and the Caribbean. Former colonies began to assert their independence, leading to the formation of new nations and the deconstruction of colonial power dynamics. This period was not only about political independence but also saw the rise of social movements that demanded justice and equality on a global scale. The social consciousness of this time broadened significantly, incorporating critical global issues such as poverty alleviation, the fight for universal human rights, environmental activism, and the pursuit of gender equality.

In the latter half of the 20th century, the emergence of identity-based movements marked a pivotal shift in social advocacy. Feminism gained momentum, spotlighting gender-based injustices and pushing for reproductive rights, workplace equality, and legal protections against violence. Simultaneously, the LGBTQ+ rights movement sought recognition, challenging societal norms and advocating for the rights of sexual and gender minorities. Indigenous rights movements emerged, emphasizing the need for sovereignty, cultural preservation, and reparations for historical injustices. Furthermore, disability rights advocates fought tirelessly for accessibility, equality, and the dismantling of societal stigma. Throughout this era, social consciousness evolved into a more nuanced understanding that embraced the concept of intersectionality, recognizing that experiences of oppression are interconnected and affect individuals differently based on their multiple identities.

Environmental and Economic Consciousness

As we moved into the 21st century, social consciousness began to incorporate an urgent focus on environmental issues that threaten the planet's sustainability. The challenges posed by climate change, pollution, and biodiversity loss have gained prominence, prompting grassroots movements and larger advocacy organizations to mobilize people globally. Groups like Greenpeace and Extinction Rebellion have been at the forefront, raising awareness and pushing for policy changes to combat environmental degradation. There is also a growing recognition of the relationship between poverty and environmental justice, as marginalized communities often bear the brunt of ecological destruction, further complicating the fight against social inequality. Economic discourse has evolved in tandem with these environmental concerns, scrutinizing the ethics of capitalism and its impact on social equity. As disparities between the wealthy and impoverished widen, the discussions around social justice increasingly encompass economic fairness and the call for systemic reform.

The 21st Century (Current Era)

The rise of the internet and the proliferation of social media platforms have revolutionized the way information is shared and consumed. This technological revolution has empowered a new generation of activists and advocates, allowing for the rapid dissemination of ideas and fostering global networks of solidarity. Movements like #MeToo, which emerged as a response to pervasive sexual harassment and assault, and Black Lives Matter, which addresses systemic racism and police brutality, have highlighted critical social issues and rallied millions around the globe. Climate activism has also surged, mobilizing a diverse array of participants connected through digital platforms to demand immediate action against climate inaction.

Social Justice and Corporate Responsibility

As social consciousness expands, there is increasing pressure on corporations and governments to adopt and implement socially responsible practices. The emergence of corporate social responsibility (CSR) initiatives and the adoption of environmental, social, and governance (ESG) criteria have become critical benchmarks for evaluating business practices. Consumers and stakeholders are now more vigilant, demanding transparency and ethical behavior from organizations. This shift reflects a broader societal expectation that businesses should not only aim for profitability but also contribute positively to society and the environment.

Intersectionality and Diversity

Modern social consciousness emphasizes intersectionality, a framework that recognizes the multifaceted nature of social identities and the ways in which they overlap. This approach asserts that various forms of discrimination, whether based on race, class, gender, sexual orientation, or disability—are interconnected and must be addressed holistically. Movements advocating for social change are increasingly focused on fostering inclusive societies that appreciate and address these complexities, seeking to create environments where diverse voices and experiences are valued and heard.

Overall, the evolution of social consciousness over time reflects a dynamic interplay of philosophical, political, economic, and cultural forces. From the elite concerns of ancient and medieval societies to the contemporary global recognition of the rights and needs of marginalized communities, social consciousness today encompasses a wide and intricate tapestry of issues—ranging from racial and gender equality to environmental sustainability— and continues to develop as our world becomes ever more interconnected. But until Teilhard de Chardin, no social scientist could create a framework or taxonomy that can become a baseline for such social consciousness to grow through guided principles, initiatives, and programs.

Teilhard de Chardin's KEM taxonomy introduces nuanced understanding of human consciousness evolution through three primary dimensions: Kinesthetic, Emotional, and Mental.

Kinesthetic: This dimension refers to the physical, biological, or instinctual aspects of human beings. It includes sensory experiences, and the basic, biological instincts tied to survival and bodily experience. In the evolutionary scheme, this is the stage where life is driven primarily by physical interaction with the world, without complex intellectual processing.

Emotional: As human beings evolved, the emotional aspect came to the forefront. Emotional experiences are tied to feelings, social interactions, and the ability to form complex relationships. This stage in human development corresponds to the growth of social behavior and empathy, and the development of emotions and feelings that help individuals relate to one another.

Mental: The mental dimension concerns intellectual functions—thinking, reasoning, problem-solving, and the emergence of culture, language, and advanced cognition. It involves the ability to conceptualize, abstract, and create meaning from the world around us. Teilhard de Chardin saw this as the highest evolutionary stage for human beings, where thought and consciousness shape and guide the course of civilization.

These dimensions illustrate the journey of consciousness evolving from simple biological forms to increasingly intricate emotional and intellectual stages. De Chardin postulated that humanity is progressing toward an ultimate convergence point known as the Omega Point. This concept symbolizes the apex of all human consciousness converging into a collective, transcendent mind or a form of global intelligence. I am firmly convinced that we stand on the brink of reaching this Omega Point, very soon. Global geopolitics are changing at a rapid speed, the world is divided into many corridors of economies, not just for economic reasons but also for all geopolitical and geostrategic reasons. The world is deeply divided with the West on one side and Russia, China, Iran, and some other Middle East Nations on the other side while countries like India decided to stick to non-alignment. The central and Eastern European nations split in their alignment decisions.

Coming to Africa, more and more African nations started loving the Chinese Belt and Road initiatives and they started supporting that China is there to help them out and their support is growing more. Coming to South America, Surprisingly Brazil and other South American countries also ditching the west and aligning more towards China and Russia with one recent exception of Argentina especially after the election of the new President Javier Gerardo Milei, who decided to totally align with the US and the west.

Some Asian countries play neutral with maintaining the strategic relationship with both corridors. One such country that is in a very delicate spot is India. India is playing the Darling of west as well as Russia until recently with some displeasure started growing from the USA and Canada. India's recent decisions after the Ukraine war made most of the countries around the world surprised to see India taking a multi-polar positioning with putting its own interest in the front and unaligned with any specific Corridor or supporting not supporting the sanctions against Russia doing trade with Russia especially the oil trade, India has its own reasons to do that and it has because the world is changing and it has been transformed a lot and with this current geopolitical, geostrategic and most importantly the geoeconomic poisoning of the world. With the Trump's second term, India might be pushed to some extreme position to take a side. Under the current geo-economic conditions where countries are chasing semiconductor chips, Lithium and oil etc. Everyone is playing Just-In game with nonalignment or alignment for specific matter or issue only. Nations are focused on protecting their sovereignty first and open for multilateral and multifaceted treaties instead of blanket ones.

In times of significant change, it is essential to maintain a vigilant and proactive stance. History serves as a valuable teacher, providing us with insights that can guide our actions today. Instead of getting caught up in trivial debates or allowing ourselves to become divided into factions, which only serve to hinder our progress, we must draw from these lessons. Such divisions can create fertile ground for negativity and, ultimately, lead to failure in our collective endeavors.

As a trader, businessman, and geopolitical strategist who passionately values the principles of humanity, I firmly believe in the immense power of economic strategies to cultivate peace across borders. Rather than resorting to warfare or confrontation with our adversaries, we have the opportunity to forge stronger bonds through the enhancement of our economies. By engaging in small yet meaningful collective actions aimed at unification—such as establishing economic corridors that promote free movement of goods and services, developing inclusive trade policies that benefit all parties, and fostering regional integration—we can construct a society that is both more powerful and harmonious.

Moreover, it is crucial for us to recognize that these economic initiatives not only boost our individual nations but also contribute to global stability. By prioritizing collaboration over competition, we can create an ecosystem that thrives on mutual benefit and understanding. This approach will not only elevate our economic standing but also build bridges between diverse cultures and communities. Therefore, we must act decisively and with purpose to shape a brighter future, not just for ourselves, but for the world at large. Together, through thoughtful strategy and unwavering commitment, we can cultivate a landscape where cooperation prevails, leading to lasting peace and prosperity for generations to come.

TOP Social System

The TOP social system, an acronym for "Tension of the Organized Whole," represents a model of social organization that emerges as societies become increasingly complex, interconnected, and integrated. This system is characterized by collaborative efforts toward a shared purpose or collective goal. As societal complexity grows, the necessity for collective organization and direction becomes paramount.

Key Characteristics of a TOP Social System:

Collective Cohesion: This system underscores the idea that individuals are integral parts of a larger, organized structure. As a result, social bonds strengthen as people recognize their interdependence.

Emerging Collective Intelligence: When individuals collaborate within complex organizations, be it societies, nations, or the global community, their collective intelligence, often referred to as the noosphere, evolves, enhancing both social and cognitive capabilities.

Centralization of Power: As societies develop greater complexity, centralized governance becomes essential for coordinating and integrating the system's various components

Cultural Evolution: The TOP system embodies an evolutionary tendency towards creating a more sophisticated global or societal framework, where everyone's actions contribute to a broader, shared objective.

TIE Social System

In contrast, the TIE social system, which stands for "Tension of Individual Element," focuses on the individual as an autonomous entity within society. While the TOP system highlights collective intelligence and integration, the TIE system emphasizes the unique contributions that each individual can make to the social fabric.

Key Characteristics of a TIE Social System:

Individual Autonomy: This system values the independence of individuals, recognizing their unique capacities, insights, and experiences that drive societal evolution.

Personal Innovation: The TIE system encourages creativity and independent thinking, allowing individuals to foster cultural and intellectual growth in society through their unique ideas and innovations.

Decentralization of Power: In this framework, power and decision-making are distributed among individuals rather than being concentrated in a central authority.

Ego and Personal Development: The TIE system emphasizes personal growth and self-consciousness, influencing the collective system in a less structured manner.

While these systems may seem distinct, they interact and complement one another in various ways, especially in the context of social and cognitive evolution. Below are some ways in which they are related:

TOP and KEM:

- The TOP system and the KEM framework are aligned in their view of the evolution of society and consciousness. As societies become more organized and complex (the TOP system), individuals evolve through the KEM stages.
- As the TOP system pushes for greater collective organization and cohesion, it can encourage the development of more sophisticated emotional (E) and mental (M) capacities in individuals. For instance, centralized power structures (e.g., governments, global organizations) may facilitate the expansion of intellectual and cultural exchanges, fostering a more advanced mental (M) state of society.

- The TOP system may require more advanced emotional (E) intelligence in individuals to navigate complex social relationships, and greater mental (M) capacities to participate in organized systems of governance, economics, and culture.

TIE and KEM:

- The TIE system, which emphasizes individual autonomy, plays a key role in the development of the KEM stages at the personal level. Kinesthetic (K) experiences are often about basic survival and personal physical experiences, and emotional (E) responses are shaped by individual relationships, desires, and personal freedoms.
- As individuals move through the KEM stages, their mental (M) capacities expand, enabling them to better express themselves, think independently, and contribute creatively to society—key aspects of the TIE system.
- The TIE system allows individuals to move beyond mere survival (K) and emotion (E) and toward complex intellectual processes (M), while still retaining their individuality within a broader societal context.

TOP and TIE:

1. The TOP and TIE systems represent the tension between the individual and the collective, a dynamic that is central to social evolution. While the TOP system strives for organization, cohesion, and the unification of human society, the TIE system champions individual rights, autonomy, and self-expression.
2. This tension drives much of social progress, as the balance between collective unity (TOP) and individual freedom (TIE) determines how societies evolve in terms of governance, values, and cultural development. For

instance, the rise of democracy can be seen as a response to the tension between these two forces, where centralization (TOP) is balanced with individual freedom and rights (TIE).

The need for Integrating the Systems is precedent to mayaNomics.

In Teilhard de Chardin's broader vision of human evolution toward the noosphere, the interplay between TOP, TIE, and KEM is essential. As humanity moves forward, collective systems (TOP) will become more integrated and sophisticated, allowing for greater emotional (E) and mental (M) awareness and development in individuals. This evolution reflects the gradual synthesis of the TIE (individual) and TOP (collective) systems, where personal autonomy can coexist with collective organization. At the same time, the evolution of KEM stages will enable individuals to develop the emotional and intellectual capacities needed for such integration.

Transition from social classes to division of labor

In Europe during the Renaissance period, which lasted from the 14th through 16th centuries, saw the lines between social classes begin to blur. This was due to wealth from international trade. However, the idea of class remained important although not mandated by the occupation. In the 18th century, Interestingly, the division of labor was introduced matching the era of Industrial revolution. This could be a turning point.

2.2 Times of Change of Social hierarchical systems

Ancient Civilizations:

Sangam Era Tamil Civilization: Sangam Period was not hierarchical in any means. There were divisions between people based on where they lived and what they did. Such divisions were called "Kudi" or "Kulam". People lived in a social system almost all modern social reformers dream of. It was a federation of many different tribes and clans coming together with decentralized power with consensus-based issue resolutions. Examples being Vettuvar, Villiyar, Irular and Pallar. As mentioned in Purananuru, Tudiyar, Panar, Paraiyar and Kadampar. Vellalar and Vanikar – Traders and Businessmen. There was a special spiritual connection with the ancestors and the demigods, Ayyanars under the Aaseevaram.

Ancient China: As we have established before, the Golden era of China between the 2800 and 2050 had a spiritual alignment and integration of people and their relationships with the demigods and ancestors. The social and hierarchy did not exist much unless for the local governance. But as seen before, this was replaced by military rules of 18 kingdoms between 2070 and 256 just before the Hans Empire that brought back the social order but through dynasty structure.

Mesopotamia (Sumerians, Akkadians, Babylonians): Unlike the ancient Tamil Era, Mesopotamia had King/Emperor being the top ruler, often considered divine or semi-divine followed by Priests and Priestesses who are religious leaders holding significant power, often guiding laws and culture. The next in the hierarchy were Nobles and Warriors enjoying equal privileges and power. They were Landowners, military leaders, and aristocrats. Merchants/Artisans were Skilled workers and traders, some of whom could gain wealth. Many of the population were farmers and were responsible for food production. During this era slavery was a prevalent practice. The slaves were usually the Captives of war, or those born into servitude, with no rights.

Ancient Egypt: In ancient Egypt, Pharaoh was Considered both a political ruler and a god, at the top of the hierarchy. The next were the Viziers, who were highest-ranking officials, often advisors to the Pharaoh. The Priests were Powerful figures responsible for religious ceremonies and maintaining divine order. Nobles were Wealthy families that controlled land and resources. Unlike the Mespot, the ancient Egyptians separated the intellectual class from Noble and kept them below the nobles called Scribes. They are Educated and literate individuals, crucial in administration and record-keeping.

Farmers and Laborers: Much of the population works the land or in other manual labor. Since there were a lot of development activities like building and constructions, a new class of people emerged during the ancient Egypt quite different from farmers but very much enjoying similar privileges.

The Slaves were Mostly war captives or debtors, serving in homes or on construction projects but enjoyed no privilege of a laborers doing the same job.

Ancient Greece: Citizens: Only free-born Greek men could be considered citizens, with political rights. Wealthy families who often held political or military power were called Aristocrats in the Greek Society. Merchants and Artisans were Skilled workers who were essential to the economy but had less political power. Another aspect of the ancient Greek is that the Women generally had limited rights and could not participate in politics, though they had significant roles in family and religion. Slaves were Owned by citizens or the state, performing labor across various sectors.

Ancient Rome:

As we have seen under the social consciousness, ancient roman who were contemporary to the Sanga Tamil Society had more inherited structures and values that allowed them to exercise the republic and decentralization of power.

This was the era between 1000 BC to 400 BC. But, almost following the footpath of Tamil kingdoms the glory of decentralization and republic started falling apart in the hands of greedy rulers who started consolidating more central powers from 250 BC that existed over the next 500-700 years. The emperor was the highest authority, often seen as a god. The Senators were the elite ruling class that governed and passed laws. Equestrians (Knights) were wealthy individuals often involved in trade or public service. Romans had more division of labor as the national building, trade, architecture and other forms of developments flourished during the era. They were called Plebeians who are Common citizens, including farmers, craftsmen, and traders, some with voting rights. Slaves were the lowest in the social hierarchy, they could be captives, criminals, or those born into slavery.

Medieval Period (5th–15th Century)

The Medieval Period gave rise to the Feudal System of Europe. For the first time, the kind started sharing power with the local/feudal lords. Some of the modern oligarchies reflect this structure including some socialism(crony). The King was the monarch who had ultimate control over the land, but often shared power with lords. It's interesting to note that the modern Techno Feudalism, as coined by Yanis Varoufakis resembles this in the name of Capitalism(crony) where the tech companies use the Tech infrastructure (like Cloud) as a tenant system like lords relacing the land with servers, internet protocols, AI equipment etc. Nobles (Lords/Barons) were wealthy landowners who swore allegiance to the king in exchange for land. They were the military and political elite. The Knights were Vassals who served nobles in exchange for land or protection, often military elites. The next class were Serfs/Peasants who were Much of the population, worked the land in exchange for protection and land to farm but had limited freedom. As religions started taking more power and influence in the state, the

Clergy class started emerging with the Church having immense power, often more than secular rulers. Bishops, abbots, and priests held influence, and monasteries were important centers of learning and charity.

Islamic Caliphates (Medieval Period)

In Islamic Caliphate period, the caliph is the political and religious leader, believed to be the successor of Prophet Muhammad. The Nobles and Military Leaders are wealthy, influential families, often in charge of regional territories or armies. Merchants and Artisans: Active in trade, which was central to the economy, particularly due to the vast caliphate trading routes.
Peasants: Farmers and workers, responsible for sustaining the economy.
Slaves are Captives from war or those born into slavery, some of whom could attain high status depending on their abilities (like military slaves known as *mamluks*).

Early Modern Period (16th–18th Century)

This is the Period of Renaissance and Early Modern Europe where Monarchs are rulers. The Kings and queens, often seen as divinely ordained, ruled over vast kingdoms. The Nobility were the next in the hierarchy who enjoyed the status as Landowners controlling vast estates and playing a key role in governance and warfare. The Clergy were Churchmen who held significant social, political, and economic power. Another unique class of the Early modern Europe is the Bourgeoisie, thanks to the Emerging middle class of merchants, bankers, and intellectuals, particularly in urban areas. In many regions, particularly Eastern Europe, the feudal system persisted with a population of Peasants/Serfs with many of them living in poverty. The transatlantic slave trade was at its height during this period, with millions of Africans forced into slavery in the Americas.

Mughal Empire of Indian Peninsula

Emperor (Padishah): The Mughal ruler had absolute power and was often considered semi-divine.
Nobles (Amirs): Powerful military and administrative elites who managed regions of the empire.
Merchants: Traders and businesspeople, particularly active in luxury goods and the global economy.
Artisans: Skilled workers, particularly in textiles, metalwork, and ceramics.
Peasants: Farmers and workers who formed the backbone of the economy.
Slaves: Some Mughal rulers The Role of Slave Armies and Slavery Throughout History. Across various historical contexts, societies have employed slave armies, composed of individuals coerced into servitude. These individuals fulfilled vital roles, both in domestic capacities and as soldiers during military conflicts, illustrating the intricate social and economic frameworks of their times.

Modern Era (19th–20th Century)
Victorian England

Monarch (Queen/King): The monarchy served primarily as a symbolic representation of the nation, fostering a sense of unity and continuity. However, substantial governmental authority and decision-making power rested with Parliament, which guided the country's affairs through elected representatives.
Aristocracy: The upper class, consisting of landowners, military leaders, and influential families, held considerable wealth and social prestige. Their involvement in politics, culture, and the economy positioned them as key players in shaping national and local policies.

Middle Class: The Industrial Revolution facilitated the emergence of a robust middle class, encompassing professionals, merchants, and bureaucrats. This group benefited from increased economic opportunities and social mobility, significantly contributing to the transformation of societal structures.

Working Class: The working class, including factory workers, laborers, and tradespeople, faced considerable challenges, often enduring lengthy hours in demanding and unsafe conditions. This situation spurred movements advocating for labor rights and social reforms aimed at improving their living and working conditions.

Women: During this period, women encountered significant limitations in rights and opportunities. Nevertheless, the rise of early feminist movements initiated important discussions surrounding women's suffrage and equality, laying the groundwork for future advancements in gender rights.

Colonial Elites: Within British colonies, a distinct hierarchy emerged based on race and class, with Europeans often positioned at the top. This structure influenced social relations and governance, highlighting the complexities of colonial power dynamics.

Caste System in British Colonial India

The caste system was never a practice by the ancient Tamils or initial kingdoms of the Indian Peninsula predominantly rules by Tamil Kings of Later Day Pandyas, Cheras and Cholas. But slowly over a period, the new settlers of norther part of Indian peninsula from Central Asia and Mesopotamia started devising mechanisms of dividing the people to gain access and enjoy some higher status for themselves, as most migrant do it to the indigenous and aboriginal on the land even to this time of the world. Such divisions are as below:

Kshatriyas: The Kshatriya caste, comprising warriors and rulers, held responsibilities related to governance and protection of their communities. They were instrumental in fostering stability and order within their regions.

Vaishyas: This group consisted of merchants and traders who actively contributed to the economic framework of society. Their roles in commerce and agriculture were integral to the livelihoods of many, underpinning economic resilience.
Shudras: Representing the working class, Shudras provided invaluable labor and services. However, they often faced social marginalization, which highlighted the need for greater inclusivity and recognition of their contributions.

Dalits (Untouchables): Dalits, considered outside the conventional caste system, have historically faced significant discrimination. Recognizing their struggles is essential for fostering a more equitable society that values the dignity of all individuals.

Brahmins: Brahmins played roles as poets, entertainers, priests, scholars, and educators. They enjoyed significant elevation of social status from poverty to prosperity during the British colonial era as British were looking for an alternate way of controlling the kingdoms and kings of the era.

Feudal Lords: Feudal lords existed and thrived as alternate power regardless of what type of government or governing structure existed. They were aligned and travelled together with the kings or sometime regardless. While there are some castes associated with feudal lords, mostly they existed(still exist) above or parallel to the caste system.

Caste System in Modern Day Union of India

The union of India, being a republic and a democratic nation, is trying to get rid of caste system over a period of 75 years since independence. But these divisions are deep rooted in the societies across the country and the special interest grounds like Political Elites, Bureaucratic elites and business elites enjoy the fruits of such division, unfortunately the caste system still exists although the discriminatory practices of hierarchical structure and superiority by birth is vanishing slowly out of society. But the Feudal lords still exist with more people joining the class with the modern tag of entrepreneurs and Financiers.

Contemporary Era (20th–21st Century)
Capitalist Societies (Global)

Corporate Elite: The corporate elite comprises top executives, entrepreneurs, and affluent individuals whose influence shapes global markets and industries. Their decision-making abilities have profound implications for economic innovation and growth.

Middle Class: Today's middle class includes professionals, technicians, and bureaucrats who generally enjoy relative economic stability. Their role in the economy is significant, contributing to social cohesion and civic engagement.

Working Class: The contemporary working class consists of laborers, factory workers, and service employees, who, despite their critical contributions, often encounter challenges related to wages and job security. Addressing these concerns is vital for fostering social equity and improved working conditions.

-Underprivileged Groups: Underprivileged groups, including racial minorities and immigrants, frequently face systemic barriers that hinder access to education, healthcare, and housing. Recognizing and addressing these inequalities is essential for promoting social justice and ensuring equitable opportunities for all members of society.

Communist Systems (e.g., Soviet Union, Mao China)

Party Elite: This group comprises the highest-ranking officials within the Communist Party, including key leaders and bureaucrats. They often hold significant sway over political decisions and policymaking. Due to their positions, they have access to various privileges, such as improved housing, exclusive stores, and benefits not generally available to the broader population. This concentration of power has occasionally raised concerns about potential corruption and a disconnect from the everyday experiences of ordinary citizens.

- Intellectuals: Intellectuals, including scholars, engineers, and scientists, are recognized as vital contributors to the state's progress and technological advancement. The regime has typically relied on their expertise to enhance industry and education while promoting the ideological foundations of communism. However, their creative autonomy is sometimes constrained, as their work must align with party doctrines. Consequently, while they play an essential role in the state's development, many encounter limitations on their intellectual exploration and expression.
- Workers and Peasants: In theory, communist ideology promotes equality among all citizens. However, in practice, disparities can arise regarding access to goods, resources, and political influence. While the state aims to eliminate class distinctions, certain groups, such as factory managers and collective farm leaders, may receive preferential treatment. This situation can create a divide that challenges the initial goals of equality and may lead to disillusionment among the working class and rural populations.
- Dissidents and Political Prisoners: Individuals who express dissenting opinions or challenge the regime may be labeled as dissidents, including activists, writers,

and everyday citizens. The state's response can be significant, often leading to social ostracization, strict surveillance, or even imprisonment. Political prisoners frequently endure harsh conditions, fostering an environment of fear that inhibits free expression and reinforces the regime's control. The experiences of these individuals underscore the broader struggles for freedom and human rights within oppressive systems.

2.3 Times of Change of Assets

The concept of **assets** and their management has evolved significantly throughout history, shaped by economic, technological, and societal changes. Assets are essentially resources that have value and can be owned or controlled to produce value over time. These can include physical items (like land, real estate, or gold) and intangible items (like stocks, bonds, or intellectual property). Below is an overview of how the understanding and types of assets have evolved historically. The concept of **assets** has evolved over time, shifting significantly as societies, economies, and technologies have developed. Throughout history, the types of assets people valued, and how they managed them, were influenced by political, economic, and social structures. Below is an exploration of **assets across different eras**, highlighting how they transformed through history.

Prehistoric Era (Before 3000 BCE)

Prehistory is typically divided into three main stages:

1. Paleolithic: The earliest period of human history, lasting from about 2.5 million years ago to around 10,000 BCE.
2. Mesolithic: A transitional phase, roughly between 10,000 BCE and 8,000 BCE, marking the shift from purely hunter-gatherer societies to the beginnings of settled life.

3. Neolithic: Roughly 8,000 BCE to 3,000 BCE, characterized by the rise of agriculture, domestication of animals, and the formation of permanent settlements.

In prehistoric times, assets were primarily tied to the essentials of survival — natural resources like water and food, tools for hunting and gathering, and social structures that allowed humans to live and thrive. The Neolithic Revolution marked a major shift, with the development of agriculture, permanent settlements, and the rise of more complex forms of economic assets.

Category	Examples of Assets
Natural Resources	Water, fertile land, forests, hunting grounds
Tools and Weapons	Stone tools, bone tools, wood implements, fire
Shelter and Housing	Caves, temporary shelters, wattle and daub houses
Clothing and Adornments	Animal skins, plant fibers, beads, and other adornments
Trade Goods	Shells, beads, flint, obsidian
Art and Symbolism	Cave paintings, figurines, carvings, ritual objects
Social and Cultural	Tribal leadership, kinship, communal bonds, sacred sites

Paleolithic:

A lot of evidence points to the existence of Tamil Race during the Paleolithic age and mostly they had unorganized groups, language, culture and trade. But it is during the Sangam Age, that started around 7000 BC, the Era of the Tamils as the predominant Cultural and Trading society started flourishing. The Key thing to be noted about the word - "Sangam". It means Society, Group and Consortium. We shall see the unique Framework of Governance through Sangam been practices throughout the Tamil Kingdom's Sangam Period spanning over 7000 years (Sangam 1 – 7000 BC – 3000 BC, Sangam 2- 3000 – 2000 BC and Sangam 3- 2000 BC to 500 AD).

1st Sangam Tamil Civilization Era (7000 BC– 3000 BC)

The First Sangam era is the prehistoric phase of Tamil civilization. Although it was widely believed to have no concrete evidence, the new archeological discoveries in Korkai, Athichanallur and other sites across the modern-day Tamil Nadu like Arikamedu suggests clearly the existence of Civilization, Culture and Trade not only existed but also flourished during this era spanning over 4000 years. The discovery of Iron tools and weapons made an astonishing revelation that the iron age needs a big correction.

Key Features of the First Sangam Era:

The First Sangam is traditionally believed to have taken place in a city called Kapatapuram, which, according to legends, sank beneath the sea. The First Sangam was reportedly composed orally, and the texts are said to have been lost when Kapatapuram submerged. As a result, the specifics of this era are speculative and rooted in myth. Consequently, there are no surviving historical records or archaeological findings from this period until recent excavations at Athichanallur began to reveal more evidence. The official dating of these findings suggests that a civilization existed in that area more than 5,000 years ago, indicating activity before 3000 BC, which aligns with the First Sangam age. The use of iron and copper artifacts from this time showcases the tools and ornaments that were part of this civilization's assets. Further excavations in the southern tip of Tamil Nadu are expected to uncover more evidence of the prehistoric civilization that partly submerged into the ocean. Additionally, the theory of the lost continent of Lemuria provides a broader context for these findings.

Nature of Assets: Iron tools, Ornamental items made of metals, weapons, grains etc., might have been used as assets. Although there is no direct evidence of documented assets from the First Sangam period, we can infer certain kinds of assets and wealth from later Tamil epics and texts, as well as traditional stories and from the evacuation sites of Athichanallur. These assets are likely to be included:

Natural Resources and Land

- Land: Land would have been a primary asset in the First Sangam era, especially since the Tamil civilization was largely agrarian, even in its early stages. The fertility of the land in the Tamil region, particularly in the river valleys (such as those of the Kaveri and Vaigai), would have made agriculture a key economic activity.
- Forest Resources: The region would have rich forest resources, including wood for building and wild games for hunting. These would have been important for the early inhabitants' survival and livelihood.
- Water Resources: Rivers, lakes, and water bodies would have been vital for agriculture, fishing, and transportation. Access to water was a crucial asset.

Livestock: Cattle, especially oxen, were likely important for agricultural work (plowing the fields) and for trade. Cattle would have also been a sign of wealth and status. While there is little direct evidence from the First Sangam era, later traditions suggest that elephants and horses were highly prized in the Tamil region, and they would have been valuable assets, especially for war and royal use.

Trade Goods: Ancient Tamils of Sanga age used Naavays (tongue like vessel) to get into and travel across oceans. The main ports being Kulasai and Korkai.

- Spices and Agricultural Products: The Tamil region was rich in spices, especially pepper, cardamom, and ginger, which became important commodities for trade in later periods. Rice, millets, and cotton would also have been key products.
- Pearls, Precious metals and Gems: The southern part of India, particularly around the Pandya kingdom, was known for its pearls and gems, which were considered valuable assets. The mythological texts of the Sangam era often mention the wealth of the Pandya dynasty, which was connected to the trade of pearls. Athichanallur produced evidence of Golden Netripattam and copper statues.
- Timber and Building Materials: Timber from forests and other materials like stones would have been important for construction, including the building of homes, temples, and fortifications. The Athichanallur site showed the evidence of Bricks during the period.
- Grains – There were evidence of Saamai Rice being cultivated and exported.

Social Assets and Wealth Indicators:

- Rulers and Chiefs: The First Sangam era was likely ruled by tribal chiefs or local kings, and the power dynamics of these early societies were defined by land ownership, military prowess, and the ability to control trade routes and resources.
- Bards and Poets: Poets, sages, and bards (such as Agastya) were significant cultural assets, as oral tradition and poetry were key to preserving history, culture, and wisdom. These individuals likely held a high status and would have been supported by the elite or ruling classes.

- Artifacts: The early Tamil civilizations may have also had small-scale production of jewelry, clay pots, and simple artifacts, which were valued as symbols of wealth and culture.

Symbolic and Cultural Assets:

- Poetry and Oral Tradition: The Sangam period is famous for its poetry, and the First Sangam would have contributed to the earliest forms of Tamil literature. While the exact works from this era are not available, it is believed that these oral compositions were treasured by the community and passed down through generations. The ability to compose poetry and participate in literary gatherings would have been a valued cultural asset.
- Religious and Spiritual Assets: Early Tamil society would have also been deeply connected to spiritual and religious practices. Gods and deities, especially those associated with nature (e.g., Murugan, Kali, Indra), would have been important cultural and social assets, with rituals and practices being passed down orally.

Military Assets:

- Weapons and Tools: Society during the First Sangam era relied on stone tools, bronze, and later iron weapons for hunting and protection. The First Sangam may have seen the beginning of weapon-making as an important craft.
- Defensive Structures: While no specific evidence of fortifications exists from this period, early Tamil kingdoms, such as the Pandya and Chola dynasties (which would later arise), were known for their strategic use of forts and defensive structures, which may have had their origins in this early period.

The First Sangam era was a time deeply rooted in mythology and oral tradition, so historical details about specific assets are largely speculative. However, based on later Sangam literature and cultural traditions, it is likely that the First Sangam era would have involved the following assets:

- Land for agriculture and settlement.
- Livestock, such as cattle and possibly elephants and horses.
- Trade goods, including spices, grains, pearls, and other commodities.
- Cultural assets like oral literature, poetry, and the wisdom of poets and bards.
- Social status is linked to land ownership, Metals like Gold, Copper ownership, military prowess, and trade.

Ancient Era (3000 BC - 500 AD)

2nd Sangam Tamil Civilization Era (3000 BC – 2000 BC) and 3rd Sangam Tamil Era (2000 BC – 300 AD)

The Sangam Tamil Civilization period, primarily associated with the Tamil-speaking kingdoms in Indian Peninsula (notably the **Chola**, **Chera**, and **Pandya** dynasties), was characterized by an agrarian economy, trade, and rich cultural life. The wealth of the Tamil kingdoms was based on the following types of assets:

1. Land

- Agricultural Land: In the Sangam period, land was a primary asset and a key source of wealth. The fertile plains of the Tamil region were ideal for cultivating rice, millet, and other crops. Land ownership, particularly fertile agricultural land, was essential for wealthy generation. Kings and local chieftains were often landowners, and the agrarian economy was structured around land cultivation.
- Irrigation Systems: In areas like the Chola kingdom, extensive irrigation systems (e.g., tanks, canals) were used to manage water resources.

These irrigation structures were critical assets that boosted agricultural productivity.

2. Livestock

- Cattle and Elephants: Livestock, including cattle, elephants, and horses, were valuable assets. Elephants were used in warfare, royal processions, and religious ceremonies, making them a symbol of power and wealth. Cattle provided milk, labor, and were used as a form of currency in rural economies.
- Horses: Horses were prized in the Tamil kingdoms, especially for use in warfare and trade. Horse trade played a significant role in the economy, and they were often seen as assets of the ruling class.

3. Trade Goods

- Spices and Textiles: The Tamil kingdoms were involved in extensive trade, both overland and overseas, with regions such as Sri Lanka, the Malay Archipelago, Persia, and the Roman Empire. Spices, especially black pepper, were highly valued as trade assets. Textiles, particularly fine cotton and silk fabrics were also important trade goods.
- Precious Stones and Pearls: South India, particularly the Pandya region, was known for its pearls and precious stones. These were traded with distant regions and were valuable assets in the economy.

4. Metals and Minerals

- Iron and Gold: Metals like iron were used for agricultural tools, weapons, and construction. Gold and silver were valuable as wealth storage and trade assets. Gold coins and jewelry were significant as symbols of wealth, especially for royalty and nobility.

5. Urban Centers and Infrastructure

- **Port Cities**: Coastal cities such as Korkai, Kaveripattinam and Nagapattinam were important trade hubs. Ports were vital for both importing goods like Roman wine and exporting local products such as textiles, spices, and pearls. These cities themselves became valuable assets in the Tamil kingdoms.

- **Fortresses and Temples**: The royal palaces and temples, often richly adorned with sculptures, jewelry, and wealth, were significant assets. Temples also played a central role in the economy, being both centers of religion and economic activity, as they accumulated land, goods, and donations.

6. Social Assets

- **Cultural Capital**: The Tamil society had a rich cultural heritage, and its literature, arts, and traditions were highly valued. Poets, scholars, and artisans had a form of social and intellectual capital that contributed to the kingdom's wealth. The Sangam poets often praised the richness of the land, the prosperity of trade, and the valor of kings, which were all reflections of the assets in society.

Roman Empire (27 BC – 476 AD)

The Roman Empire was one of the largest and most sophisticated civilizations in ancient history, and its wealth and economy were based on various forms of assets, both material and intangible. Below are the key assets during this period:

Land:

- Agricultural Land: Like the Tamil kingdoms, land was a critical asset in ancient Rome. Large estates (called latifundia) were owned by wealthy Roman elites, often worked by slaves or peasants. These estates produced a variety of goods, including grains, olives, grapes (for wine), and livestock.
- Roman Colonies: The Roman Empire expanded through colonization, and land in newly conquered territories became an asset for the Roman state

and its elite. The government would often distribute land to soldiers, particularly veterans, in exchange for loyalty.

- Public Land: In the later years of the Republic and during the Empire, public land (known as ager publicus) was controlled by the state but granted to private individuals. This system created significant wealth for Rome's elite class, who controlled vast amounts of this public land.

Slaves:

- Slave Labor: The Roman economy was highly dependent on slavery, and slaves were considered significant assets. They were used in agriculture, mining, construction, domestic service, and even in gladiatorial games. The wealthy Romans often had large households with numerous slaves, and slave traders played a key role in the Roman economy.
- Slave Markets: Slaves were bought and sold in markets across the empire, and their labor was essential to the production of goods and services.

Currency and Precious Metals

- Gold and Silver: The Romans minted coins (e.g., denarii, aurei) made from gold, silver, and bronze. These coins were not only a form of currency but also a symbol of imperial power. The wealthy Romans held large amounts of precious metals in the form of coins and bullion.
- Wealth Storage: Gold and silver were stored in Roman treasuries (e.g., the aerarium), and the Roman elites often held gold and silver as part of their personal wealth.

Trade Goods and Commodities

- Luxury Goods: Romans were avid consumers of luxury items, which were often imported from distant parts of the empire or beyond. These included silk (from China), spices (from India), wine, oil, gems, and exotic animals (e.g., lions, elephants).

- Grain: The Roman Empire was heavily reliant on grain production, particularly from Egypt and North Africa. Grain was crucial to feeding the large urban populations of Rome and other cities. The control of grain-producing land was thus a vital asset for Roman rulers.

Infrastructure and Urbanization

- Roads and Aqueducts: Roman infrastructure was one of the empire's greatest assets. The Romans built an extensive system of roads and aqueducts, enabling efficient trade, communication, and water distribution. These were assets that enhanced both military mobility and economic productivity.
- Public Buildings and Cities: Cities in the Roman Empire were often centers of wealth and power, with monumental architecture such as the Colosseum, Baths of Caracalla, and temples. The construction and maintenance of these structures were significant assets, showcasing the empire's power and facilitating commerce, tourism, and civic pride.

Military Assets

- Legions: The Roman legions were among the most formidable military forces in history. Roman military power was a critical asset, as it enabled the empire to expand and maintain control over vast territories. The legions were also crucial for protecting Roman assets, including trade routes, agricultural land, and cities.
- Weaponry and Armaments: Roman soldiers used advanced weaponry and armor, which were valuable assets. The Romans were also skilled in siege technology and military engineering, which were used in warfare and in building infrastructure.

Intellectual Property and Culture

- Roman Law and Governance: Roman legal systems and political institutions became one of the empire's enduring assets. Roman law, which included property rights, contracts, and citizenship laws, became a foundation for modern legal systems.
- Cultural and Artistic Assets: Romans valued cultural assets, including architecture, sculpture, literature, and philosophy. Roman artworks and literature were not only expressions of wealth but also tools for maintaining cultural and political power.

Medieval Era (500–1500 AD)

Key Assets:

- Land: In medieval times, land remained the most critical asset. The feudal system, particularly in Europe, was centered around land ownership and control. Lords held vast estates, and peasants (or serfs) worked the land in exchange for protection and basic rights.
- Manorial Estates: These were large, self-sufficient agricultural estates that formed the economic backbone of medieval societies. Lords controlled the land, and peasants or serfs cultivated it.
- Livestock: Livestock continued to be valuable, as animals provided food, labor (plowing fields, transporting goods), and raw materials like wool and leather.
- Precious Metals and Currency: Coins made from precious metals like gold and silver were widely used. The Church also held significant assets, often in the form of land, treasures, and relics.
- Military Assets: Weapons, armor, and horses for knights were essential to nobility and became key assets for maintaining power and status.

Major Changes:

- The feudal system and manorial economy meant that land was still the foundation of wealth, but wealth was also increasingly tied to military power, especially for the nobility.
- Precious metals (gold and silver) began to take on a more standardized form in coinage.
- The rise of the Church as a dominant economic and political force meant that religious institutions owned vast amounts of land and wealth, adding a significant new layer of assets.

Early Modern Era (1500–1800 AD)

Key Assets:

- Land: Land remained a primary asset, but its role shifted as monarchies and early forms of capitalism began to take hold.
- Trade and Commercial Goods: With the rise of global exploration and trade (such as the Age of Discovery), merchants started accumulating wealth in the form of trade goods—spices, silk, sugar, and other valuable commodities.
- Stocks and Bonds: The early modern period saw the emergence of joint-stock companies. The Dutch East India Company (founded in 1602) is often considered the first publicly traded company, and owning shares in such ventures became an asset.
- Real Estate: Urbanization increased, and real estate in cities became valuable as commercial centers grew.
- Gold and Silver: These continued to be important, especially as European nations mined vast quantities of precious metals from the Americas, further fueling the growth of European economies.

Major Changes: Capitalism began to emerge, with an increasing shift from land-based wealth to merchant and commercial assets. The rise of banking, investments in global trade, and the growth of joint-stock companies marked a shift in how wealth was accumulated. Shares and bonds became a new type of financial asset as trading and investment practices evolved with the expansion of global commerce.

Industrial Revolution (1800–1900 AD)

Key Assets:

- Factories and Machinery: The Industrial Revolution dramatically shifted the focus of valuable assets from land and agriculture to capital goods—factories, machinery, and industrial infrastructure. These new forms of wealth allowed nations to industrialize and produce goods at unprecedented scales.
- Railroads and Infrastructure: With the expansion of railroads and infrastructure, assets like rail lines, ports, and factories became highly valuable.
- Stocks and Bonds: The financial sector grew rapidly, and corporate stocks became an increasingly important asset. Stock markets (like the New York Stock Exchange) became more established.
- Real Estate: As cities grew due to industrialization, urban real estate became a significant asset class, especially in burgeoning commercial centers.
- Natural Resources: Industrialization also led to a demand for raw materials—coal, iron, oil, etc.—which became valuable assets for industrial enterprises.

Major Changes:

- The shift from agrarian-based wealth to capital goods and industrial production marked a key transformation. The growth of factories, machinery, and the railroad industry created new forms of wealth.
- Stocks, bonds, and corporate assets became increasingly important, marking the rise of modern capital markets.
- With the growth of industrial production, the accumulation of natural resources (such as coal, oil, and iron) became central to the wealth of industrialized nations.

20th Century (1900–2000 AD)

Key Assets:

- Stocks and Bonds: The 20th century saw the growth of global financial markets, where stocks and bonds became fundamental assets in wealth accumulation, especially with the rise of multinational corporations.
- Real Estate: Residential and commercial real estate continued to be a primary asset, particularly with the rise of suburbanization in the post-World War II era.
- Intangible Assets: The concept of intellectual property (IP) began to emerge as a key form of wealth. Patents, trademarks, and copyrights became highly valuable assets, particularly for companies in the technology, entertainment, and pharmaceutical industries.
- Human Capital: Education and skills began to be recognized as forms of human capital, increasingly important in a knowledge-based economy.
- Digital Assets: By the late 20th century, data, and the emerging digital economy began to redefine what constituted assets, especially in the tech sector.

Major Changes:

- Intangible assets such as intellectual property and brand value have become increasingly important, especially in the technology and entertainment sectors.
- The growth of global financial markets, multinational corporations, and digital economies reshaped how assets were defined and accumulated.
- Real estate continued to be a critical asset, but now in both commercial and residential sectors.

21st Century (2000–Present)

Key Assets:

- Digital and Virtual Assets: The rise of the internet, cryptocurrencies (e.g., Bitcoin, Ethereum), data, and non-fungible tokens (NFTs) have introduced new forms of assets that exist primarily in the digital realm.
- Intellectual Property: Patents, copyrights, trademarks, and other forms of IP are now critical to the success of many businesses, especially tech firms, and have become highly tradable assets.
- Stocks and Bonds: These remain foundational in modern wealth management, but they are now traded globally and include a wide array of complex financial instruments (e.g., ETFs, derivatives).
- Environmental and Sustainability Assets: Assets related to green energy, carbon credits, and sustainable infrastructure have grown in importance due to global concerns over climate change.

Major Changes:

- The emergence of **cryptocurrencies** and **digital assets** marks a fundamental shift in how people store and trade wealth.
- **Data** has become a critical asset for tech companies, reshaping entire industries like advertising, healthcare, and finance.

- The increasing importance of **sustainable assets** reflects broader societal shifts toward environmental responsibility and sustainability

The Future of Assets

- Environmental and Sustainable Assets: As concerns over climate change and sustainability grow, environmental assets (like carbon credits, renewable energy infrastructure, and sustainable agriculture assets) are becoming increasingly important. Investments in green technologies and sustainable practices are rising.
- Social and Digital Assets: The digital transformation continues to redefine assets, with data becoming a highly valuable asset. Data ownership, data privacy, and how personal and corporate data are used for business and profit are likely to be key considerations in future asset management.
- Artificial Intelligence and Automation: AI and automation are likely to change the nature of assets as well, making AI-driven assets, such as algorithms and machine-learning models, valuable resources in the economy.

The historical evolution of assets has gone from primarily physical and tangible resources (land, gold, machinery) to an increasingly complex and intangible mix (stocks, bonds, intellectual property, digital assets). Technological progress, globalization, financial innovations, and cultural shifts have continuously transformed what is considered an asset, the ways assets are valued, and how individuals and institutions interact with them. In the future, assets will likely continue to evolve with trends in digitalization, environmental sustainability, and shifting economic models.

2.4 Times of Change of Money

Money is not simply created through the act of printing; rather, the physical printed money symbolizes only the initial level of its intrinsic value. Many people harbor the misconception that the government and central banks are the sole entities responsible for the creation of money. In reality, they serve as facilitators, providing the necessary frameworks and systems through which money is produced and circulated. Therefore, it is important to recognize that the US dollar, for instance, is not the ultimate representation of money itself but rather a foundational platform upon which various forms of additional money can be generated.

Money exists in multiple forms, one of which is the profit generated by businesses. It is a common misbelief to attribute negative consequences solely to the printing of fiat currency while at the same time aspiring to considerable profits from commercial ventures. To illustrate, when the monetary supply is either completely absent or significantly constrained, the dynamics of purchasing goods become disproportionately aligned with their selling prices. This scenario can lead to stagnation or complete erasure of profits, plunging the business environment into what can be referred to as a "non-profit" state. The consequence of such a situation is detrimental; companies may begin to deplete their own resources, eroding the capital essential for compensating their executives and employees, which could ultimately result in closures and layoffs.

This understanding helps clarify why Wall Street and its economists often voice criticisms regarding the practice of money printing. They are acutely aware that their sector, especially those involved in financial services, relies heavily on a continuous influx of revenue and profits which stem from various activities. These activities include asset management, debt servicing, and credit provision.

For consumers to access the additional funds necessary to pay for these services, it is crucial that these service providers generate sufficient profits to not only cover their operational costs but also create surplus capital for reinvestment and growth. This cycle is essential to prevent the depletion of available resources and to sustain an ongoing trajectory of economic expansion.

In summary, the interplay between money creation, business profitability, and economic health illustrates the intricate web that supports a thriving financial system. It emphasizes the need for a balanced approach to money supply management, ensuring that profits and resources remain aligned to foster sustainable growth.

I Owe You Money: Understanding the Nature of Government and Central Bank Currency. At first glance, it may seem obvious that the currency issued by governments and central banks—whether it be the U.S. Dollar, Euro, Yuan, or Rupee—is simply money. However, a closer examination reveals that these printed currency notes serve a different function. Rather than being money in the truest sense, they represent a form of legal tender that can be understood as an "I Owe You." This concept implies that, when a high-ranking official—such as the Chairman of the Federal Reserve or the governor of a central bank—inscribes a note with the words, "I promise to pay you a sum of...," they are not asserting the value of the currency itself. Instead, they are issuing a promissory note, which indicates a promise to exchange that particular amount for a recognized currency at a future date.

The labels we commonly associate with currency—Dollar, Euro, Yuan, or Rupee—are merely identifiers for a medium of exchange. They do not encapsulate the intrinsic value of money itself. This leads to a perplexing question: if these notes are essentially IOUs, where do we find the 'real' Dollar, Euro, Yen, Yuan, or Rupee?

The reality is that they exist as promises that can only be fulfilled under certain conditions, making their true nature a subject of deeper economic inquiry.

"The Role of Contracts Between Businesses in Creating Money"

When one business enters into a contractual agreement with another, stipulating the payment will be made in a specific currency at a defined future date, this transaction initiates the creation of money in a functional sense. Such contracts establish a foundation for economic activity, as they are based on the expectation of the successful exchange of goods or services in the future. Once the contract is ratified, the economic clock starts ticking, and the transaction functions in a manner similar to money, even though it has yet to be executed.

This form of money creation hinges on the assumption that the product or service will be delivered in a satisfactory manner and within a specified timeframe. However, it is essential to note that unless the agreement includes an escrow arrangement—where the buyer deposits an agreed-upon amount of actual money into a secure account—both parties are engaging in a process of money creation through the stipulation of their contract. In effect, these contracts can expand the money supply by establishing obligations that will eventually convert into tangible currency upon fulfillment.

"Credits and Loans in the Fractional Reserve Banking System are money"

Within the framework of modern economies, banks operate under a system known as fractional reserve banking. This system allows banks to lend out a significant portion of their deposits while maintaining only a small fraction of their reserves. The specific percentage deemed necessary to be kept in reserve is referred to as the reserve requirement. This requirement plays a crucial role in determining how many times a bank can multiply its lending capabilities based on its reserves. For example, if a bank is subject to a reserve requirement of 10% (0.1), it means that for every dollar deposited, the bank is required to keep only ten cents in reserve. The remaining ninety cents can be loaned out, effectively allowing the bank to lend ten times its actual reserves. This process not only fuels lending and borrowing but also influences the overall money supply within the economy, as each loan creates additional money through deposits made by the recipients of those loans.

"Leverage Created by Banks, Financial Institutions, Funds, and Corporations is Money"

Leverage is a financial strategy that involves using borrowed funds to increase the potential returns (or losses) of an investment. This practice allows individuals and corporations to control a greater volume of assets than they could solely with their own cash reserves. The implications of leverage are significant as it can enhance both profits and risks associated with investment activities.

As of 2023, a remarkable 13 of the 15 largest U.S. banks reported a Tier 1 leverage ratio exceeding five percent. This ratio serves as an important measure of a bank's capital relative to its total assets, reflecting its ability to absorb losses. Capital One topped the list with an impressive Tier 1 leverage ratio of 11.2 percent, indicating a strong capital foundation. Closely following are Citizens Bank and First Republic, each showing a ratio of 9.3 percent. Furthermore, in the second quarter of 2024, TD Bank's U.S. operations—part of the Canadian Toronto-Dominion Bank—boasted the highest common equity Tier 1 (CET1) capital ratio among major U.S. banks, as ranked by total assets. With a CET1 ratio of 16.77 percent, TD Bank significantly exceeded the regulatory minimum requirement of 4.5 percent, highlighting its strong capital position and risk management capabilities.

Corporations frequently utilize leverage to finance expansion projects, acquisitions, or day-to-day operations. By borrowing funds at lower interest rates, these organizations can amplify their return on equity, which is the profit generated from their shareholders' investments. However, it is crucial to approach leverage with caution; an excessive amount can lead to financial distress if the firm fails to generate sufficient revenue to cover its debt obligations. Companies experiencing downturns may struggle to meet interest payments or repay principal amounts, potentially resulting in bankruptcy or significant operational cutbacks. In the realm of real estate investment, leveraging is a common practice where investors secure mortgages to acquire properties. By doing so, they aim to generate rental income or benefit from appreciation in property values that surpass the costs associated with their mortgage payments. This strategy can create substantial wealth over time; however, it also carries risk, especially in fluctuating real estate markets where property values may decline. In the stock market, individual investors can access leverage to purchase more securities than their cash holdings would allow. This can be accomplished through margin accounts, where investors borrow funds from brokerage firms. While this method magnifies potential returns, it also heightens the risk, as losses can similarly be amplified. A decline in stock prices can rapidly erode equity in the margin account, leading to margin calls where investors must either deposit additional funds or sell off securities to maintain their position.

“Bonds Created by Governments and Businesses are Money”

Although bonds are not legally categorized as money, they perform a vital role within the money supply and the broader financial system, effectively acting as a form of money. Bonds are debt securities issued by governments or corporations to raise capital. Investors who purchase bonds essentially lend money to the issuer in exchange for periodic interest payments and the return of the bond's face value upon maturity. The liquidity and security associated with bonds contribute to their function within the financial landscape. As they are often viewed as safer investments compared to stocks, many individuals and institutions include bonds in their portfolios to mitigate risk. In times of economic uncertainty, bonds can serve as a haven, preserving capital while also providing a steady income stream through interest payments. Overall, the interplay of leverage and bonds within the financial infrastructure illustrates the complexities of modern investing and the importance of careful risk management in both corporate finance and personal investment strategies.

"Bonds in the Financial System is money"

Although bonds are not classified as money in the traditional sense, they play a crucial role in shaping the broader financial system by influencing various economic dynamics.

Debt and Credit Creation: Bonds provide a mechanism for governments and corporations to raise capital by borrowing from investors. When a government issues bonds, it is effectively soliciting funds to finance public projects, such as infrastructure development, healthcare, and education. Similarly, businesses issue bonds to fund expansion, research and development, or to refinance existing debt. This access to credit is vital for stimulating economic growth, as it allows for increased investment in both public and private sectors. The funds raised through the issuance of bonds can lead to job creation, improved services, and the enhancement of overall economic activity.

Investment Vehicles: For individual investors and institutional funds, bonds represent a critical component of diversified investment portfolios. Bonds are often viewed as safer investments compared to stocks, particularly government bonds, which are generally considered low risk due to the backing of government credit. This characteristic makes bonds an attractive option for conservative investors seeking stable income streams. The fixed interest payments, known as coupon payments, provide predictability and can help investors manage cash flow in their financial planning.

Market Liquidity: The bond markets, especially those focused on government debt, are among the most liquid in the global financial landscape. High liquidity means that investors can easily buy and sell bonds without significantly impacting their prices. This flexibility contributes to the overall stability of the financial system, as it allows for quick adjustments to changing economic conditions and facilitates the flow of capital. Liquidity in the bond market also influences interest rates and exchange rates, as fluctuations in bond prices can signal shifts in investor sentiment and economic outlook.

"Stock Market Gains is Money"

As of the time of this writing, Apple Inc. has a market capitalization of approximately $3.83 trillion, with its stock trading at a valuation of 10 times its revenue rather than its profit. This high valuation underscores how the stock market can be perceived as a form of money, where investor confidence and future growth potential significantly impact stock prices. In 2024, Apple's revenue is projected to be USD 400 billion, highlighting the company's substantial financial performance as a key driver of its market value.

Additionally, other forms of money creation can occur through formal agreements between governments that are denominated in specific currencies. These contracts can facilitate trade and investment across borders, contributing to liquidity and economic activity. Furthermore, when governments bail out failed or non-performing assets, they inject capital into the economy to stabilize financial systems and prevent crises. Such interventions not only reflect a form of monetary policy but also illustrate the government's role as a backstop in maintaining economic stability during challenging times.

2.5 Times of Change of Trust & Custodian

The concepts of trust and custodianship have undergone profound transformations throughout human history, shaped by the intricate interplay of societal, economic, legal, and governance changes. Below, we delve into a more detailed examination of how these ideas have evolved across various historical periods:

Ancient Civilizations (Pre-Common Era): Sangam Tamil Civilization Era

- Trust: In the early centers of civilization, such as Mesopotamia, Egypt, and Greece, trust was fundamentally a personal affair, deeply embedded in the relationships and social structures of the time. It was heavily influenced by religious beliefs and familial ties, with community leaders, elders, and priests playing crucial roles in mediating disputes and managing economic affairs. Trust was characterized by a sense of loyalty, mutual respect, and reciprocity, forming the cornerstone of social interactions and community cohesion. Individuals relied on each other's integrity and reputation, understanding that their standing within the community was tied to their ability to uphold these unspoken agreements.

- Custodianship: During this epoch, custodianship was closely intertwined with the stewardship of property and communal resources. The ruling elite and religious authorities assumed the roles of custodians, with temples functioning as safe havens for wealth and resources, meant for both sacred and social purposes. In this system, royal families and nobility-maintained control over land and assets, ensuring their appropriate use and preservation for future generations, often acting under divine or royal mandates that reinforced their authority.

Unfortunately, the later day after the Sangam period was followed by Kings and a Circle of Insiders become more and more powerful, breaking from the great Sangam Periods. For the next thousand years, Tamil Civilization went through many transformations through glorious kings and kingdoms with expansion of the kingdoms like cholas through the vast land and oceans across Asia but the assets and custodianship very much stayed within kingdom's authority although the local village level traditions continued under different forms and formats. Even now one can witness the power of Sangam's (union of people) prevalent over the central powers in the Tamil civilization (and rest of the Union of India).

Medieval Era (5th–15th Century)

- Trust: The medieval period saw a transformation in the notion of trust, particularly as it became intertwined with the feudal system, where social hierarchies were established through allegiances, oaths, and fealty. Trust was then focused on the relationships between lords, kings, and the clergy, with individuals expected to demonstrate loyalty through personal and socio-political commitments. Oaths of loyalty were not mere formalities; they represented binding agreements that dictated the behavior and expectations between rulers and their subjects, leading to a deeper recognition of the legal dimensions of trust within this context.

- Custodianship: The church played a central role during this period, emerging as a key custodian of knowledge, culture, and economic wealth. Monasteries and cathedral schools became vital centers for preserving literature, manuscripts, and religious teachings, serving as repositories of collective memory and wisdom. Feudal lords managed land on behalf of monarchs or engaged in reciprocal arrangements with vassals, illustrating a complex web of power dynamics and accountability that defined custodianship as both a privilege and a responsibility.

Renaissance and Early Modern Period (14th–18th Century)

- Trust: The Renaissance sparked a significant evolution in the perception of trust, particularly as commerce and trade flourished across Europe. The development of commercial law illustrated a shift where trust expanded beyond individual relationships into institutional frameworks. The rise of the written contract and formal agreements became vital, emphasizing that trust could now be substantiated and secured through legal avenues. This transition enabled greater economic growth, as people could engage in transactions with more confidence, knowing that their interests were legally protected.
- Custodianship: Throughout this period, significant wealth and resources became increasingly concentrated in the hands of the elite, including the church, aristocracy, and affluent merchants. Early banking institutions began assuming formal custodial roles, managing monetary assets and facilitating transactions. The rise of colonial empires introduced another dimension of custodianship, where nations exercised control over vast overseas territories, managing

resources often without regard for the indigenous populations, which raised ethical questions about stewardship and exploitation.

Industrial Revolution (18th–19th Century)

- Trust: The Industrial Revolution ushered in a new era of professionalization regarding trust, driven by the rise of corporations and expansive institutions. Joint-stock companies and state-operated entities necessitated structured systems of trust affirming fiduciary duties and ethical governance. This era emphasized meticulous auditing practices and implemented legal frameworks to protect shareholders' interests and ensure responsible management of resources, reflecting a societal shift toward institutional trust as opposed to personal trust.
- Custodianship: As economic activities proliferated, custodianship increasingly transitioned to institutional entities. Financial institutions such as banks, insurance companies, and professional trustees became common stewards of personal and corporate assets, illustrating the growing complexity of financial systems. Moreover, governments started to take active roles in managing public resources and infrastructure, fostering a landscape ripe for the establishment of various trusts, such as land trusts and charitable organizations, which highlighted the expanding importance of custodianship in safeguarding community interests.

20th Century

- Trust: The rapid evolution of financial markets and the growing complexity of corporate structures in the 20th century led to the establishment of robust regulatory frameworks designed to uphold trust. Legal and financial professionals, including fiduciaries, investment managers, and trustees, became essential figures within wealth management systems. Trust law evolved significantly, particularly within Anglo-Saxon legal systems, as corporate governance structures became critical for maintaining stakeholder confidence and sustainability in business practices.

- Custodianship: The forces of globalization and technological advancements in the 20th century reshaped custodianship into a highly regulated and specialized domain. Financial institutions like custodial banks emerged, tasked with the safeguarding of substantial assets, including pension funds, investment portfolios, and securities. As financial markets became more sophisticated, the responsibilities of custodial banks expanded dramatically, formulating comprehensive frameworks for the custody and management of both tangible and digital assets, ensuring that these entities acted in the best interests of their clients.

6. 21st Century

- Trust: In the current digital era, trust remains fundamental to social exchanges, yet it faces an array of new challenges and complexities. The advent of digital technologies, social media, and cryptocurrencies has transformed the landscape of trust, introducing both opportunities and vulnerabilities. Issues surrounding data privacy, cyber security, and the rise of misinformation call for new frameworks that address the nuances of trust in an interconnected and fast-evolving digital world. As we navigate these challenges, the quest for transparency and accountability in both personal and institutional relationships continues to shape modern perceptions of trust.

- Custodianship: Today, custodianship is not only about managing traditional assets but also encompasses a wide array of digital and intangible resources. The introduction of blockchain technology and decentralized finance (DeFi) has begun to revolutionize how custodianship is perceived, challenging established norms around asset management and ownership. This complex landscape requires new approaches to custodianship, balancing innovation with the need for oversight and protection to safeguard assets and maintain public trust. Through these historical developments, we see that trust and custodianship are not static concepts but rather dynamic constructs that have evolved to meet the needs of changing societies, economies, and technologies.

Age	**Division Of Labor**	**Economy**	**Value Proposition**	**Trust**
Ancient				
Sangam Age				
Pre-Industrial	Very Less Division of Labor	Food/ Exchange of food.	Need for survival	Commitment: Oral Commitment Mediators: Community and Personal
Industrial	Larger division of Labor	Goods production	Higher production	Commitment: Centralized Paper Mediators: Government, Representational Groups
Enterprise/ Information Age	Aggregated division of labor based on skills & knowledge	Mass production & customization	Specific and faster production	Commitment: Decentralized Computer + Paper. Mediators: Government, Representational Groups, Computer Managers
Extended Enterprise /complex information	Distributed division of Labor	Information and service	Mass customization, flexibility, time-market, security,	Commitment: Decentralized Computer + Centralized

Age				Computer + Paper. Mediators: Government, Representational Groups and Computer Server Managers
Artificial Intelligence & Internet of Things Age	Interconnected Division of Labor	Automation-to-Autonomous, Creativity & Artificial Intelligence	Integrated Supply Chain, Smart Assets, time-to-market, time-to-sale	Commitment: Crypto network backed by Thousands of Decentralized & distributed computers Mediators: No Mediators necessary as commitments are embedded within network and visible to all nodes.

2.6 Times of Change of Technology & Innovation

Ancient:

Sangam Tamil Civilization Era

- Medicine: The Siddha system of medicine, one of the oldest in the world, originates from Tamil Nadu. It integrates spirituality, philosophy, and a deep understanding of human anatomy and herbal remedies. Ancient Siddhas significantly contributed to herbal medicine, with foundational texts like the

Thirumandiram highlighting holistic health principles. The system emphasizes balance among body, mind, and environment, mirroring contemporary holistic health concepts, and showcases advanced chemical knowledge through alchemical practices.

- Architecture and Construction: Cities such as Korkai and Madurai exemplified meticulous planning, featuring advanced urban layouts with streets and reservoirs. Temples from this era demonstrated architectural precision and included intricate stone carvings representing various narratives.
- Maritime Technologies: The Sanga Tamil Kingdoms were innovators in shipbuilding and maritime technology, constructing large vessels for extensive trade across the Indian Ocean using sophisticated techniques.
- Metallurgy and Weaponry: The ancient Tamils excelled in metallurgy, producing high-quality iron and steel for various purposes, including weaponry, exemplified by the renowned Vikramaditya sword.
- Agricultural Technology: Ancient Tamils developed efficient irrigation systems, including tanks and canals, to enhance agricultural productivity in the seasonal climate, along with advanced drainage systems for effective water management during monsoons to support crop cultivation.

Europe

Some of the European Innovations are:

- **Invention of horseshoes:** The earliest recorded mention of horseshoes is attributed to St. Eligius, an Irish monk from the 7th century, who is often credited with their invention. However, similar methods likely emerged in other regions simultaneously. As horses became essential for transportation, farming, and warfare, the use of horseshoes became widespread. By the 12th century, horseshoeing was well established in Europe, with blacksmiths improving the design for greater durability and effectiveness.

- **Three field agriculture:** The three-field system was an agricultural method used in medieval Europe - that improved crop yields and soil health. Emerging between the 8th and 10th centuries, it gained popularity by the 11th to 13th centuries. Its main benefits were increased crop production, better soil fertility, and reduced soil erosion.
- **Steamboats:** The creation of the steamboat unfolded like a captivating tale of innovation, marked by the contributions of various inventors, with Robert Fulton standing out for his remarkable achievements. This groundbreaking vessel transformed the landscape of transportation in the 18th and 19th centuries, ushering in an era where the movement of goods and people became swifter and more efficient, particularly across the winding rivers and serene lakes. The steamboat's influence extended far beyond mere logistics; it reshaped the very fabric of society. It became a powerful catalyst for trade, dramatically enhancing commerce while also leaving its mark on military engagements—most strikingly during the turbulent years of the American Civil War. This marvel of engineering not only facilitated rapid communication but also played a crucial role in the relentless wave of industrialization sweeping through both the United States and Europe, forever altering the course of history.
- **Innovation in accounting practices:** The dawn of double-entry bookkeeping marked a revolutionary turning point in the annals of accounting history, fundamentally reshaping the landscape of financial record-keeping. This groundbreaking method was immortalized by Luca Pacioli, an astute Italian mathematician often hailed as the "father of accounting." In the year 1494, Pacioli unveiled his seminal work, "Summa de Arithmetica, Geometria, Proportioni et Proportionalita," a compendium that laid the cornerstone of modern accounting practices. As the world navigated through the bustling corridors of trade and commerce during the Medieval and Renaissance eras, a palpable demand for sophisticated record-keeping emerged. Merchants, with ambitions of grandeur, ventured into cross-border trade, where the intricacies of

complex financial transactions required a meticulous approach to documenting their dealings. This evolution in accounting not only polished the standards of financial practices but also significantly bolstered the enforceability of contracts across nations, endowing European businesses with a competitive edge that propelled them forward in the marketplace.

- **Financial institutions for Credits and Insurances:** The development and evolution of financial institutions for credit and insurance in Europe represent a pivotal economic transformation in history. These institutions have been instrumental in shaping contemporary economies by providing businesses and individuals with access to capital, managing risks, and addressing various financial needs. Their emergence has established the groundwork for significant economic shifts throughout the Renaissance, the Industrial Revolution, and beyond. In the realm of credit, advancements such as double-entry bookkeeping, the rise of merchant banks, and the establishment of central banks, including the Bank of England, have contributed to the development of more sophisticated systems for lending and capital allocation. Simultaneously, the insurance sector has evolved to effectively manage the myriad risks associated with trade, property, and health as industrialization progressed, leading to notable advancements in marine life, and fire insurance. Furthermore, the rise of commercial banking, the issuance of corporate bonds, and the establishment of stock exchanges have stimulated the growth of industrial economies and significantly influenced the structure of modern financial markets. Collectively, the expansion of these financial institutions has played a vital role in propelling contemporary economies, fostering increased investment, mitigating risks, and enhancing economic mobility across society.
- **Assessment of Risk:** Blaise Pascal and Pierre de Fermat played crucial roles in the early development of probability theory, especially through their letters discussing gambling problems in the mid-1600s. Their exchanges helped create new ways to think about how likely different outcomes were in games of chance,

paving the way for better understanding of risk. In 1662, John Graunt, a merchant in London, began one of the first systematic studies of demographic data, focusing mainly on mortality rates. His important work, *Natural and Political Observations Made upon the Bills of Mortality*, used statistical methods to shed light on public health issues and improve strategies for managing risks, particularly during outbreaks of disease. In the 18th century, Jacob Bernoulli made significant strides in probability with his introduction of the Law of Large Numbers. This idea states that as more trials are conducted, the average result will get closer to what is expected. This principle has major implications for fields like insurance, where understanding risk and predictability is essential. It has since become a fundamental part of modern statistics and how we analyze data today.

- **Printing Press:** The printing press stands as one of the most pivotal inventions in European history, fundamentally transforming the ways in which books and ideas were disseminated and reshaping society, culture, and the economy in profound ways. This revolutionary technology played an indispensable role in catalyzing major movements such as the Renaissance, the Protestant Reformation, and the Scientific Revolution, all of which collectively contributed to the emergence of the modern world as we know it today. Prior to the advent of the printing press, the production of books was an arduous and labor-intensive process, relying on the painstaking hand-copying of texts by scribes. This made books both scarce and excessively expensive, accessible only to the privileged elite. The earliest methods of printing, including woodblock printing, involved the meticulous carving of images and text into wooden blocks. These blocks were then inked and pressed against paper or fabric to create prints. While Johannes Gutenberg, a German inventor and metalworker, is prominent for developing the movable type printing technology in the mid-15th century, it is essential to recognize that similar printing techniques had been utilized in China long before. For instance, woodblock printing was already established during the Tang

Dynasty (618-907 AD), and around 1040 AD, the innovator Bi Sheng introduced movable clay type. However, despite these advancements, early Chinese printing did not facilitate widespread literacy to the extent that was later seen in Europe. In the Islamic world, there were also early forms of printing that utilized techniques such as stamped paper and engraving methods, further showcasing the region's contributions to the evolution of printed text. Yet, it was the European innovations that ultimately revolutionized the field on a much larger scale. The breakthrough moment arrived in the 1440s with Gutenberg's invention of the movable printing press, which marked a significant leap forward in printing technology. This system allowed for the composition of text by arranging and rearranging individual metal letters, effectively overcoming the limitations inherent in traditional woodblock printing. Gutenberg was not only a skilled blacksmith and printer; he was also a visionary publisher who developed a new oil-based ink that adhered better to paper and a special metal alloy that was uniquely suited for the mass production of printing plates. His most renowned accomplishment, the Gutenberg Bible—completed around 1455—stands as one of the earliest major books produced with this innovative method. This remarkable work not only exemplifies the technical advances of the printing press but also underscores its monumental impact on European society, paving the way for an explosion of literacy, the spread of new ideas, and the eventual cultural shifts that characterize the modern era.

Other innovations are: Advanced ship building and navigation systems. Example, circumventing Africa to reach Asia, Magnetic compass showing 32 directions, Arab lateen rig, Portlands, Vellum etc.

Portuguese technological innovations over the period in history are: Better navigation systems, better charts, Astronomy etc.

China technology over the history: Printing Technology invented in China in 900AD, Invention of pound-locks in 10th century Song dynasty helped in upstream river navigation of ships that drastically helped in trade and war. The Grand canal ran 1776 km which was primarily used in transporting grains.

Nazi Germany era technology: Rocket missiles, Acoustic torpedo etc.,

Britain Technology over the period: Cotton mills, Wireless radar etc.,
United States technology innovations over the period in history: Rail Roads, Cotton , Steel, Atom bomb, Internet, Software technologies, Electronics, Financial, Credit, Insurance and Risk Products

So, Technology innovations always moved the needles and shifted the balance of power from one civilization to the other. With the current geoeconomic conditions, innovation takes primary place in Geopolitical and Geostrategic Power Play.

Chapter 3. Economic State Craft and Geoeconomic Cooperation

In contrast to market economies, state-controlled economies, often referred to as command economies, feature substantial government oversight and regulation regarding the production, distribution, and pricing of goods and services. The dichotomy of market and state economies underscores the stark contrasts between two predominant models of economic organization: market economies and state-controlled economies. Each system employs a unique methodology in the allocation of resources, production processes, and distribution mechanisms for goods and services. Here is a comprehensive exploration of each side of this economic dichotomy.

2.1 State Economy:

The critical characteristics of state-controlled economies include:

Public Ownership of Resources: In a state-controlled economy, the government possesses and governs the primary means of production, encompassing essential industries and frequently extending to consumer goods. This often leads to diminished or entirely absent private ownership rights, as resources are managed with the goal of serving the collective interests of society rather than individual profit.

Centralized Economic Planning: A centralized authority, which is typically a government agency, exerts control over economic activities. This agency decides the types and quantities of goods and services to be produced and dictates pricing structures accordingly. Additionally, the government may regulate wages and employment levels to achieve macroeconomic objectives, aiming for stability and predictability.

Limited Market Competition: The dominant role of the government in managing industries leads to a reduction in competition. Most businesses are state-owned or operate under significant governmental constraints, which can inhibit innovation and responsiveness to market demands. This environment may lead to inefficiencies as businesses have less incentive to improve their services or products.

Emphasis on Social Equity: Promoting social equity is an overarching goal of state-controlled economies. The government often endeavors to minimize economic disparities and ensure that all citizens have access to essential goods and services. However, the emphasis on equity can sometimes undermine economic efficiency and lead to resource misallocation.

Historical Examples: Nations that have exemplified state-controlled economies include the former Soviet Union, North Korea, and Cuba, each demonstrating varying degrees of government involvement and control over economic life. These systems have experienced challenges related to inefficiency and limited consumer choice.

2.2 Market Economy (Capitalist System)

A market economy, often referred to as a capitalist system, is defined by economic decisions made primarily by private individuals and businesses rather than through central planning. In this framework, market forces such as supply, and demand significantly influence the configuration of production, distribution, and pricing. The defining characteristics of a market economy include:

Private Ownership: In a market economy, individuals and corporations own and manage varying resources, including land, labor, and capital. This principle of private property permits owners to make independent choices motivated by profit maximization and personal interests. Ownership rights empower individuals to innovate and invest in resources, driving economic activity.

Supply and Demand Mechanism: Prices within a market economy fluctuate based on the continual interaction between supply and demand. When there is increased consumer demand for a specific product, prices tend to rise. This price signal incentivizes producers to increase output to capitalize on potential profits. Conversely, when supply surpasses demand, prices fall, prompting producers to reduce production or diversify their offerings to remain viable in the market.

Competition as a Catalyst: The competitive landscape in a market economy stimulates businesses to vie for consumer patronage and sales. Competition drives innovation, spurs efficiency, and enhances service quality, as firms seek to differentiate their products and offer superior value. This environment encourages continuous improvement and responsiveness to consumer needs, fostering economic progress.

Limited Government Intervention: An idealized market economy favors minimal government interference in economic activities. The government's role is primarily to enforce contracts, protect property rights, and maintain the rule of law. This laissez-faire approach encourages entrepreneurship, allowing markets to self-regulate based on participants' decisions and behaviors.

Examples of Market Economies: Countries with market economies include the United States, Canada, Australia, and most Western European nations. These regions implement free-market principles, where economic decisions arise from individual actions rather than centralized directives, resulting in diverse economic landscapes.

Key Differences Between Market and State Economies:

"Private Capitalism makes Steam Engines; State capitalism makes Pyramids"

- Frank Chodorov

Ownership Structure: In a market economy, resources and means of production are predominantly controlled by private individuals or enterprises, whereas, in a state-controlled economy, the government maintains ownership over the major resources.

Decision-Making Processes: Economic decisions in a market economy are informed by private choices and market dynamics, while a state-controlled economy relies on directives from a central authority.

Government's Role: The government's role in a market economy is typically minimal, focusing on regulatory functions, while in a state-controlled economy, governmental involvement is extensive and all-encompassing.

Resource Allocation Mechanisms: The allocation of resources in a market economy is driven by the principles of supply and demand, whereas a state-controlled economy allocates resources based on a centralized plan established by the government.

Operational Efficiency: Generally, market economies display a higher degree of operational efficiency due to competition and innovation, while state-controlled economies often suffer from inefficiencies linked to bureaucratic management and potential corruption.

<u>Social Outcomes:</u> The focus on profit and wealth accumulation in market economies can lead to pronounced inequalities, while state-controlled economies prioritize wealth redistribution. However, this can result in inefficiencies, low productivity, diminished motivation, instances of corruption, and the emergence of elite classes.

2.3 Hybrid Economies

Modern economies predominantly function as hybrid systems, seamlessly integrating both market-driven mechanisms and state-controlled elements. These mixed economies are designed to enhance overall efficiency and spur innovation through the principles of a competitive market. At the same time, they address critical issues related to social welfare and equity by employing a variety of government regulations and interventions. The objective of overarching is to create an economic environment that fosters individual dynamism while simultaneously upholding collective social responsibility. As these economies evolve, the intricate interplay between market forces and state intervention plays a crucial role in shaping their trajectories, often reflecting the shifting societal values and priorities of the times.

Historically, governance frameworks resembling the republican system established by the Roman Empire can also be traced back to the Sangam Tamil kingdoms, which existed from approximately 5000 BC to 300 AD in what is now modern-day India. This governance model was marked by local groups working within organized administrations, with the monarch serving primarily as a facilitator and mediator, rather than as an autocratic figure wielding absolute power. Although the United States has since transitioned into a form that many see as a diminished version of its original republican ideals, it continues to stand as a beacon of hope for individuals and societies around the world seeking to reclaim fundamental freedoms such as expression, individuality, and the right to trade.

In the context of what is known as the **Social Triad system**, capitalism can be viewed as representative of individualism, where personal achievement and self-reliance are paramount. In contrast, social democracy aligns more closely with collectivism, emphasizing the role of the community and government in ensuring equitable outcomes for all. This ideological dynamic creates a significant political divide that warrants examination and discussion. The concept of human evolution, particularly regarding societal development and consciousness, encourages constructive dialogue and mutual understanding between these differing perspectives. With the rapid emergence of artificial intelligence in contemporary society, both economic systems face unique challenges, especially as issues like cronyism threaten to undermine their effectiveness. Additionally, the evolution of the populace itself has faced considerable challenges in recent decades, raising concerns about stagnation. This is particularly alarming for nations such as the United States, where a combination of irresponsible governance and growing complacency among citizens has contributed to a perceived decline in global status.

The notion of self-belief and the intrinsic trust in one's personal greatness is a critical element in this discourse. Many admirers of the United States, especially immigrants seeking a new life, are drawn to the country not just for the opportunities it offers, but for a reward system that prioritizes creativity, innovation, and productivity. This intrinsic value is fundamental; the term "opportunity" can sometimes obscure the very essence of capitalism that has historically fueled America's extraordinary success.

Spiritualism also plays a significant role in this complex discussion. From a spiritual perspective, the pervasive belief is that no physical borders or mental barriers were instituted on humanity by a higher power. Historically, access to the essentials for prosperity has been available regardless of the geographical confines of nations. While countries may be distinct in their borders and governance, there are no inherent limits to trade or education, enabling each nation to function as a self-contained economy. This arrangement provides its citizens with diverse career opportunities across various sectors, including healthcare, technology, education, and agriculture.

Taking the sobering context of poverty, such as that found in Somalia, it becomes evident that significant opportunities exist that could address challenges like child hunger — an issue that harbors immense potential for societal progress. For instance, the concept of "billion calories" suggests that if one were to equate the need for calorie-rich food with a monetary value, there would likely be a surge of entrepreneurial ventures aimed at establishing food-related businesses within the region. This analogy underscores the reality that while substantial opportunities may be present, the necessary systems for fully capitalizing upon these prospects are often lacking. Ultimately, opportunity can be analogized to potential energy; unless an effort is made to harness that potential, it remains dormant. The distinguishing factor that positioned America as a great nation is its unique capacity to provide the essential framework and support necessary to transform inherent potential into tangible success while rewarding individual efforts and contributions along the way.

Modern economies predominantly function as hybrid systems, seamlessly integrating both market-driven mechanisms and state-controlled elements. These mixed economies are designed to enhance overall efficiency and spur innovation through the principles of a competitive market. At the same time, they address critical issues related to social welfare and equity by employing a variety of government regulations and interventions. The objective of overarching is to create an economic environment that fosters individual dynamism while simultaneously upholding collective social responsibility. As these economies evolve, the intricate interplay between market forces and state intervention plays a crucial role in shaping their trajectories, often reflecting the shifting societal values and priorities of the times.

Historically, governance frameworks resembling the republican system established by the Roman Empire can also be traced back to the Sangam Tamil kingdoms, which existed from approximately 5000 BC to 300 AD in what is now modern-day India. This governance model was marked by local groups working within organized administrations, with the monarch serving primarily as a facilitator and mediator, rather than as an autocratic figure wielding absolute power. Although the United States has since transitioned into a form that many see as a diminished version of its original republican ideals, it continues to stand as a beacon of hope for individuals and societies around the world seeking to reclaim fundamental freedoms such as expression, individuality, and the right to trade.

In the context of what is known as the Social Triad system, capitalism can be viewed as representative of individualism, where personal achievement and self-reliance are paramount. In contrast, social democracy aligns more closely with collectivism, emphasizing the role of the community and government in ensuring equitable outcomes for all. This ideological dynamic creates a significant political divide that warrants examination and discussion. The concept of human evolution, particularly regarding societal development and consciousness, encourages constructive dialogue and mutual understanding between these differing perspectives. With the rapid emergence of artificial intelligence in contemporary society, both economic systems face unique challenges, especially as issues like cronyism threaten to undermine their effectiveness. Additionally, the evolution of the populace itself has faced considerable challenges in recent decades, raising concerns about stagnation. This is particularly alarming for nations such as the United States, where a combination of irresponsible governance and growing complacency among citizens has contributed to a perceived decline in global status.

The notion of self-belief and the intrinsic trust in one's personal greatness is a critical element in this discourse. Many admirers of the United States, especially immigrants seeking a new life, are drawn to the country not just for the opportunities it offers, but for a reward system that prioritizes creativity, innovation, and productivity. This intrinsic value is fundamental; the term "opportunity" can sometimes obscure the very essence of capitalism that has historically fueled America's extraordinary success.

Spiritualism also plays a significant role in this complex discussion. From a spiritual perspective, the pervasive belief is that no physical borders or mental barriers were instituted on humanity by a higher power. Historically, access to the essentials for prosperity has been available regardless of the geographical confines of nations. While countries may be distinct in their borders and governance, there are no inherent limits to trade or education, enabling each nation to function as a self-contained economy. This arrangement provides its citizens with diverse career opportunities across various sectors, including healthcare, technology, education, and agriculture.

Taking the sobering context of poverty, such as that found in Somalia, it becomes evident that significant opportunities exist that could address challenges like child hunger — an issue that harbors immense potential for societal progress. For instance, the concept of "billion calories" suggests that if one were to equate the need for calorie-rich food with a monetary value, there would likely be a surge of entrepreneurial ventures aimed at establishing food-related businesses within the region. This analogy underscores the reality that while substantial opportunities may be present, the necessary systems for fully capitalizing upon these prospects are often lacking. Ultimately, opportunity can be analogized to potential energy; unless an effort is made to harness that potential, it remains dormant. The distinguishing factor that positioned America as a great nation is its unique capacity to provide the essential framework and support necessary to transform inherent potential into tangible success while rewarding individual efforts and contributions along the way.

The current state of the nation invites critical examination regarding the underlying factors that have led to its present condition. The United States has increasingly rewarded individuals, businesses, and institutions based on potential rather than actual performance. This trend is exemplified by the substantial bailouts provided to major corporations, justified by their prospective job creation capabilities, with insufficient consideration given to their historical performance results. In this context, both large businesses and government entities have functioned as conduits for financial distribution from the Federal Reserve to the populace. This approach aligns with principles of state capitalism.

Moreover, America—along with numerous other nations—has adopted a practice of granting substantial salaries to individuals based solely on their academic qualifications rather than their actual productivity. It is essential to recognize that every human being is endowed with the potential for knowledge acquisition and skill development, yet we often impose limitations on ourselves. This critique is not intended to undermine formal education or the role of large businesses. Rather, the concern arises when these entities operate without the imperative of producing measurable results.

The economic vitality of a nation should not be gauged by the sheer volume of money in circulation but rather by its velocity and the intrinsic value of that currency. Additional factors influencing economic health include the effective circulation of money throughout society. In a robust economic framework, currency should retain substantial value and circulate efficiently across all societal strata—including blue-collar workers, white-collar professionals, service providers, manufacturing sectors, religious institutions, agricultural producers, and daily laborers. Challenges emerge when monetary resources are concentrated in one area, fail to circulate across diverse economic classes, or experience devaluation due to excessive printing.

To mitigate these challenges and foster a healthy economy, the adoption of geoeconomics becomes imperative. It is crucial to abandon the mindset of wealth redistribution. The government should not distribute wealth to individuals without a foundation of productive output. Instead, all citizens must leverage their potential to generate tangible economic results, utilizing their physical labor (blue-collar) or cognitive skills (white-collar), or a combination of both. This level of engagement will only occur if the government refrains from perpetuating unrealistic expectations of wealth distribution. While some degree of wealth redistribution is necessary for a thriving economy, it must stem from rewards for productive work and deliverables.

Wealth is a relative concept, often recognized by its ability to be exchanged for significant monetary value. Thus, affluent individuals consistently shift their wealth across different forms to realize its true market value. Regrettably, many citizens—both natives and immigrants—have become complacent with the distribution system, which does not derive from the productivity of human resources. Consequently, the sustainability of this system is jeopardized. The existing model of channeling resources from the upper echelons of society to broader distribution through financial institutions and large corporations has been entrenched for years. However, the funds generated at the upper tier frequently do not permeate to the lower strata. Individuals at the base of the economic pyramid are increasingly aware that this financial mechanism, initially instituted by Nixon, marginalizes them. Regardless of their willingness to work diligently, monetary circulation often remains confined to the upper half of the economic spectrum. It is essential for political, business, and social leaders to comprehend the true role of private capitalism within a healthy economic framework. While state capitalism possesses merits as a tool, it must be crafted and applied with a constructive ethos to foster healthy competition among nations, consistent with geoeconomic principles.

A hybrid economic model, as proposed by mayaNomics, is warranted to establish a balance between private and state capitalism. Nations should prioritize geoeconomic engagement over military might in their pursuit of geopolitical and geostrategic advantages. Such a balanced approach would ensure that the volume, velocity, and value of money align cohesively, allowing monetary flow to reach all sectors of society, rewarding individuals and enterprises for their productivity, dedication, and risk-taking endeavors. MayaNomics aims to provide a structured framework to facilitate this balance.

Economic statecraft refers to the use of economic means to achieve geopolitical and national objectives. In the past, it primarily involved traditional tools such as trade agreements, sanctions, tariffs, foreign aid, and investments. However, in the digitally transformed world, economic statecraft has evolved, incorporating a new set of tools and strategies facilitated by technological advancements in digital infrastructure, data, and blockchain technologies, among others. As the digital world continues to reshape global economies and political landscapes, economic statecraft now includes cyber capabilities, digital currencies, and the influence over data flows, online platforms, and tech ecosystems. This shift presents both new opportunities and challenges for nation-states in their efforts to maintain or enhance their global influence.

2.4 Impact of Digital Transformation on Economic Statecraft

The digital transformation has fundamentally altered the nature of global economic interactions by introducing new tools, platforms, and networks for statecraft. These changes are transforming both the instruments used in economic statecraft and the dynamics of economic power on the global stage.

New Tools for Economic Statecraft

- **Cyber Diplomacy and Cyber Sanctions:** States are increasingly using cyber tools in foreign policy, including cyberattacks, hacking, or cyber espionage to achieve political or economic goals. Cyber sanctions can be imposed on states or entities that engage in malicious digital activities, such as influencing elections or stealing intellectual property.

- **Digital Currencies and Central Bank Digital Currencies (CBDCs):** Countries are exploring or launching their own digital currencies, and CBDCs are gaining traction as a tool for economic sovereignty and international influence. Digital currencies could reshape the global monetary system and provide states with more control over cross-border transactions, especially by bypassing existing financial systems (such as SWIFT).

- **Data as an Economic Asset:** Data has become a valuable commodity in the digital age, and its control has significant geopolitical implications. States with the ability to regulate, control, or restrict data flows—through regulations such as GDPR in Europe or China's Cybersecurity Law—can use data governance as an instrument of economic statecraft.

- **Digital Trade Agreements**: As the global economy becomes more digitalized, traditional trade agreements now include provisions for cross-border data flows, e-commerce, and digital intellectual property protection. Countries that can shape these agreements to their benefit can gain competitive advantages in the global marketplace.

- **Influence Over Tech Ecosystems:** Major tech firms such as Google, Amazon, Facebook, and Tencent play pivotal roles in global digital commerce and communications. Countries can use their influence over these companies to pursue strategic goals, such as economic dominance, cultural export, or even restricting foreign tech companies to favor national champions.

- **Digital Infrastructure and Global Connectivity:** The global digital infrastructure, including the internet, cloud computing services, and global communication networks, is a crucial enabler of economic statecraft. Control over this infrastructure allows countries to:
  - Influence the flow of capital and information
  - Shape international norms and standards
  - Imposing digital tariffs or cybersecurity barriers to protect domestic industries

For example, China's Belt and Road Initiative (BRI) has increasingly involved the expansion of digital infrastructure, positioning China as a leader in global digital trade and connectivity. Similarly, countries like the US and EU are working on digital trade policies to reinforce their positions in the global digital economy.

2.5 Geopolitical Shift: Digital Divide and National Sovereignty

The digital transformation has led to new economic divides based on digital access and technological capabilities. These divides have significant implications for economic statecraft:

- Developed vs. Developing Nations: Countries with advanced technological infrastructure (such as the US, China, and the EU) have the advantage of controlling global digital networks, platforms, and data flows. In contrast, developing nations with limited access to digital resources may struggle to engage fully in the global digital economy.

- Digital Sovereignty: Nations are increasingly concerned with protecting their sovereignty in the digital realm. As such, countries are establishing policies to assert control over data, tech infrastructure, and digital platforms within their borders. For instance, countries like India and Russia have discussed data localization laws to ensure that data generated within the country stays under local control.

2.6 Techno-Nationalism and Strategic Competition

Digital technologies are also central to the growing techno-nationalism seen in global geopolitics:

- US-China Rivalry: The competition between the US and China for dominance in fields such as 5G technology, AI, and cloud computing has become a central axis of geopolitical tension. This rivalry is part of a broader economic statecraft, where each country is using technological advancements to gain global influence and economic power. For instance, China's Made in China 2025 initiative and AI policies aim to make China the global leader in key emerging technologies.

- Decoupling in Technology: Countries may seek to decouple from global digital systems that are perceived as too dependent on foreign technology. For example, the EU is working on initiatives to reduce dependence on US tech giants, and India is exploring alternatives to Chinese infrastructure providers like Huawei.

2.7 Role of Technology and Digital Platforms in Economic Statecraft

Digital Platforms as Global Economic Levers: Global digital platforms such as Facebook, Amazon, Google, and Alibaba play significant roles in global economic power dynamics. These platforms facilitate global trade, communication, and content distribution, and their control or influence can be an instrument of economic statecraft:

- Platform Sovereignty: Countries are becoming increasingly concerned with the power these platforms wield over their economies and societies. Governments are imposing stricter regulations on platform monopolies (e.g., antitrust investigations in the US and EU against big tech companies) to maintain control over their digital landscapes.
- Global E-commerce: E-commerce platforms have become essential to global trade. Governments use digital trade agreements to set the rules for international online commerce, from tariffs to data protection. Countries like Singapore and South Korea are leaders in negotiating digital trade agreements to secure their position in the growing global e-commerce market.

Digital Services as Statecraft Tools

- Social Media Diplomacy: Social media platforms have become tools for soft power, allowing governments to engage directly with foreign populations. The use of social media for propaganda or promoting political agendas is a form of economic statecraft in the digitally transformed world. For instance, Russia's use of social media for political influence or China's censorship and control over digital platforms exemplify the increasing role of digital media in shaping global politics.
- Tech Export Control: Countries may use restrictions on technology exports as part of economic statecraft. The US ban on Huawei and restrictions on chip sales to China reflect how nations use tech policy to curb geopolitical rivals' access to critical digital infrastructure.

Digital Asset Control: Cryptocurrencies, Blockchain, and Tokenization

The rise of digital assets such as cryptocurrencies, tokenization of funds, and blockchain technology has further transformed the landscape of economic statecraft:

- Cryptocurrencies and Economic Sovereignty: Governments are exploring Central Bank Digital Currencies (CBDCs) to maintain control over their monetary systems in a world increasingly dominated by decentralized digital currencies like Bitcoin and Ethereum. By issuing CBDCs, states can ensure monetary sovereignty, enable cross-border transactions, and monitor financial flows more effectively.
- Blockchain for Transparency and Trade: Blockchain technology is being explored for its ability to provide transparent and efficient trade systems, reducing friction and enhancing trust in transactions. Countries are adopting blockchain-based

solutions for everything from supply chain management to secure digital identities.

- Sanctions and Digital Asset Tracking: Digital currencies present challenges to traditional sanctions regimes, as cryptocurrencies can facilitate anonymous cross-border transactions. Governments are developing blockchain and cryptocurrency monitoring tools to track illicit financial flows and enforce economic statecraft strategies.

As digital technologies continue to evolve, so too will the tools and strategies of economic statecraft. Countries will need to adapt their policies to address the opportunities and challenges created by the digital revolution. This involves balancing digital sovereignty, technological competition, and global cooperation to maintain economic power in an increasingly digital and interconnected world. Governments will continue to use digital means of economic influence, from regulating data flows and implementing digital sanctions to fostering innovation in digital assets and blockchain technologies. The digital world offers new pathways for countries to assert economic dominance, but it also raises complex issues related to cybersecurity, digital inequality, and global governance.

Ultimately, economic statecraft in the digital age will require nations to be agile, technologically savvy, and collaborative, with a strong emphasis on maintaining control over critical digital assets while navigating the broader implications of a digitized global economy.

2.8 Mechanisms of Geoeconomic Cooperation

Geoeconomic cooperation encompasses the strategic employment of various economic tools, policies, and practices by nations or international entities to further geopolitical or strategic objectives. This concept highlights the intricate relationship between economic power and political or security aims, revealing how economic interactions can serve as vehicles for broader geopolitical influence. Below, we delve into several essential mechanisms of geoeconomic cooperation:

Trade Agreements and Economic Partnerships

Bilateral and Multilateral Trade Agreements: Nations engage in negotiations to establish trade agreements that can significantly alter their economic landscapes. By lowering tariffs, eliminating trade barriers, and harmonizing regulatory frameworks, these agreements incentivize increased trade and investment flows. Not only do these deals foster economic growth, but they also act as tools of geopolitical influence that strengthens political and economic ties among countries.

Examples:

The European Union (EU): A prime example of multilateral cooperation, the EU facilitates trade among member states promoting economic stability and political unity.

The United States-Mexico-Canada Agreement (USMCA): This agreement replaced NAFTA, reinforcing trade relationships and addressing modern trade challenges.

The Regional Comprehensive Economic Partnership (RCEP): This is the world's largest free trade agreement, linking 15 Asia-Pacific countries to enhance economic integration.

Free Trade Zones (FTZs): These designated areas allow goods to be landed, handled, manufactured, or reconfigured without the intervention of customs authorities, promoting cross-border investment and economic collaboration. By reducing or eliminating trade barriers and standardizing regulations among member countries, FTZs can enhance economic interdependence and facilitate political cooperation.

Economic Sanctions and Incentives

Sanctions as Geoeconomic Tools: Economic sanctions serve as punitive or coercive measures imposed by one state or group of states against another to compel a change in behavior, often related to issues of peace and security. These sanctions can take various forms, such as comprehensive trade embargoes, targeted financial restrictions, or sector-specific bans that focus on critical industries like energy or technology.

Examples:

The U.S. Sanctions on Iran: Targeting Iran's oil exports to exert pressure over its nuclear program.

EU Sanctions Against Russia: Enacted in response to the annexation of Crimea, which aimed to curtail financial and military access to the Russian economy.

Incentives and Economic Aid: Conversely, states may utilize economic incentives such as foreign aid, investment guarantees, and development assistance to achieve diplomatic objectives. These incentives often serve to stabilize regions, foster democratic reforms, or secure alliances.

Example: The Belt and Road Initiative (BRI), led by China, exemplifies this approach, where infrastructure loans and investments are extended to participating countries in return for political and economic alignment with Beijing's strategic interests.

Investment and Infrastructure Projects

Foreign Direct Investment (FDI): The strategic allocation of foreign direct investments is crucial in fostering economic integration and reinforcing bilateral relations. Nations may promote investment opportunities as a way to attract strategic partners, which, in turn, helps to cultivate mutual economic benefits and strengthen diplomatic ties. For Example: The China-Pakistan Economic Corridor

(CPEC) is a monumental infrastructure initiative that underscores China's intent to increase its geopolitical influence in South Asia while fostering economic growth in Pakistan.

Infrastructure Development Initiatives: Large-scale infrastructure projects, often spanning multiple countries or backed by international organizations, align diverse economic interests with overarching geopolitical objectives. These initiatives enhance regional connectivity, improve trade routes, and foster interdependence among countries. For Example: The Trans-European Transport Network (TEN-T) is a European Commission project aimed at creating an integrated transport network across EU member states, enhancing both economic integration and collaborative strategic efforts.

Currency and Financial Cooperation

Currency Alliances and Currency Swap Agreements: In an attempt to stabilize trade or reduce dependence on dominant global currencies, countries may form currency alliances or engage in swap agreements. Such arrangements enable nations to trade using their respective currencies, mitigating risks associated with currency fluctuations and fostering economic resilience. For Example, The China-Russia Currency Swap Agreement, which allows both nations to conduct trade using their own currencies rather than the U.S. dollar, thereby promoting greater financial autonomy.

Multilateral Development Banks: Various financial institutions like the World Bank, Asian Infrastructure Investment Bank (AIIB), and European Investment Bank (EIB) are pivotal in facilitating geoeconomic cooperation. These banks not only provide funding for development projects but also enable member countries to collaborate on initiatives that yield both economic dividends and geopolitical influence. For Example, the AIIB, spearheaded by China, serves as a platform for financing infrastructure projects, reinforcing China's position in Asia and extending its influence across the region.

Energy and Resource Cooperation

Energy Partnerships: Collaborative agreements between nations focused on the development, transportation, and consumption of energy resources can offer significant political leverage and enhance security. Such alliances are often essential for ensuring energy security, cooperation on mutually beneficial initiatives, and influencing regional stability. For Example, the Nord Stream 2 Pipeline Project, which links Germany directly to Russian gas supplies, underscores the intersection of energy trade and geopolitical strategy in Europe.

Resource Sharing and Agreements: In regions rich in natural resources but fraught with geopolitical tensions, nations may enter into agreements for the joint exploration and management of these shared resources. For Example, the ongoing disputes in the South China Sea over resource exploration highlight how countries engage in both cooperative agreements and contentious confrontations regarding oil and gas deposits, showcasing the complexities of geoeconomic interests.

Strategic Alliances and Economic Cooperation Forums

Regional Economic Integration Groups: Nations frequently establish regional organizations to bolster trade relations and political cooperation. These forums facilitate dialogue, negotiation, and collaboration on various economic issues, ultimately enhancing regional stability and prosperity. For Example, the Association of Southeast Asian Nations (ASEAN) promotes regional integration

and cooperation among its ten member countries, focusing on both economic growth and political collaboration.
The African Union (AU) aims to achieve continental unity and development, incorporating economic objectives within its political framework.

In conclusion, geoeconomic cooperation represents a vital intersection of economic strategies and geopolitical ambitions. Nations leverage a variety of economic mechanisms to forge strategic relationships, enhance political leverage, and navigate complex international environments, highlighting the critical role economics plays in global politics today.

I started to develop mayaNomics and parallelly started writing the book in 2022 with a target of publishing by 2023. But I started realizing that during the covid times most people started riding on the quantitative easing around the world and free distribution of money and availability of cheap capital. Even though Covid ended by 2023, the economy did not hit the recession as expected majorly due to two reasons. 1. A large pile of fiat money printed and distributed during the covid was still available in market 2. Most people who were supposed to get back to work had withdrawn from the labor market as they could still spend money and or the earning from the assets like the government bonds. That gave a pseudo job market boom which in turn kept the positive economic indicators alive for 2 more years. So, among other reasons I decided to publish mayaNomics by early 2025 when I believe surely a correction going to happen either through market crash or through a quick market uplift, although I believe it will be temporary and will be an indication of the future big crash the way the light burns big before it dies. Acceptance of any need for a new economic model happens through a painful adjustment process as everyone is busy during the boom cycle. It's the Economic spiraling down or spirally up make people nervous and be prepared or look for alternate models.

Chapter 4. Economy as a "State-Machine"

According to the Business Cycles theory all economic activity occurs over specific periods of time. The measurement of business cycles is always attributed to Westley Mitchell and Burns. According to them, Business Cycles are types of fluctuations found in the aggregate economic activity of nations. Such a cycle consists of expansions occurring at about the same time in many economic activities, followed by similar, general contractions. Hayek's work in Austrian economics emphasized the role of information in the economy and the use of prices to communicate information and coordinate economic activity. Hayek applied these insights to both the advancement of Mises' theory of business cycles and the debate over economic calculation under central planning. Hayek was awarded the Nobel Prize in 1974 for his work in monetary and business cycle theory. But business cycles theory can only be best understood and applied in the real-world scenarios with the fundamental understanding of the economy as a State Transition Machine.

MayaNomics fundamentally asserts that the economy operates as a state machine within a defined market or region, consistently evolving from one state to another. The rate of change (Delta) and its classification as either positive (+) or negative (-) cannot be accurately assessed through conventional tools like demand-supply analysis or the equilibrium principle. While these methods may provide some insights into the current state, they are inadequate for predicting future developments. The economy is best characterized as the rate of change of various factors and must be analyzed through time and state functions, specifically utilizing integral and differential calculus.

The intrinsic value of assets within the economic framework is minimally influenced by external factors, and this relationship is vital in determining their true value. The real intrinsic value must be discerned through the historical trends of past values and the influencing factors that shaped them. By pinpointing minute differential values (Delta) and applying these insights, we can effectively map and forecast future values through the integration of time factors from point X to point Y.

The key challenge as we progress beyond theoretical discussions is the difficulty of applying static analytical methods to markets that are fundamentally dynamic. In economic terms, "static" refers to a state of equilibrium that exists at a specific moment, while in the physical sciences, it describes a position of rest without any motion. Simon Kuznets highlights that economic statics studies relationships and processes under the assumption of stability and continuity. Notably, Professor Clark outlined five types of change that are often considered absent in economic statics: (a) population size, (b) capital supply, (c) production methods, (d) forms of business organization, and (e) human wants. Economic statistics capture the relationships between two economic variables at a single point in time, providing a snapshot of the economy that, while insightful, lacks a comprehensive view of its dynamic nature.

Conversely, "economic dynamics" focuses on understanding economic changes over time, emphasizing the critical role of temporal factors in shaping the relationships among economic variables. Professor Hicks aptly described economic dynamics as a framework where every quantity is time sensitive. Similarly, Ragnar Frisch conceptualized economic dynamics as a system comprising variables that evolve across different temporal intervals. As a result, this field examines how expected changes in one variable, such as price, can influence the demand and supply of a commodity. The extent of this influence is contingent on the changes occurring in related variables.

A pioneering figure in promoting institutional economics, Thorstein Veblen challenged the limitations of traditional static economic theory. He advocated for a broader perspective that recognizes individuals as shaped by evolving customs and institutions rather than merely as economic decision-makers. Veblen emphasized that the predominant motive in the American economic system was the pursuit of wealth accumulation, suggesting that profit often took precedence over the production of goods. Another influential thinker in the institutionalist school, John R. Commons, made significant contributions through his labor research, emphasizing the collective actions of various groups within the economy and their interplay within a continuously evolving framework of institutions and laws. Other notable economists associated with institutionalism include Rexford Tugwell, John M. Clark, and Wesley C. Mitchell.

While institutionalism may not be the leading school of thought in economics today, its impact endures, particularly among economists seeking to address economic issues through lenses that consider social and cultural dynamics. This comprehensive approach proves especially valuable when analyzing the challenges faced by developing countries, where the modernization of social institutions can be pivotal for industrial advancement.

While the state-machine can be theoretically applied to analyze an unlimited possibility of economic states and functions, the most applied arena is to model the business/investment cycles dating with respect to GDP and Recession. The purpose of this chapter is to give simplified introduction to most complex economic State-Machine. So, in the context of Business Cycle Dating, we limit ourselves to the two most important rules. 1. Calculus Rule and Two-Quarter Rule.

Calculus Rule: a simple method for locating turning points, and it might be called the calculus rule. This said that a peak in a series y_t occurs at time t if $\Delta y_t > 0$ and $\Delta y_{t+1} < 0$. The reason for the name is the result in calculus that identifies a maximum with a change in sign of the first derivative from being positive to negative. A trough (or local minimum) can be found using the outcomes $\Delta y_t < 0$ and $\Delta y_{t+1} > 0$. In this special case the states S_t are defined as $S_t = 1(\Delta y_t > 0)$, so that S_t depends only on contemporaneous information. This rule has been popular for defining turning points in economic activity when y_t is yearly data—see Cashin and McDermott (2002) and Neftci (1984)

The Two Quarters Rule for Dating Business Cycles: The rule that two quarters of negative growth initiates the transition from an expansion to a recession is often cited in the media. This rule is different from the other rules considered here because it requires knowledge of both the current state and the future evolution of y_t when defining what constitutes a local peak or trough. Extended symmetrically so that the beginning of an expansion is signaled when there are two successive quarters of growth produces the "two quarters rule":

$\wedge_t = 1(\Delta y_{t+1} < 0, \Delta y_{t+2} < 0)S_t$ ....(2.6)

$\vee_t = 1(\Delta y_{t+1} > 0, \Delta y_{t+2} > 0)(1 - S_t)$. ....(2.7)

In (2.6) we see that a peak occurs at time t ($\wedge t = 1$) if the growth rates at $t+1$ and $t+2$ are negative *and* $St = 1$, that is, an expansion held at time t. A similar interpretation can be given to (2.7). Although the NBER Dating Committee has been quite explicit that they do not define a recession in this way
one still sees it used in academic work, for example, Mazurek and Mielcová (2013, 185) who state that "A recession itself is defined by GDP declining for at least two consecutive quarters from the preceding period."

Although the economists try to give simplified measures of the health of the economy around Growth and Recession, mostly they are flawed due to the fact the predictive aggregates like GDP, CPI, PPI etc that are used in modeling them are highly manipulated and biased. Furthermore, when it comes to the global scale, the economy operates as a state machine that triggers and influences other state machines. Economic changes affecting one set of factors in a market inevitably impact different factors in another market. Therefore, without the creation and rigorous analysis of a comprehensive integral state machine, accurate economic predictions are unachievable. Although constructing such a model presents a significant challenge, advancements in deep tech AI, distributed computing, and digital asset technologies herald a promising future for developing robust economic models, provided the process is executed correctly.

4.1 Creative Destruction and Market Continuum

Economic State Machine and the transition of market elements (companies, assets, commodities, products, services, credit instruments, equities, etc.) cannot be fully formulated without the art and science of creative destruction. According to Joseph Schumpeter, Creative destruction is the process by which new products and processes replace outdated ones, leading to the destruction of existing economic structures. This destruction paves the way for new structures to emerge, which can create long-term economic growth and progress. This gets even more amplified with the new innovations in business and technology guided by digital transformation. So, to be successful in the digitally transformed world, one must have a deeper understanding of the factors of the past, present and future, clearly connected through state machine models and have the mechanism to build, protect and grow the assets within the economic systems.

Another major factor one must keep in mind is, how much role Innovation plays in the building the State-Machine and transformations. Many would tend to believe that innovation can create magical transformations. But in the economic state machine, innovation alone fails to produce enough profit or automatic value generation or capital to move the economy to another state. While most Innovation provides the tools and mechanisms for disruption of existing markets and destruction of older structures and components, it does not guarantee creative destruction, meaning, the innovation may simply have a negative impact rather than positive. As we have seen before, the economy is interconnected with state machines involving multiple industries and multiple markets having both forward feed and backward feeding to one another. Still each one of them is influenced by their own things, factors and the driving forces. So, as with any control system, the economic state machine system must carefully choose and introduce innovative technologies taking into consideration the processes, inputs, controls, feedback, feedforward and other variables that might have adverse effect on it. Like how doctors are doomed to fail if he/she approaches the human body without having to surrender to the Principle of Evolution, by clearly understanding he/she is not the creator but only a doctor to cure, every Economist should understand the Architecture of the Market Existence. The market ecosystem is the extension of the human imagination. It's an extension of multiple human thoughts coming together. That means the Market Pre-Existed in abstraction. The thoughts are tied to DNA. And DNA has the roots where everyone is Wired-together. With more and more people become Part of the market, new dynamics are getting added with Market as a Continuum. Economy is at the mercy of market behavior and market behavior is at the mercy of human psychology and human psychology is deeply influenced by the Brain-DNA-Neural systems trifactor. That's why it is so important to model the market cycle based on Psychology.

4.2 Market Cycle

One of the most referenced Market cycle diagrams was created by Wallstreet Cheat Sheet. The cheat sheet explains the market cycle and conditions in Eight phases: 1) Disbelief, 2) Hope 3) Optimism and belief, 4) Total Euphoria, 5) Complacency, 6) Anxiety & Panic, 7) Capitulation/Anger/Depression and 8) Disbelief once again. The Wall Street Cheat Sheet serves as a valuable framework for understanding market psychology. While each situation may present unique characteristics, the emotional factors that influence traders tend to remain stable across diverse markets and timeframes. A fundamental principle to recognize is that emotions significantly impact buying and selling decisions, ultimately driving price movements. This principle is essential for comprehending market dynamics driven by the state transitions.

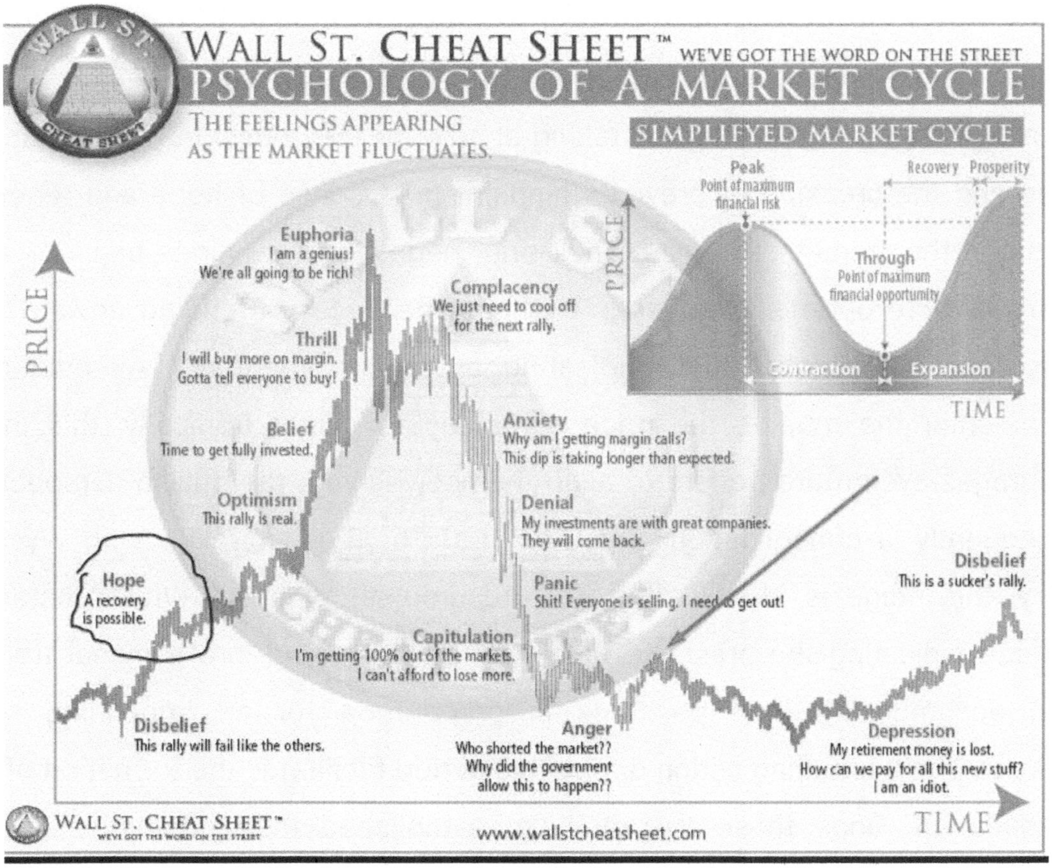

Figure 1

Phase 1, Disbelief: The initiation of every new trend is often accompanied by a prevailing atmosphere of skepticism and doubt. Traders who have previously incurred substantial losses may exhibit reluctance to acknowledge the emergence of a new trend. They frequently convince themselves with statements such as, "I have encountered this before," or "It is improbable that I will fall for this again." This phenomenon is not uncommon. Many novice traders struggle to accept the possibility that a new trend may be developing. In an effort to cope with the potential for upward market movement, they tend to dismiss the situation, trivializing the trend by asserting, "It is not possible," which may protect them from potential disappointment. However, this mindset simultaneously hinders their ability to engage with the trend, representing a significant oversight.

Phase 2, Hope: During the second phase, prices begin to rise further. At this juncture, some previously disenchanted traders start to reconsider the notion that a new trend may, in fact, be taking shape. As they observe the increase in prices and the breaking of previous highs, a faint sense of hope and renewed interest in the markets emerges. Their prior negative perceptions begin to shift toward a more optimistic outlook: "Perhaps the price is trending upward?" or "Observe, a new higher high—indicating upward momentum." As additional buyers enter the market, the price continues to climb. Ironically, this influx encourages even more traders to align themselves with the bullish perspective. Subsequently, a consolidation phase occurs. For those familiar with Wyckoff theory, this stage is identified as the Accumulation phase. With substantial evidence indicating the presence of a new upward trend, professional traders begin accumulating long positions in preparation for an impending price breakout. The fluctuating action during this period facilitates the formation of the consolidation. Once these traders have established their positions, a price breakout occurs, advancing us to phase 3.

Phase 3, Optimism and Belief: At this stage, market activity becomes increasingly dynamic. Following the consolidation, prices surge significantly. This upward movement is remarkable to observe. Traders, previously filled with hope, evolve into staunch optimists, further invigorating the upward trend and attracting additional buyers—both retail and professional traders who have missed the earlier consolidation—eager to capitalize on the nascent trend. This progression leads us into phase 4.

Phase 4, Total Euphoria: In this final phase, often characterized as the Fear of Missing Out (FOMO) phase, retail traders who were previously hesitant finally succumb to the temptation of joining the long side of the upward trend. Their decision to enter at this moment stems primarily from FOMO; they are apprehensive about missing potential gains. The rapid price increase convinces them that a new uptrend is indeed underway. Their negative experiences associated with prior trends diminish, supplanted by euphoric aspirations for success. Consequently, they hasten to enter the market, anticipating a profitable journey and potential financial rewards. However, it is important to note that a shift in the price trajectory may be imminent.

Phase 5, Complacency: After an initial period marked by optimism, complacency may begin to manifest among traders. In the event of a price decline, certain traders may respond by increasing their long positions, perceiving the decrease as a buying opportunity in anticipation of a trend reversal. This viewpoint is prevalent, as many participants in the market believe that prices will recover and continue their upward trajectory.

Phase 6, Anxiety and Panic: After a temporary rebound, should prices decline sharply, numerous traders may undergo a phase of panic. This sudden drop can signal a possible conclusion to the prevailing uptrend, particularly for those who have entered positions later in the cycle and are now confronted with losses. The circumstances may lead to the activation of stop-loss orders and margin calls, prompting a swift exit from positions to mitigate losses. Unfortunately, this often results in liquidation at prices lower than the initial purchase point. The collective actions of many traders exiting their positions, in conjunction with some initiating short positions, can exacerbate the downtrend within the market.

Phase 7, Capitulation, Anger, and Depression: As the market trend unexpectedly shifts, many traders may express confusion regarding the change in trajectory. Over time, traders may capitulate, coming to terms with the downtrend and responding to the rapid price decline. Emotional reactions may encompass frustration and disappointment, as individuals process their prior positions and overall performance. Some may opt to retain their investments, harboring hopes for a market recovery.

Phase 8, Disbelief (Cycle Repeats): As the market begins to stabilize following a period of consolidation, prices may initiate an upward trend once more. Despite this upward movement, many traders, still recalling the recent downturn, may approach this rise with caution, often interpreting it as a potential false rally. The market reveals a cyclical pattern wherein emotions significantly impact traders' decision-making processes. Emotional states profoundly influence the buying and selling behaviors of traders, leading to price oscillations. This, in turn, alters traders' perceptions of the market, potentially impacting their future decision-making regarding buying and selling, thereby perpetuating price fluctuations. This cyclical nature encapsulates the market's functioning as interconnected feedback loops.

Chapter 5. Social Conscience, Collectivism and Individualism

In this chapter, we are going to see perspective about individualism and about collectivism that has been spinning and growing around the human social conscience evolution. In the last 15 to 20 years of politics in the USA, I have been witnessing the three sides of the political spectrum, the liberal side, the conservative side, and the libertarian on the right side (I belong to this) having a deep divide and fights regarding what is the best. Though it seems to be a biparty system in the USA when it comes to election machinery, the actual spectrum has Six segments – Extreme Right, Right Wing, Right to Center, Center to Left, Left wing and Extreme Left. The Libertarians are the third significant population but mostly Right to Center. Pretty much across the world one can see such kind of divide in various forms. When it comes to ideology, the major divides that make both sides are Collectivism and Individualism and differ in their intensity of the spread based on the compromises in Social, Economic and Political interests. The republic leaning people are supposedly the individual liberty-loving people while the democrat leaning people stand for collectivism and government control. In a republic, an individual is more powerful than a collective group of people including the governments; BUT on the other hand, democracy works this way where at least in the liberal democratic group in America a group is more powerful than an individual right. It is obvious to me and most of you as well, a group cannot be powerful than an individual but they look at from a different perspective as they say that they are protecting the interest of an individual a less powerful individual by making them part of a bigger community to increase their power so that they can go and fight with the other side.

Basically, we are going to make one small to fight a big bully by making his powerful by providing the support of a larger group by lending more hands to fight, i.e. Collectivism. So, the small guy can go to a group of people and attach himself to the majority or 51 percent of the people who can come together to force something upon the big guy who belongs to the 49 percent. Essentially, they claim to collectively increase the power of an individual. That's the way democratic liberalism defines and defends its ideology.

In the current America (and all over the world), these social democratic liberals are doing a fundamental mistake creating a crony liberalism and crony socialism as the special interest groups utilize this opportunity to create a phony collectivism while silently playing capitalism under the carpet. Such private crony capitalists use collectivism to their advantage by bringing in a lot of people under them to make a majority force upon things against the other side.

Most governments around the world do not encourage individualism because they want to force things on their citizens. No corporation is going to like consumers who are powerful enough to stand up and fight them. They wanted consumers who simply follow and become consuming things. They don't like contractors and independent consultants because they need more confirming and tax paying workers. They don't like small businesses because small businesses will be very independent, very individual, they can put terms with the big guys so they would like to trash the small businesses. Everything that is happening around the world right now will indicate clearly a major shift towards individualism as the generations of people learnt the conspiracy of special interest in the name of collectivism and they take back control. But we have seen this wave shifting in the past as well probably every 100 years in the last 600 years ever since the world started liberating themselves from the grips of Kingdoms and colonizers either through republics or through democracy.

There were two factors that were throwing the balance in favor of collectivism verses individualism, they are: 1. Individuals work against each other many times in the race of individual social, economic and political elevation and it seems too difficult for them to come together for common cause or goal. This is there mayaNomics comes as a framework of balance through the introduction of the system of consensus and common minimum agenda etc. for two or more individuals to come together for a specific cause or benefit under a minimum **"Cause Level Agreement"**

Though collectivism might have won the initial argument of fighting powerful people who need the collective power of individuals, it fails to hold water when the other side is a collective force. Now it comes to the matter of which collective force is better than the other. And of course, the group that has strong individuals as their members will win the fight. But what happens to the collective group of good people who have a good cause, right argument, on their side failed and outsmarted by the other group just because fewer members of that group are way smarter, abled and skilled? This brings back the point, which is better, Collectivism or Individualism. As I had mentioned in the second chapter, this infight between collectivism and individualism continues with no side really wins at any given time. That's because, it's not the time factor that judges the superiority, it is the Cause and the situation driven by multiple factors that determines the superiority of the system at that given point for that cause. So, it is essential to have a blended system of these two evolutionary social systems along with human evolution. This argument shall become more and more clear to the reader as we close into defining the mayaNomics framework in the later chapters.

It's time to create unique frameworks like mayaNomics as a model of engagement for people of liberty and people of collectivity on a common platform with Cause level Agreements, Common minimum Agenda, forming consortium styled entities that will facilitate the consensus mechanisms of engagement between the participating individuals and groups. Institutions that give all the power that an individual requires still bring them together through consensus. In the social democratic system one cookie cutter rule applicable to all the people in the system will leave a lot of people unrepresented or underrepresented i.e. the majority's (say 51%) view, the cookie cutter rule will be forced upon the remaining 49 percent.

But in the consortium style society everything shall be driven by cause-level agreement, consensus-based rules. The governance model under discussion operates within a complex framework that diverges from a purely rule-based consensus mechanism, instead placing significant emphasis on the vital importance of collectivism. This suggests that while individuals may initially come together independently, there is strong encouragement for them to collaborate and build a consensus on critical issues that affect the collective. In some instances, they might reach a unified decision on a particular matter, while in others, their shared perspective may evolve dramatically over time. Ideally, this system is designed to function synergistically through consensus; nevertheless, there exists a pronounced deficiency in achieving this ideal state. This lack of effective consensus-building significantly hampers their ability to compete against larger, more entrenched entities that often engage in practices associated with cronyism, such as the well-known tech giants Google and Facebook.

The current legal framework, particularly as it relates to the lawsuit system, does provide individuals with a platform to express their grievances. Yet, a more pressing need has emerged for robust collective actions, especially in the form of class action lawsuits. These allow numerous individuals to join forces and bring forward their collective rights and shared concerns. A societal framework that encourages and nurtures such unity is essential; harnessing the collective strength of society can yield far greater influence and outcomes than individuals acting alone. This foundational concept emphasizes the need for a society that harmoniously balances individualistic pursuits with collectivist efforts; it is imperative to preserve individualism while simultaneously cultivating an atmosphere where collaboration and consensus among individuals are both valued and encouraged.

Examining the contrasts between collectivism and individualism reveals that collectivism fosters an environment where individuals are motivated to unite in the pursuit of common goals or needs. In contrast, within an individualistic framework, there may not always be a shared necessity that binds people together, leading to the challenge of effectively rallying individuals under a unified collective banner. My mentor, Zig Ziglar, astutely pointed out that the idea of a self-made person is fundamentally flawed. From the very moment you awaken—whether you're brushing your teeth, using the restroom, choosing your outfit, or commuting to your workplace, you are benefitted by the contributions and efforts of others in society. The undeniable truth is that no one navigates through life entirely alone; a vast network of individuals supports you in various ways throughout your daily experiences.

While some may adamantly maintain that their achievements are solely the result of their own endeavors, this perspective often overlooks the multitude of contributions from others that facilitate individual success. For instance, the government frequently claims credit for providing essential infrastructure, such as roads that enable businesses to flourish; however, we do not fully subscribe to that extreme view. Nevertheless, we must acknowledge a crucial kernel of truth in the assertion that no one can claim to achieve success in complete isolation. In our daily lives, we are surrounded by countless individuals who play significant roles—both overtly and subtly—in our personal and professional advancements.

Within an individualistic paradigm, it is perfectly valid for individuals to assert their independence and demonstrate their capability to succeed without external assistance, and this autonomy must be respected. However, in a societal structure—such as the concept proposed by Mensch Force—we deliberately choose not to impose rigid, inflexible rules. Our members are given the freedom to operate independently of the collective framework when they choose. We strongly encourage them to pursue their individual aspirations while simultaneously fostering the belief that collaborative efforts can lead to greater achievements and opportunities for all involved.

To further illustrate this principle, let's consider the scenario of a solo consultant seeking business insurance. As an independent practitioner, this consultant may find themselves facing significantly higher insurance premiums due to their limited bargaining power when approaching insurance providers individually. However, when consultants unite as a collective group, they can leverage their combined strength to negotiate more favorable rates and terms with insurance companies. In this case, the collective essence of the organization yields tangible benefits to individuals that often remain inaccessible if they were to operate in isolation.

Though the actual negotiations with insurance companies occur on a one-on-one basis, the foundational strength and advantages derive from the consultants' affiliation with a collective entity. This situation exemplifies the effectiveness of a consensus mechanism in action. Unlike traditional democratic systems where rules may be dictated by a small group of corporate leaders, within this model, all consultants are active participants in the consensus-building process. This inclusive approach ultimately leads to more favorable outcomes for every participant involved, showcasing the potential benefits of harnessing both individual talents and collective action in navigating the complexities of modern society.

The management of responsibility within a decentralized structure raises important questions about accountability and individual performance. In such systems, individuals operate independently, which can lead to instances where one might express that their efforts were insufficient. This perceived vulnerability can impact on the overall framework. A fundamental aspect of this discussion is the recognition that individuals maintain their uniqueness regardless of the environment—be it corporate or societal. Often, personal freedoms can be limited by external forces, and this understanding underscores the persistence of individuality, even in collaborative settings.

In corporate environments, employees do not amalgamate into a singular entity. For instance, the distinct roles of consultants and their clients illustrate this separation. The dynamic between managers and team members also reflects this individuality, where each role retains its own identity within a project. Thus, project delivery effectiveness does not rely solely on a top-down hierarchical command. Rather, it is influenced by individual contributions beyond the basic requirements. True value creation occurs when individuals exercise discretionary effort. In contrast, if individuals feel compelled to act, the outcomes may not reflect adequate performance levels. Research indicates that a significant percentage of IT projects exceed their budgets, with many ultimately failing. Various studies report failure rates as high as 80% for specific technological initiatives.

The concept of "delivery" is often equated with the expenditure of funds, where resources are used with minimal added value. Addressing the core question of value delivery when empowering individuals requires exploration of underlying principles. In many corporate structures, individual liberties can be restricted through the enforcement of management rules and guidelines. Employees may face financial repercussions for underperformance, which can create a motivating atmosphere based on the fear of loss. In contrast, the absence of such threats in a decentralized framework can foster a different approach. Individuals are encouraged to leverage their skills for tangible results without the burden of job insecurity.

The principle of profit-sharing is also emphasized in decentralized models. By reducing unnecessary intermediaries in both organizational and project contexts, individuals may benefit significantly from their contributions. Each consultant can become a stakeholder in their projects, participating in creating smart contracts with the organization. This structure is designed to provide opportunities for individuals to gain from wise investments of their time. Today, companies are undergoing a profound transformation in their operational ecosystems, which allows any business—regardless of size or industry—to evolve into an ecosystem-centric entity in a significantly reduced timeframe. This shift has ignited what we refer to as exponential growth, a phenomenon that is becoming increasingly achievable for organizations that embrace innovative strategies and adapt to changing market dynamics.

Reflecting on the past two decades, the idea of achieving exponential growth often appeared elusive to many organizations. While a select few demonstrated the courage and vision to adopt this ambitious mindset, the majority clung to traditional, incremental growth strategies that prioritized gradual improvements over bold innovation. It is critical to understand that those who stubbornly adhere to these conventional approaches face a heightened risk of failure as we progress further into 2025 and beyond. The landscape of business and the geoeconomic ecosystem has fundamentally changed due to rapid technological advancements, shifting consumer preferences, and increased competition. Consequently, an organization or nation's strategic focus must prioritize pathways to achieve exponential growth. Building a robust ecosystem, whether for an enterprise or a larger national framework—is not just advantageous; it is essential for survival and prosperity. The role of the ecosystem is particularly significant; it not only facilitates substantial growth but also plays a vital part in ensuring that the entities and institutions within a specific economic zone can thrive in an increasingly competitive market. Therefore, the primary strategic focus for organizations should be on transforming every entity into an ecosystem-oriented establishment. This transformation entails diversifying across various sectors, fostering innovation, and deliberately crafting opportunities that encourage the emergence of exponential growth.

To deepen our understanding of this concept, we must recognize that the definition of value is being increasingly reframed through the lens of the participant's experiential journey within the ecosystem. In today's marketplace, consumers and buyers are highly discerning and demand more from the organizations they engage with. If a business does not align its services and offerings with the overarching objective of driving ecosystem growth, those products and services risk being perceived as outdated and irrelevant. From a business perspective, it would be unwise for clients to invest premium prices in offerings that do not deliver tangible value. Conversely, when an organization can position itself as an incremental value producer, articulating clearly and effectively how it will contribute meaningfully to both the ecosystem as a whole and the pursuit of exponential growth—clients are much more likely to be willing to invest heavily in those services. This dynamic is equally applicable at the national and global levels, where geoeconomic strategies play a crucial role in shaping and leveraging economic relationships and opportunities in a rapidly changing world. In conclusion, the imperative for organizations and nations alike is clear: an active commitment to fostering an ecosystem-centered approach is vital for enabling exponential growth. As we navigate the complexities of modern business environments, only those who adapt, innovate, and build collaborative ecosystems will thrive in the face of future challenges.

Human Capital Crisis and AI adoption

Throughout history, free trade was fueled by innovations and those innovations are driven by Free Mind. Liberation of mind Needs social, individual and economic systems liberation. The dignity of an individual should be at the highest point so as the Self Respect. Political liberty is the single most important thing to the other liberties, but people in power or aspiring to be in power do not like and tend to take away freedom and liberty. Since even a dictator needs People's vote to be in power, most politicians around the world indulge in the act of making the citizens consumers of government freebies.

AI as a division of Labor Manager.

"Perform White collar Job the Blue-collar Way - or you don't deserve any $ollar"

There are two fundamental units of life: 1. Love and 2. Work. They represent the two sides of the same coin. It's not just humans; every living being around us teaches us the importance of these two elements. Human society cannot thrive without the act of giving and receiving love and work.

The framework of karma Yoga, the guiding principle I advocate and embody, explains the why, how, and what work. To be a karma Yogi, one must focus on work with a clear goal—an aim to achieve. This goal should yield something beneficial to society, while also allowing you to capitalize on it. As my mentor Zig Ziglar said, "If you are something to somebody, you are somebody." Recognizing that you are designed for success in life, it is essential to adopt the necessary skills, tools, and techniques to pursue such goals. You can roam freely with aspirations, but you cannot simply wander through life without any objectives. Choosing that path means declaring that you are not part of society and, therefore, do not deserve to reap its benefits.

I often share the story of Yogi with my listeners. In an Ashram, the Yogi lived and taught classes about life and spiritualism. He also maintained a small garden, where he worked diligently every day. His protégés always encouraged him to toil hard in the garden, but he resisted. One day, the protégés took matters into their own hands and hid all the tools he used for gardening. As usual, the ashram staff served food to Yogi. When the protégés returned later to check on him, they were shocked to find that he had not eaten and was deep in meditation. After some time, they decided to interrupt the meditation, as it was getting late and nearly time for dinner. They asked the Yogi why he had not eaten. With tears in his eyes, he replied, "Students, I don't deserve this food because I did not contribute anything today to this world." He continued, "I am upset because I failed as a teacher today. After all this time as my protégés, you haven't grasped the fundamentals of life. You cannot take without having the heart and labor to give." This story encapsulates the essence of karma Yoga and the principles by which we should all live.

As society has evolved over time—with advancements in technology, business, and education—many people have shifted from physical work to mental work, transitioning from blue-collar to white-collar jobs. However, economic upturns across various regions globally often do not lead to significant changes in the mindsets of white-collar employees in corporations. This workforce, primarily made up of professionals in managerial, administrative, and technical roles, tends to focus on superficial aspects of their work environment, such as office aesthetics, social status, or casual dress codes—elements that do not add substantial value to their professions.

For many individuals, the job search begins on a challenging note, clouded by societal and familial sarcasm that erodes their confidence, compounded by unnecessary competition and comparisons with peers. Once these individuals secure a position, they often encounter a disheartening mindset shift, adopting a negative outlook as if it were a predetermined part of their job search experience. It's essential to understand that climbing the corporate ladder requires adhering to a series of specific steps and milestones. Attempting to circumvent these necessary steps through office politics—such as networking solely for self-advancement, engaging in egocentric conflicts with colleagues, or wasting precious work hours scrolling through social media—only detracts from genuine progress. Instead, it's vital to remember the fundamental meaning of "employment," which, regardless of context, translates to "work." Merriam-Webster defines work as "the exertion of energy by natural phenomena; the outcome of such exertion; the transference of energy that occurs through the motion of the point where force is applied, calculated by multiplying force by displacement along the line of action." This definition reflects the principles of natural physics that we learn from a young age.

Let's turn our attention to the blue-collar workforce within various corporations. Over the years, straightforward and concrete metrics have been established to gauge job performance in these roles. For example, a blue-collar worker's efficiency can be quantitatively measured by how well they transport an object from one location to another or how effectively they assemble two components together. Consider a common scenario, if a process worker were to leave their designated area to log into a social media platform for a casual chat, there could be significant repercussions. A responsible operations officer would prefer to avoid worrying about such unprofessional conduct during work hours. If such behavior were to occur, the likely immediate response would be to swiftly dismiss the employee for their irresponsibility.

Now, let's broaden this discussion. Imagine the implications if a pizza delivery person took hours to arrive because they prioritized chatting with friends instead of fulfilling their delivery duties. Similarly, consider a truck driver who halted their journey to watch YouTube videos while stranded on the road. The key point to emphasize here is the disparity in performance metrics between blue-collar and white-collar workers. If the blue-collar workforce is held to stringent accountability measures, why do we often allow white-collar workers to operate under less scrutiny? Why do we tolerate unproductive behavior and lackluster outcomes from those in white-collar roles, especially when they are compensated five times more than their blue-collar counterparts?

Let me clarify that I do not advocate for socialism; I firmly align myself with capitalist and free market principles as a Libertarian. My primary focus is on highlighting the issue of irresponsible work ethics among professionals. At its core, work should represent productivity and yield positive results, whether through physical labor (as seen in blue-collar roles) or intellectual contributions (expected of white-collar jobs). While I recognize that the human mind is an asset requiring various skills, I cannot help but question whether white-collar workers are genuinely producing sufficient results to justify their elevated salaries.

My conclusion is stark and compelling: "No." Based on my view of rewarding work—essentially the principle of "work harder, earn more"—many white-collar workers fall short of earning even half of what they are compensated for. This shortfall ultimately places additional responsibilities on their blue-collar counterparts, which is inherently unjust. It is crucial for white-collar workers to undertake a candid self-assessment of their contributions to their organizations. My unequivocal message to this demographic is clear: cease irresponsible behaviors, produce tangible results, and abandon any illusion of self-satisfaction derived from underperformance. Otherwise, you may face significant consequences that will adversely affect your career trajectory. The essence of this message cannot be overstated: "Dear white-collar workers, if you wish to maintain substantial salaries and secure job stability, it is high time you pull up your socks and commit to delivering the results that your compensation demands."

"Fair Share is not always Fair" without contributing for it.

<u>Why is Equality a Myth?</u> Throughout history, the quest for genuine equality within societies has proven to be a multifaceted and often elusive pursuit. Various forms of evidence suggest that even in contexts where equality seems to exist, it often comes at a significant price, affecting individual freedoms and impeding overall human development. One of the earliest illustrations of this can be traced back to the Stone Age, a time when early humans displayed a remarkable range of skills that influenced their contributions to their communities.

For instance, some individuals emerged as exceptional hunters, developing advanced tools and weapons that allowed them to excel in procuring food. Others specialized in different areas, dedicating their efforts to creating implements that facilitated the gathering and preparation of food. This diversity in contributions stemmed from a variety of factors, including each person's unique set of skills, knowledge, and life experiences. Consequently, these differences led to varying levels of recognition, remuneration, and status within the group, illustrating that absolute equality is an unrealistic goal in human societies.

In any given society, the respect and values assigned to individuals often hinge on their ethical, moral, and responsible contributions to the community. This is further complicated by the fact that, while some individuals may contribute less than their peers in certain areas, whether it be through physical labor or intellectual input, they might still provide significant value through their avoidance of harmful actions, such as theft, violence, or deceit. This distinction clarifies that the concept of equality may be more of an abstract theoretical ideal rather than a tangible reality capable of being uniformly applied across different contexts. The notion of a "fair share" can often be misleading, fraught with misconceptions and varying interpretations among individuals. At its core, sharing is an act motivated by generosity and should ideally remain a discretionary choice rather than a mandatory obligation imposed on people. While acts of kindness and generosity are generally viewed positively in society, the decision to withhold such actions should not carry a stigma or be viewed as a moral failing. The idea of fairness is inherently subjective, influenced by cultural, social, and individual contexts, thereby complicating the establishment of a standardized definition that could apply universally.

Moreover, societal narratives frequently oversimplify the roles of individuals within the economic ecosystem, often casting those who invest as villains and those who work as heroes. Individuals who possess confidence in their own skills and talents commonly choose to offer their labor and services to support others' endeavors. At the same time, those who possess capital—whether accumulated through savings, investments, or inheritance—play a crucial role in fostering innovation by financially supporting the talents and initiatives of skilled individuals.

When individuals possess both talent and capital, they often become entrepreneurs, skillfully blending their abilities to create new products, services, and businesses that can lead to substantial advancements in society. This synergy can drive economic growth and foster an environment in which new ideas flourish. Each role within this framework, whether it involves hard work, investment, or creative innovation, holds intrinsic value and is vital for the progress and development of society. In conclusion, the pursuit of equality, while noble in intent, often overlooks the complexities of human nature and societal structures. Recognizing the varied contributions of individuals and the intricate web of relationships that bind society together allows for a more nuanced understanding of what it means to promote fairness and equity, rather than striving for an unattainable ideal of equality.

The journey of building wealth is deeply rooted in a core principle: production must precede consumption. Those who successfully accumulate wealth possess a keen understanding of this truth. They recognize the vital importance of reinvesting their financial gains into new ventures or innovative products, thus initiating a sustainable cycle of growth that not only enriches their own lives but also uplifts the broader community. Each transaction in this complex web of economic activity involves participants who emerge as winners or losers. However, viewing these exchanges solely through the lens of equality risks obscuring the intricate reality of individual agency and the larger economic framework at play. Such a limited perspective may lead to significant misunderstandings regarding the unique contributions each participant makes to the energetic pulse of the economy.

Human nature reveals its own duality, embodied in a constant interplay between "laziness" and "activeness." This intrinsic conflict can result in a lack of drive for some individuals, while for others, it ignites an unyielding pursuit of their ambitions. When society inadvertently rewards complacency, it can stifle the determination and diligence of those who consistently strive to make meaningful contributions. Therefore, it becomes imperative to acknowledge the efforts of individuals who demonstrate exceptional resolve—through intellectual engagement, skill cultivation, or sheer hard work—by offering them due recognition, incentives, and rewards. Such acknowledgment is essential for nurturing an environment that values the impact of their labor on society.

The quest for stability versus prosperity reveals a profound personal choice, one that varies greatly from individual to individual. Stability arises when people feel they have reached a contented point in their lives, where further growth seems unnecessary or even daunting, or when they consciously decide against pursuing additional advancement. Opting for the path of stability often signifies a profound acceptance of one's current reality, allowing individuals to focus on their personal journeys while acknowledging the ambitious pursuits of others striving for greater prosperity. This approach fosters an atmosphere of respect and understanding, enabling diverse ambitions to thrive within society. Such acceptance not only nurtures personal growth but also cultivates a community where various paths and aspirations can intertwine harmoniously.

Exploring the intricate dynamics of ecological systems, we uncover the complex lives of various animals and insects, each playing distinct roles within their habitats. Among these roles, the position of the hunter shines notably. Hunters embark on perilous journeys, constantly navigating an array of risks and adversities all in the unyielding quest for sustenance for themselves and their communities. They devote immense amounts of time and energy to these endeavors, often venturing far from the comfort and safety of their homes in search of prey. It is vital to recognize that drawing comparisons between the efforts of hunters and those of individuals who remain behind—typically caring for their young or maintaining their nests—can be intrinsically unfair. Hunters, through their courageous and often hazardous undertakings, create a stronger claim to the spoils resulting from their hard-earned labor. While the act of sharing these rewards is ultimately a matter of personal choice, it should not be misconstrued as a societal obligation.

It is essential to understand that the primary motivation for hunters goes beyond simple survival instincts. It includes a deep-rooted desire for the significant rewards that often come with their efforts—rewards typically greater than what non-hunters gain from their contributions. This understanding encourages us to shift our focus from past achievements to a future-oriented perspective, highlighting the importance of upcoming hunting endeavors. If a hunter decides to stop their pursuits for any reason, it's important to recognize that the idea of a fair share becomes less relevant; without active participation in hunting, there is no bounty to distribute. In this sense, the complex relationships and roles within ecological communities reflect the intricacies of human interactions within our economic systems, emphasizing the significant impact of individual contributions and the delicate balance between cooperation and competition.

"Larger Trees Should Care for Small Mushrooms"

As mentioned before, the nature of life is inherently unequal, and fairness often remains an elusive concept. Many individuals, especially those less fortunate, find themselves marginalized and struggle to carve out their place within society. A lot of these individuals adapt to their circumstances as best they can, much like small mushrooms thriving in the shade of a large tree; these mushrooms face constant threats such as being washed away by rain or overshadowed by the tree's canopy. Therefore, it is crucial for those with greater creativity, skills, ambition, and proactivity to offer their support and protection to those less fortunate, almost as if it were a matter of divine intention.

Regardless of whether you identify as an entrepreneur, a self-employed individual, or an employee within an organization, it is vital to acknowledge that your inherent design is one of success. Your nature is geared toward achieving both spiritual fulfillment and overall happiness in life. You are presented with numerous opportunities to acquire skills through the process of mastery, which you can leverage to create pathways for growth and advancement.

However, it is unfortunate that many individuals experience a restriction of their freedom, often hindered by systemic barriers or personal circumstances. In this book, we will address the complexities surrounding this issue. I am eager to share a solution aimed at helping you break free from the cycle that keeps you trapped, allowing you to fully realize your potential and embrace the opportunities that lie ahead.

"Liberate Yourself from Robotic Society"

In my journey, I embrace the role of a liberator of systems, a notion that profoundly shapes both my personal beliefs and professional pursuits. My vision is expansive, reaching into the myriad interconnected systems that define our lives. These include the complex machines of large business enterprises, the intricate layers of social structures, the often-confounding frameworks of government, the rapidly shifting terrains of social media, and corporate environments profoundly impacted by individual contributions. At the heart of my mission lies a sense of urgency: a deep commitment to emancipate not just individuals but the very systems that shape their existence. My primary clientele—successful entrepreneurs operating in the eight-figure realm, self-employed consultants, and esteemed investors—turn to me to navigate through the complexities that stifle their potential. Together, we peel back the layers of systemic barriers, empowering them with frameworks that enable, rather than constrain.

To grasp my perspective fully, one must delve into the reasons behind my use of the term "social robotic systems." This phrase draws a stark contrast to the pre-Industrial Revolution era, when individuals were primarily engaged in self-sustaining practices for their families. Back then, people utilized their unique skills to create meaningful goods within contexts like agriculture and various forms of self-employment. However, the Industrial Revolution marks a significant turning point in history—a profound reconfiguration that curtailed individual freedoms and spurred a radical reshaping of societal frameworks. Fueled by distinct philosophical doctrines and agendas, this era set in motion a transformation that redefined societal values and structures. In this new reality, society began to recognize that the industrial systems at play were not aimed at uplifting and empowering individuals; instead, they were meticulously designed to cultivate a workforce that was disciplined and compliant, ultimately serving the interests of a small, powerful elite.

The evolution from the loosely organized feudal systems of the past to the more structured and organized societies we recognize today is often celebrated as a step toward liberation. Yet, the Industrial Revolution twisted this noble pursuit into the formation of a new social order—one increasingly focused on discipline, efficiency, and conformity, often at the cost of individual freedom and creativity. This systemic overhaul fostered a disturbing cycle in which control became the dominion of a concentrated elite, who manipulated societal frameworks and structures to enforce adherence. The result? People became conditioned to function more like components within a vast machine—social robots—rather than as unique, self-determining individuals.

Because of this systemic conditioning, individuals increasingly find themselves shaped by pervasive cultural norms, rigid societal behaviors, and an educational system that prioritizes conformity over creativity. These systems, designed to cultivate compliance and consumerism, align with the agendas of those in power. In this unforgiving environment, the pursuit of liberation transforms into a momentous collective endeavor—an urgent quest to reclaim agency, individuality, and a true sense of purpose amidst a landscape that increasingly favors mechanical uniformity over personal expression.

Throughout history, labor rights movements have achieved remarkable progress over the past three centuries, yet it is crucial to acknowledge and confront the pervasive negative consequences that have accompanied these advancements. Presently, we find ourselves facing a profoundly concerning widening of the social divide, epitomized by a small, privileged elite who deftly navigates and extracts value from a broad spectrum of laborers. This exploitation is glaringly apparent in the lives of countless individuals who, despite their inherent potential to engage in creative endeavors or leverage their unique talents, encounter formidable barriers that severely restrict their opportunities for growth and self-expression.

Many among these individuals yearn to reclaim their autonomy and articulate their creative visions; however, they are often beset by relentless challenges that threaten their very existence within an environment that frequently feels stifling and inhospitable. These obstacles manifest in diverse and insidious forms, through the convoluted maze of bureaucratic red tape, the oppressive weight of economic pressures, or the constrictive bounds of societal expectations. Together, these forces create a daunting wall that impedes the pursuit of personal and professional fulfillment.

My mission within these intricate dynamics is to illuminate pathways to liberation—both for individuals yearning to break free from constraints and the broader systems that keep them shackled. I aspire to facilitate a transformative shift towards environments that genuinely foster creativity, innovation, and personal fulfillment. This pursuit transcends mere individual empowerment; it is fundamentally about reshaping the systemic structures that thwart potential and stifle growth. I envision myself as a liberator of systems, a principle that is intricately woven into the fabric of my personal and professional journey. My focus encompasses a myriad of interrelated systems, spanning business organizations, societal frameworks, governmental institutions, the complexities of social media, and the corporate cultures sculpted by collective individual contributions. My mission is both clear and urgent: to liberate individuals and these constraining systems in a meaningful way. The primary clients I serve include visionary eight-figure entrepreneurs, insightful self-employed consultants, and distinguished investors. I guide them through the intricate nuances of these complex systems, offering instruction on how to leverage these frameworks to their advantage while adeptly maneuvering through the often rigid and unforgiving structures that dominate today's landscape.

To fully appreciate my perspective, it is vital to explore why I characterize these environments as **"Social Robotic Systems".** This phrase is not a nostalgic nod to the era before the Industrial Revolution when individuals primarily worked for their families and harnessed their distinct skills to produce meaningful goods through agriculture and various forms of self-employment. The Industrial Revolution fundamentally altered the landscape, dramatically curtailing individual freedom and instigating systemic shifts driven by specific philosophical ideologies and agendas. This transition led society to an important realization: the industrial framework was not crafted to empower individuals, but to cultivate a compliant workforce that primarily serves the interests of a narrow elite.

The historical journey from feudal kingdoms to organized, structured societies was largely envisioned as one of liberation and empowerment. Yet, the consequences of the Industrial Revolution diverted this noble pursuit into the establishment of a new social order—one that emphasized discipline and conformity, often at the expense of individual freedom. This systemic shift birthed a destructive cycle in which control was wielded over the masses by a concentrated cadre of elites, who adeptly manipulated social structures to enforce compliance and mold individuals into functioning more like social robots than autonomous, creative human beings. In essence, my exploration of these dynamics is driven not only by a desire to critique the existing systems but also to actively pursue the liberation of both individuals and the institutions that confine them, fostering environments that are genuinely conducive to authentic creativity and personal fulfillment.

As a result of long-standing cultural norms, pervasive social behaviors, and rigid educational systems, individuals today find themselves conditioned to conform to expectations that primarily serve the interests of those in power. This cycle of conditioning promotes a lifestyle centered around consumption and adherence to conventional standards, often at the expense of personal authenticity. Consequently, many individuals develop identities that are largely shaped by external pressures, leading to an abundance of job positions that offer limited avenues for personal expression or creative engagement.

While it's important to acknowledge the remarkable progress that labor rights movements have made over the past three centuries—including improved working conditions, fair wages, and legal protections, it's equally crucial to highlight the adverse effects that accompany these developments. In contemporary society, we increasingly witness the emergence of a stark social divide. A small elite class continues to manipulate economic opportunities, extracting value from a vast pool of workers whose potential remains untapped. Numerous individuals possess the ability and desire to engage in creative pursuits or to apply their unique skill sets, but they often encounter significant barriers that restrict these opportunities. These restrictions have only been tightened over time, leaving many feelings trapped in roles that do not align with their passions or aspirations.

Despite this challenging landscape, there exists a resilient community of self-employed individuals who are actively working to reclaim their autonomy and pursue their creative ambitions. However, their journeys are fraught with obstacles, as they struggle to maintain stable positions and sustainable livelihoods amid an increasingly competitive and demanding economic environment. Ultimately, I find a profound sense of purpose within these intricate dynamics. My aim is to illuminate the pathways to liberation—not only for individuals seeking to break free from societal constraints but also for the broader systems that inhibit creativity and innovation. By highlighting these pathways, I aspire to facilitate a transformation toward environments that genuinely nurture personal fulfillment, encourage innovative thinking, and allow for the exploration of one's true potential thereby elevating the entire society around the individual.

Let me elaborate on the current condition of our robotic systems and the underlying mechanisms at play. A complex and nuanced framework has been carefully constructed by individuals entrenched in positions of power and affluence. Their primary aim appears to be the maintenance of control over the broader population, ensuring that their positions remain unchallenged. This has led to the establishment of a cultural, social, and educational environment meticulously designed to shape individuals into predetermined identities that align with the status quo. This manipulation is not merely incidental; it is a deliberate effort that allows those in power to exploit our innate potential. As a result, many individuals find themselves molded into personas that fit specific job role positions that often bear little resemblance to their true skills, passions, or aspirations. This disconnect can lead to a profound sense of dissatisfaction and frustration, as individuals grapple with the reality of their assigned roles.

In this intricate web, many people find themselves caught in a relentless cycle. They may pursue jobs solely to meet their financial obligations and to sustain a comfortable livelihood. This pursuit often leads to the acceptance of positions that do not tap into their true abilities or interests. Opportunities for greater fulfillment and financial success frequently slip away, leaving them feeling stagnant or unfulfilled. It's particularly disheartening to observe colleagues in their forties coming to the sobering realization that they have grown deeply entrenched in a system that suppresses their professional growth and personal evolution. This situation serves as a significant warning for those in their twenties and thirties: it is paramount that they awaken to the current reality and question the status quo. Individuals are not inherently fated to operate merely as cogs in a vast, impersonal machine. Despite the often-repeated reassurances from employers and societal narratives, the truth is that many occupations will not foster our passions, nor will they align with our natural skills. Allowing oneself to traverse this path for several decades carries the risk of complacency, leading to a disengaged existence where one becomes increasingly disconnected from one’s own life and aspirations.

The entrenched system appears to thrive on cultivating compliant workers; it perpetuates a societal divide that primarily benefits a small, privileged segment of the population while leaving many behind. This cycle is meticulously designed to uphold the status quo, reducing individuals to mere components of a labor force that follow directives without question, surrendering their autonomy and creativity.

However, amidst this challenging landscape, there exists a glimmer of hope. It is essential to proactively identify and support those exceptional individuals and organizations genuinely committed to challenging this prevailing paradigm. The imperative is not only to recognize these change-makers but also to actively engage with their efforts, seeking to dismantle the institutions that have conditioned us to become compliant employees, particularly those deep-rooted in outdated industrial-age practices. To effect meaningful change, we must work toward cultivating an environment where creativity, innovation, and mastery are highly valued. This cultural shift is vital for fostering opportunities that create greater value—not just for a select few, but for society. Such an endeavor requires collective effort, dialogue, and a commitment to envisioning and building a future that contrasts sharply with the limitations of our current system.

We find ourselves at a pivotal juncture in historical moment that demands our acute attention to the myriad challenges posed by capitalism. This economic system, which often prioritizes the relentless pursuit of profit over the fundamental well-being of individuals, has led to several pressing concerns. One particularly troubling phenomenon is crony capitalism, characterized by the growing trend of machines and automated systems replacing human workers under the guise of efficiency and profitability. This alarming shift not only jeopardizes a significant number of jobs but also undermines the intrinsic value of work itself—a value that is crucial not only for personal fulfillment but also for the social cohesion that binds communities together.

Amidst this upheaval, there shines a beacon of hope. Everyone possesses the inherent capacity to transcend the confines of this mechanized existence and reclaim their aspirations and dreams. It is imperative that we actively pursue our individual ambitions and goals before opportunities dissipate into the void of technological advancement and market volatility. Having championed the transformative changes brought about by the fourth industrial revolution, I am acutely aware of their profound implications on all aspects of our lives—from employment to personal identity. To carve out a brighter and more promising tomorrow, we must engage in proactive, deliberate measures to defend our opportunities while simultaneously igniting our passions. We should resolutely refuse to accept a life stripped of meaning, instead choosing to strive toward realizing our true potential and envisioning a future that authentically reflects our core values and aspirations.

My commitment is to support initiatives that empower individuals to actively participate in the creation of improved systems that cater to human needs rather than simply prioritizing capital. Such structural transformations not only enhance the framework through which we navigate our daily lives but also improve the quality of life for all involved stakeholders. Currently, my focus lies in supporting innovative startups dedicated to developing social robots and autonomous workers that align with this compassionate vision of human-centric progress. My approach is centered around delivering tangible, practical outcomes while fostering voluntary engagement and implementing thoughtfully crafted systems. These systems aim to enable individuals to ascertain their own worth in the marketplace—an essential component for attaining authentic economic freedom. This empowerment allows people to shape their destinies on their terms, fostering a culture of innovation and creativity. While many initiatives have sought to cultivate these transformative changes, numerous efforts have faltered, often due to insufficient frameworks or inadequate tools. For a significant number of individuals, the path toward transformation is gradual and requires considerable resilience and commitment. In our increasingly interconnected world, the job market is evolving at a breakneck speed, fueled by advancements in technology and shifts in global dynamics. Nations are reimagining their borders and redefining what it means to work, prompting substantial shifts in traditional employment patterns. The concept of outsourcing, for instance, is being redefined as more individuals traverse the globe to conduct business and secure livelihood, thereby opening new avenues for economic participation.

This evolution also presents a distinctive opportunity for individuals to embrace independence—transitioning into roles as consultants, freelancers, or entrepreneurs. By harnessing their unique skills, knowledge, and creative potential, they can develop valuable products and solutions that not only generate income but also serve to enhance their career trajectories and improve their overall quality of life. Such ventures have the potential to lay the foundation for highly successful enterprises and fruitful collaborations, thereby creating a ripple effect that benefits both individuals and communities at large. However, many people grapple with the distinctions between being self-employed, working for an organization, and embarking on the transformative entrepreneurial journey. I perceive these roles as deeply interconnected and essential, each representing a vast landscape of human potential and opportunities waiting to be explored and realized. Ultimately, the decision to follow a career path as an employee, self-employed individual, or entrepreneur is a deeply personal choice—one that each person must navigate independently, weighing their unique circumstances, aspirations, and values.

Potential Risks Related to Human Talent:

- A noticeable decline in the quality of education, which can diminish skill acquisition and adaptability among the workforces.

- Evolving knowledge requirements may leave segments of the population behind, contributing to widening disparities.
- Ethical dilemmas arising from technological advancements that could contribute to a fragmented and harmful society.
- Prejudice and systemic biases that hinder fair opportunities and perpetuate inequality in the marketplace.
- An over-reliance on specific tools and narrowly defined skill sets, which can stifle creativity and adaptability, hampering personal and professional growth.

Sovereignty and Identity Crisis in the digital world.

The concepts of sovereignty and identity are becoming increasingly relevant in today's world, as the forces of globalization, technological progress, and evolving political and cultural landscapes redefine international relations. Sovereignty encompasses the authority and autonomy of a state to govern itself and make decisions without external interference. This principle is foundational to international law, which acknowledges the intrinsic right of each nation to oversee its territory and affairs. Sovereignty is a nation's prerogative to establish its internal governance systems, enacting laws and policies that reflect its political aspirations, regardless of the governing framework. The territorial integrity involves a state's jurisdiction over its geographical space, including land, airspace, and maritime boundaries. Territorial disputes, often shaped by historical claims and geopolitical considerations, can lead to complex challenges and international tensions. But with the complex global economic systems and integration of various subsystems to achieve the goals at the global scale, economic sovereignty takes the front seat to all. Economic sovereignty refers to a nation's ability to regulate its economic environment, including fiscal policies, trade agreements, and resource management. This empowerment enables states to navigate their economic trajectories and manage financial resources effectively. Considering the digital age, this concept addresses a state's governance over its cyber domain, which includes data sovereignty and cybersecurity measures. Nations are increasingly aware of the implications of digital surveillance and international technological influence, prompting initiatives to regulate digital engagement. For instance, China's structured internet policies exemplify efforts to safeguard national interests and foster local enterprises.

Finally, Cultural Sovereignty is the nation's ability to preserve and promote its cultural heritage, practices, and values amid the influences of dominant global cultures. Cultural sovereignty is vital for sustaining identity and continuity in the face of globalization. So, a comprehensive understanding of these dimensions of sovereignty is essential for appreciating how states navigate their rights and identities within an increasingly interconnected global landscape. The ongoing process of globalization represents an intricate web of interconnectedness across economic, cultural, and political spheres. While globalization facilitates enhanced trade and cultural exchanges, it significantly challenges traditional sovereignty frameworks. Institutions like the World Trade Organization (WTO) and the International Monetary Fund (IMF), alongside various trade agreements and the activities of multinational corporations, exert considerable pressure on nation-states to harmonize domestic policies with international standards. This dynamic often compromises national autonomy as states attempt to balance the imperatives of adhering to global norms with the imperative of addressing local exigencies.

Interventions by External Powers: The sovereignty of nation-states is frequently undermined by interventions from more dominant powers, manifesting through military action, economic sanctions, or diplomatic coercion. These interventions are often motivated by geopolitical considerations, humanitarian imperatives, or economic interests. For instance, powerful nations may impose sanctions on weaker states as punitive measures or as leverage for behavioral shifts, consequently creating geopolitical tensions and multifaceted dilemmas within international relations. Such external actions have the potential to destabilize governmental structures, disrupt social cohesion, and impair a nation's capacity for independent action on the global stage.

Technological Advances: The swift evolution of digital platforms and the omnipresence of the internet introduce profound challenges concerning digital sovereignty. Major multinational tech corporations, such as Amazon, Apple, and Google, wield significant control over vast datasets and possess the technological influence to shape social and political behaviors across national boundaries. This raises pivotal questions about governance in digital environments and the capacity of national governments to effectively regulate these powerful entities. As users increasingly rely on online platforms for information dissemination, social interaction, and economic transactions, the interplay between state sovereignty and corporate influence becomes increasingly intricate.

Globalization vs. National Control: The inherently international character of the internet, coupled with pervasive digital technology adoption, engenders a complex discourse surrounding national control versus international collaboration. Many states endeavor to regulate their digital landscapes to enhance security, privacy, and economic stability; however, the borderless nature of the internet often subverts these regulatory efforts. Jurisdictions face challenges enforcing domestic laws in virtual spaces where activities transcend sovereign borders, resulting in an ongoing struggle to reconcile local regulatory frameworks with the necessity for cooperative global governance in the digital sphere.

Digital Colonialism: An emerging discourse on sovereignty critiques the phenomenon of digital colonialism, highlighting the disproportionate influence exercised by major multinational (often U.S.-based) corporations over the global digital environment. Companies such as Facebook and Amazon not only serve as market leaders but also act as significant architects of the digital landscape, influencing user behaviors and shaping national policies regarding data governance and privacy. This raises critical discussions on digital imperialism, where the pervasive dominance of these corporations threatens to erode national sovereignty by controlling vital information flows and dictating terms to sovereign governments. Renowned Economist and former finance minister of Greece, Yanis Varoufakis coined the word Cloud Capitalism to describe such digital colonialization. For states intent on asserting digital sovereignty, the path is laden with challenges, particularly concerning the requisite economic and technological investments. Developing robust digital infrastructure, advancing technological capabilities, and nurturing a competent workforce demand substantial resources that smaller or developing nations may lack. This economic disparity creates a competitive disadvantage vis-vis larger tech enterprises, which often dominate markets and policy frameworks. As a result, these nations may find it increasingly difficult to implement effective strategies for managing their digital environments, leaving them vulnerable to corporate influence and external pressures. An identity crisis signifies a profound and often tumultuous period of confusion and self-reflection. During such crises, individuals, communities, or entire nations struggle to define or reaffirm their identity, purpose, or societal role in a rapidly changing world. This phenomenon is typically marked by feelings of disorientation, uncertainty, and a tangible loss of direction. Various life transitions, changing societal norms, or external pressures can trigger identity crises, compelling individuals and groups to reevaluate their sense of identity and their place in the world.

A personal identity crisis unfolds when an individual encounters significant ambiguity about their self-concept, values, and societal role. Personal identity crises often emerge during critical life transitions—such as adolescence, where one navigates the shift from childhood to adulthood; midlife, when individuals reflect on their life achievements and future goals; or following substantial personal losses, such as the death of a loved one, divorce, or serious illness. During such crises, individuals may engage in deep introspection, scrutinizing their belief systems, aspirations, and relationships with others to establish a clearer sense of self. Cultural Identity crisis arises within groups or communities facing dislocation or conflict concerning their cultural values, traditions, and social norms. Such crises can be precipitated by rapid changes in the sociopolitical landscape, technological advancements that alter communication and connection, or the erosion of cultural heritage due to migration, colonization, or globalization. Communities may feel torn between preserving ancestral practices and adapting to newfound influences, resulting in tensions and a loss of cohesion. The mingling of cultures through migration and globalization generates pressures to assimilate, often prompting crises surrounding cultural identity. Individuals from minority backgrounds may struggle to maintain their traditional identities while navigating the demands and expectations of the dominant culture. Striking a balance between preserving one's heritage and embracing new practices or beliefs presents considerable challenges, leading to conflicts of allegiance and identity.

National Identity Crisis: A national identity crisis represents a collective struggle among citizens to define their shared identity, core values, and aspirations for the future. Such crises can occur in the wake of political turmoil, economic instability, or wars, and may worsen with the challenge of integrating diverse ethnic, cultural, and religious groups within a single national framework. As citizens grapple with questions of allegiance, belonging, and cultural heritage, the

result can lead to societal fragmentation and unrest. Globalization has significantly expanded interactions among various cultures, economies, and nations, often leading to identity crises at individual and communal levels. As traditional norms and values are challenged by external influences—ranging from global media to international migration, individuals may find themselves wrestling with conflicting identities. Particularly among youth, there is a tendency to gravitate towards more globalized cultural expressions, which can create friction as established traditions encounter modern practices and worldviews. Dramatic shifts and transformations in social, political, and economic landscapes can provoke feelings of insecurity, fear, and confusion regarding personal or collective identities. The rapid pace of technological advancements and the emergence of significant social and political movements compel individuals or groups to reassess their sense of self or the roles they occupy in society, fostering a climate ripe for identity crises. While sovereignty and identity crises are conceptually distinct, they frequently overlap in significant ways, particularly when exploring themes of national identity, globalization, and the challenges posed by the digital age. The following interrelations elucidate the complexity of these intersections:
Sovereignty and National Identity: A nation may experience a crisis of identity when it loses sovereignty over critical aspects of its territory, resources, or governance due to external pressures or internal conflicts. This loss can manifest when a state struggles to assert its sovereignty or protect its cultural values from foreign influences, as seen historically in instances of colonialism, imperialism, and foreign interventions.

Cultural Assimilation and National Identity: Countries that face cultural imperialism or significant foreign influences due to globalization may confront identity crises that challenge their core cultural identities. The influx of foreign languages, lifestyles, and ideologies can create tensions within a nation regarding the preservation of its traditions and cultural integrity. This often sparks nationalist movements aimed at asserting cultural sovereignty and resisting assimilation.

Digital Sovereignty: In today's digital landscape, the concept of digital sovereignty has emerged as pivotal for national identity. The monopolistic control exercised by global technology giants—like Google, Facebook, and Amazon—over personal data and information can substantially undermine a nation's ability to protect its citizens' privacy and security. Such conditions can instigate feelings of cultural and political vulnerability. Nations must navigate the complexities of their roles within an increasingly digital ecosystem dominated by multinational corporations, raising critical questions about autonomy and identity. As nations become entwined with international markets, migration flows, and cultural exchanges, individuals often face identity crises while negotiating their national identities in the context of global influences. For example, young people growing up in rapidly globalizing societies may find themselves at a crossroads, trying to reconcile local customs and identities with broader global trends. This duality can lead to feelings of displacement, alienation, and conflict as they wrestle with competing notions of selfhood and community. Ultimately, understanding the multifaceted nature of identity crises requires a nuanced appreciation of how personal, cultural, and national identities interact and evolve, particularly in an era defined by swift change and interconnectedness.

Chapter 6. New World Order, Innovation and National Wealth

As we explore the multifaceted realm of geoeconomics, the complexities extend far beyond the mere understanding of core economic principles and technical skills. The concept of the geoeconomic spectrum encompasses the strategic methods through which nations seek to enhance their influence on a global scale, employing fundamental economic tools and strategies that evolve over time.

This spectrum reveals the intricate and often interdependent relationship between a nation's economic decisions and its broader global aspirations. It underscores the notion that economic strategies are not isolated endeavors; instead, they are integral facets of a country's overarching foreign policy framework. By effectively intertwining economic initiatives with diplomatic efforts, nations can create a harmonious synergy that may bolster their international standing or, conversely, destabilize existing power structures. This interplay can lead to significant alterations in international relationships, sometimes prompting realignments or shifts in alliances based on shared economic interests or conflicts.

The effectiveness and longevity of strategies within this economic spectrum hinge not only on the array of available geoeconomic tools—such as tariffs, trade agreements, investments, and sanctions—but also on a nation's proficiency in harnessing these instruments. Mastery in leveraging these tools requires a combination of political acumen and resource management, particularly concerning crucial assets like energy resources (including oil and natural gas), essential minerals, and cutting-edge technologies.

Furthermore, market leverage plays a pivotal role in this dynamic. A nation's influence over global markets is fundamentally linked to its capacity to dictate trade practices, safeguard trade routes, and establish economic partnerships that enhance its strategic position. Countries that can effectively navigate the complexities of both domestic and international markets are better positioned to assert their geoeconomic strategies, thereby driving the agenda on various global platforms and influencing the rules of the game in international relations. As we analyze these components, it becomes evident that the pursuit of geoeconomic strategies is not merely about economic gain; it is fundamentally about power, influence, and the desire to shape the global order in alignment with a nation's interests.

As established in the earlier chapter of Geoeconomic cooperation, the countries or regions are becoming increasingly interconnected through trade, investment, and technology exchanges. In geoeconomics, this integration can be a tool for both cooperation and competition. Multilateral trade agreements like **World Trade Organization**, regional agreements like the **European Union, NAFTA** etc., or bilateral like the **US-China trade deals** are instruments of economic strategy that affect relations between countries and create interdependencies. Nations strategically connect through supply chains to reinforce economic power or exert influence. The manipulation of these chains can be used for geoeconomic leverage, as seen in China's control over rare earth elements. Control over the global financial system, including currency, international lending, and banking systems, is a central element of the geoeconomic spectrum. States like the **US** and **China** can use their currency as a tool of influence. The **US dollar**, for instance, is the dominant global reserve currency, and its centrality in global trade allows the US to exert considerable financial power.

SWIFT and Financial Networks: The **SWIFT** system, a global network for cross-border payments, has been used as a geopolitical tool, notably when sanctions are imposed on countries like Iran and Russia. The rise of **technology** and **data** has added new dimensions to the geoeconomic spectrum. Control over technology, innovation, and data flows is now central to global influence. The US, China, and the European Union are competing to dominate the global tech landscape through intellectual property, innovation, and market control. **5G networks**, **artificial intelligence**, and **cybersecurity** are now considered critical geoeconomic battlegrounds. Data is often referred to as the "new oil," and controlling data can provide a state with significant geopolitical power. For example, nations that dominate the tech industry (such as the US with **Google** or **Facebook**) also control vast amounts of global data.

6.1 Capital Flow

Capital flow across national and regional boundaries refers to the movement of money for investment, trade, and financing across countries or regions. This flow is a central element of globalization and plays a significant role in shaping global economies. Capital flows are essential for facilitating economic growth, financing projects, and promoting innovation. They can take many forms, including foreign direct investment (FDI), portfolio investment, remittances, loans, and trade-related financial transactions. **Capital flows across national and regional boundaries** are vital to the global economy, driving growth, innovation, and economic integration. They are influenced by a wide range of factors, including interest rates, political stability, and global economic conditions. However, the movement of capital also brings risks, including financial instability, dependency, and social inequality. Managing capital flows through appropriate policies and regulations is crucial to ensure that they contribute to sustainable development and the broader economic well-being of countries and regions.

Factors Influencing Capital Flow:

1. **Interest Rates**: Higher interest rates in a country typically attract more capital inflows, as investors seek higher returns. Conversely, lower rates can result in capital outflows, as investors look for better returns elsewhere.
2. **Exchange Rates**: The value of a country's currency relative to others impacts capital flow. A stronger currency makes investments in that country more expensive for foreign investors, potentially reducing inflows. However, a weaker currency can make it more attractive to invest in the country due to cheaper assets.
3. **Political and Economic Stability**: Countries with stable political systems and strong economic growth tend to attract more capital. Political instability, corruption, or financial crises may lead to capital flight as investors seek safer environments.
4. **Market Opportunities and Investment Climate**: A country's level of development, industrial structure, and openness to foreign investment determines how attractive it is to international capital. Emerging markets with high growth potential often receive significant capital inflows.
5. **Regulatory Environment**: Government policies on foreign investment, tax laws, and trade regulations play a critical role in determining the flow of capital. Policies that promote ease of doing business and offer incentives for foreign investors typically encourage greater inflows.
6. **Global Economic Conditions**: Events such as economic recessions, global financial crises, or changes in global commodity prices can influence capital flow. During times of global uncertainty, capital often flows toward perceived safer assets, such as government bonds in developed countries.

Regional Capital Flows:

Capital flows are not only global but also regional. In some cases, countries within specific regions may have more robust financial relationships with each other than with the rest of the world. These regional flows can be influenced by several factors:

Regional Economic Integration: The **European Union (EU)**, **ASEAN (Association of Southeast Asian Nations)**, and **Mercosur** (South American trading bloc) are regional economic organizations that facilitate capital flows within member countries through trade agreements, common currency areas, and investment treaties. Regional capital flows often occur more smoothly due to shared regulations, similar legal frameworks, and reduced barriers to cross-border investments.

Currency Union: The **Eurozone** (which uses the Euro) allows for easier movement of capital between member states because of a single currency and shared monetary policy. In currency unions, capital can flow freely across borders without exchange rate risks, thus promoting investment and economic integration.

Infrastructure and Trade Connectivity: Regional infrastructure projects (e.g., roads, ports, energy pipelines) often require cross-border capital investment. For instance, projects under **China's Belt and Road Initiative (BRI)** are examples of capital flowing to build infrastructure in Asia, Africa, and Europe.

Investment in regional infrastructure can enhance connectivity, stimulate trade, and create an environment conducive to capital inflows.

Impact of Capital Flow:

Positive Impacts:

- **Economic Growth**: Capital flows can spur economic development by funding infrastructure, business expansion, and innovation. They can provide developing countries with much-needed resources to enhance their growth potential.

- **Job Creation**: Investment, particularly FDI, can create jobs, improve productivity, and introduce new technologies in the host country.
- **Market Efficiency**: The movement of capital across borders encourages market efficiency, as investors seek the best returns. This often leads to the optimal allocation of resources across the global economy.

Negative Impacts:

- **Volatility and Financial Crises**: Large, sudden movements of capital can destabilize economies, especially in emerging markets. Capital flight during periods of financial instability or policy uncertainty can trigger economic crises, as seen during the **Asian Financial Crisis** (1997) and the **European Sovereign Debt Crisis** (2010).
- **Dependency**: Countries that rely heavily on foreign capital may face risks of becoming too dependent on external sources of financing. A sudden withdrawal of capital can leave the country financially vulnerable.
- **Income Inequality**: In some cases, capital inflows may disproportionately benefit wealthy individuals and multinational corporations, exacerbating inequality within the host country.

6.2 Intrinsic value and moat exploration

Intrinsic value refers to the true, inherent, or essential value of an asset, company, or investment, based on fundamental analysis rather than its market price. The intrinsic value is what an asset is worth, regardless of what people are willing to pay for it in the open market. For businesses, intrinsic value is often associated with a company's underlying financial health, future earnings potential, assets, and liabilities.

Key Aspects of Intrinsic Value:

- Discounted Cash Flow (DCF) Analysis: This is one of the most common methods used to calculate the intrinsic value of a business. It involves estimating the future cash flow of a company (such as profits, dividends, etc.) and discounting them back to the present value using a discount rate (often the company's cost of capital). The sum of these discounted cash flows represents the intrinsic value.

- Earnings Growth: A company's ability to grow its earnings over time is a major factor in determining intrinsic value. Companies with higher growth prospects tend to have higher intrinsic value.
- Asset-Based Valuation: This approach calculates the value of a company by assessing the value of its tangible and intangible assets, such as physical properties, patents, trademarks, or brand value.
- Comparable Analysis: Investors may also use the intrinsic value calculation by comparing similar companies in the same industry and adjusting for unique factors of the company in question.

Formula for Intrinsic Value (via DCF):

Intrinsic Value=∑CFt(1+r)t\text{Intrinsic Value} = \sum \frac{CF_t}{(1 + r)^t}Intrinsic Value=∑(1+r)tCFt

Where:

- CFtCF_tCFt = Cash flow at time ttt
- rrr = Discount rate (often the company's cost of capital)
- ttt = Time period in the future

Intrinsic Value vs. Market Value:

- Market Value is the price at which an asset or stock is currently trading in the open market. It is determined by market supply and demand forces.
- Intrinsic Value, on the other hand, is more objective and based on the true value derived from underlying fundamentals.

When the market value of an asset is lower than its intrinsic value, it may present a buying opportunity. If the market value exceeds the intrinsic value, it may suggest the assets are overvalued and potentially risky.

Moat Exploration

The term moat in business and investing refers to a company's competitive advantage, the unique attributes that allow it to maintain a dominant position in the market and protect itself from competition over the long term. The concept of the "moat" was popularized by legendary investor Warren Buffett, who described it as something that "protects a business from the ravages of competition." A company with a strong moat can maintain high profit margins, generate consistent revenues, and sustain its competitive edge even as the market changes.

Types of Moats:

Brand Moat:

Companies with strong brands can create customer loyalty that is difficult for competitors to replicate. Coca-Cola, for example, has a brand that consumers trust, and this brand recognition gives it pricing power and customer loyalty advantage. Examples: Apple, Nike, Coca-Cola.

Cost Advantage Moat:

Companies that can produce goods or services at a significantly lower cost than competitors often enjoy a cost advantage. This allows them to lower prices and still maintain higher profit margins, or to survive price wars. Examples: Walmart, Costco, Southwest Airlines.

Network Effects Moat:

Companies with network effects benefit from an expanding user base that increases the value of their product or service. As more users join, the service becomes more useful or valuable to each individual user, creating a self-reinforcing cycle. Examples: Facebook, LinkedIn, eBay, Visa.

Switching Costs Moat:

Some companies have products or services that are integral to their customers' lives, making it difficult or expensive for customers to switch to a competitor. The higher the switching costs, the stronger the moat.

Examples: Microsoft Windows (many businesses rely on Microsoft software, making switching expensive and time-consuming), Adobe (with its suite of creative software).

Intangible Assets Moat:

Intellectual property such as patents, trademarks, and proprietary technologies can give companies a long-term competitive advantage. These legal protections prevent competitors from entering the same market or offering the same products.

Examples: Pharmaceutical companies (e.g., Pfizer, Johnson & Johnson) with patented drugs, Disney with its iconic characters and franchises.

Regulatory Moat:

In some industries, government regulations create high barriers to entry, effectively protecting incumbent firms from competition. These regulations can create monopolies or limit competition.

Examples: Utility companies, telecommunications companies, and banking institutions that operate in highly regulated environments.

Economies of Scale Moat:

Companies that can scale their operations efficiently tend to have a cost advantage over smaller competitors. Larger companies can spread their fixed costs across a greater number of units, driving down per-unit costs.

Examples: Amazon (due to its vast global supply chain and distribution network), Tesla (with its manufacturing scale).

The Relationship Between Intrinsic Value and Moat: The intrinsic value of a company is significantly influenced by the presence and strength of its moat.

Companies with wide moats typically have more predictable and sustainable earnings, which can lead to a higher intrinsic value.

Why does Strong Moat Matters for Intrinsic Value?

- Sustainability of Profits: A strong moat helps a company maintain high returns on capital, even in competitive environments, ensuring that its intrinsic value remains high over time.
- Lower Risk: Companies with a competitive moat face fewer risks from market volatility or competitive pressures. This reduced risk increases their intrinsic value by making future cash flows more predictable.
- Pricing Power: Companies with moats have the ability to raise prices or maintain margins without losing customers, which contributes to long-term profitability and higher intrinsic value.
- Valuation Multiples: Investors often assign higher price-to-earnings multiples to companies with strong moats because they expect them to continue to generate consistent profits.

Consider Apple, Its strong brand, network effects (iOS ecosystem), and switching costs (customers loyal to iPhones and other Apple devices) create a robust moat. This moat allows Apple to sustain high margins and continue to generate significant cash flows, boosting its intrinsic value. Therefore, Apple's intrinsic value is considered high relative to its market value, making it an attractive investment for those who believe in its future growth and resilience.

Both intrinsic value and moat are critical concepts in assessing the long-term viability and attractiveness of an investment. Understanding intrinsic value helps investors determine whether a stock is undervalued or overvalued based on fundamentals, while the moat provides insight into how well a company can protect its profits from competitors. In essence, companies with strong moats tend to have more sustainable intrinsic value, making them prime candidates for long-term investment strategies.

6.3 digital Assets for global business and economic growth

Digital assets are any type of asset that exists in a digital form and can be traded, transferred, or owned electronically. In the context of global business and economic growth, digital assets are becoming increasingly central to modern economies. These assets range from cryptocurrencies to digital currencies, tokens, and data, and they play an essential role in driving innovation, enhancing efficiencies, and shaping the future of business and finance.

Here's a breakdown of the key types of digital assets and their implications for global business and economic growth:

Types of Digital Assets

Cryptocurrencies: Cryptocurrencies are decentralized digital currencies that use cryptography for security, which makes it difficult to counterfeit or double-spend. They operate on a technology called blockchain. Examples: Bitcoin (BTC), Ethereum (ETH), Ripple (XRP), Litecoin (LTC).

- **Role in Economic Growth**:

Decentralized Financial Systems: Cryptocurrencies provide an alternative to traditional banking systems, offering financial services to the unbanked, especially in developing regions.

Cross-Border Payments: Cryptocurrencies enable faster, cheaper, and more secure cross-border transactions without the need for intermediaries, reducing costs and improving efficiency in international trade.

Investment Opportunities: Cryptocurrencies attract global investors, encouraging investment in new technologies, projects, and decentralized finance (DeFi) platforms.

Central Bank Digital Currencies (CBDCs): These are digital forms of a country's official currency issued by a central bank. Unlike cryptocurrencies, CBDCs are controlled by governments and central banks. Examples: Digital Yuan (China), Digital Euro (European Union), Digital Dollar (U.S.).

- **Role in Economic Growth**:
    - **Monetary Policy and Financial Inclusion**: CBDCs provide governments with more direct control over monetary policy, enabling more effective economic management. They also increase access to financial systems in regions with low banking infrastructure.
    - **Reduction of Transaction Costs**: They can reduce the cost and time associated with international transactions, improve efficiency, and lower barriers for businesses and consumers.
    - **Tracking and Transparency**: CBDCs could reduce illegal activities like money laundering and tax evasion by providing traceable digital money.

Tokenized Assets: Tokenization refers to converting real-world assets into digital tokens on a blockchain, making it easier to transfer and trade these assets. Examples: Real estate tokens, art tokens, stocks and bonds tokens.

- **Role in Economic Growth**:
    - **Liquidity and Accessibility**: Tokenizing assets like real estate or commodities allows for fractional ownership, enabling more people to invest in high-value assets that were previously out of reach. This increases liquidity in traditionally illiquid markets.
    - **Global Investment**: Tokenized assets allow for global investors to participate in markets that were previously geographically

restricted, promoting global capital flow and investment diversification.

Non-Fungible Tokens (NFTs):

NFTs are unique digital tokens that represent ownership or proof of authenticity of a specific item, typically artwork, music, videos, or virtual real estate, using blockchain technology. Examples: Crypto Kitties, Bored Ape Yacht Club, virtual real estate.

- **Role in Economic Growth**:
  - **New Market Creation**: NFTs create new economic sectors, such as digital art and virtual real estate, allowing for new revenue streams and business models.
  - **Incentivizing Creators**: NFTs offer creators and artists new ways to monetize their work, increasing the value of intellectual property.
  - **Digital Collectibles Market**: The rise of digital collectibles, such as rare art, gaming items, and other memorabilia, has spurred an entire industry of buying, selling, and trading.

Digital Data:

Digital data refers to the vast amount of information generated from a variety of sources such as social media, user behavior, transaction logs, sensors, and more. **Big Data** is used by companies like Google, Facebook, and Amazon to optimize their services.

- **Role in Economic Growth**:
  - **Data-Driven Decision Making**: Companies leverage data to make more informed decisions, improve customer experiences, and streamline operations. This data-driven approach enhances productivity, reduces waste, and drives efficiency.
  - **Innovation and R&D**: Data fuels innovation by providing businesses with insights into customer behavior, market trends, and new

opportunities. It is critical for the development of AI, machine learning, and automation technologies.

- **Digital Transformation of Industries**: Data is central to transforming industries such as healthcare, finance, education, and retail, promoting economic modernization and growth.

Role of Digital Assets in Global Business Growth

Boosting Financial Inclusion:

- Digital assets, especially cryptocurrencies and CBDCs, offer a significant opportunity for financial inclusion, particularly in underserved regions. For many people in developing countries, traditional banking services may not be accessible. Digital assets provide an alternative, enabling easier access to financial services, savings, loans, and remittances.

Enhancing Efficiency and Reducing Transaction Costs:

- **Blockchain Technology** (underlying digital assets) allows for more efficient and transparent financial transactions. By eliminating intermediaries (such as banks or payment processors), blockchain reduces transaction costs, accelerates settlement times, and increases transparency.
- For global business, this is especially important for industries like cross-border trade, remittances, and supply chain management. The ability to conduct instant, low-cost, and secure transactions helps to drive global commerce and economic growth.

Creating New Investment Opportunities:

- The advent of digital assets has led to the creation of new investment avenues such as cryptocurrencies, tokenized assets, and NFTs. These new investment opportunities open doors for global investors to participate in markets that were previously inaccessible. For instance, tokenized real estate or stocks allow fractional ownership, democratizing access to high-value assets.

- Digital assets, particularly blockchain-based securities, also enable more liquidity and faster trading, leading to the development of decentralized financial markets (DeFi) that compete with traditional financial institutions. Specifically, digital equity assets with clearly measurable intrinsic value that represents the Real World Assets(RWA) are going to thrive in the digitally transformed world.

Fostering Innovation:

- Digital assets are directly tied to cutting-edge technologies like **blockchain**, **artificial intelligence (AI)**, **Internet of Things (IoT)**, and **smart contracts**. These technologies are driving innovation across various industries, including finance, healthcare, supply chain management, and entertainment.
- By investing in digital assets, companies and countries can leverage new tools to build more efficient, transparent, and secure systems, leading to greater economic growth and competitive advantages on the global stage.

Enabling Digital Economies and Virtual Business Models:

- As the world moves toward digital transformation, digital assets are key to supporting virtual economies. The rise of metaverse, **virtual real estate**, and digital goods has created new business models that are contributing to economic growth.
- Additionally, digital assets like NFTs and blockchain-backed tokens provide new ways for businesses to monetize products, services, and intellectual property. For example, in the gaming industry, NFTs represent in-game assets, enabling new revenue streams through ownership and trading.

Global Trade and Supply Chain Optimization:

- Digital assets and blockchain can revolutionize global supply chains by providing real-time tracking, reducing fraud, and enhancing transparency in international trade. Blockchain-based solutions allow businesses to track goods across borders, authenticate product quality, and automate payment systems.
- Digital currencies and tokens also simplify cross-border payments, enabling faster and more secure international transactions. This supports the growth of global trade and reduces costs associated with currency exchange and international banking.

6.4 Challenges and Considerations

While digital assets offer numerous benefits, there are challenges and risks that must be addressed to fully harness their potential:

- **Regulatory Uncertainty**: The regulatory landscape for digital assets, especially cryptocurrencies, is still evolving. Governments and regulators are grappling with how to classify and regulate these assets, which may impact adoption and business models.
- **Security Risks**: Digital assets are often targeted for cyberattacks, theft, and fraud. Ensuring robust cybersecurity measures and protecting digital wallets and exchanges is critical to maintaining trust and stability in the market.
- **Volatility**: Cryptocurrencies are known for their volatility. This can make them challenging to use as a stable store of value or medium of exchange in certain circumstances.
- **Digital Divide**: While digital assets have the potential to foster financial inclusion, access to the internet and digital devices remains a barrier for some populations, especially in developing countries.

Conclusion

Digital assets are increasingly integral to global business and economic growth, driving innovation, enhancing efficiency, and creating new investment opportunities. Cryptocurrencies, tokenized assets, CBDCs, NFTs, and data are reshaping industries, enabling faster transactions, and contributing to the development of digital economies. However, the full potential of digital assets will depend on addressing challenges such as regulatory uncertainty, security concerns, and access issues. By overcoming these hurdles, digital assets could significantly enhance global economic integration and growth, offering businesses and countries new pathways to prosperity in the digital age.

- Shifting to an asset-centered economy
- Wealth as standard deviation
- Economic potential to kinetic
- Aggregate demand curve
- Generating wealth with modern assets at national levels
- Recognizing digital Asset Champion Organizations
- Achieving Integrated economic systems using digital assets

6.5 Champion Organizations and Winning with Ecosystem

The geopolitics of champion organizations explores the complex relationships between political influence, economic power, and social dynamics shaped by dominant entities across various fields, including sports, business, and international governance. These "champion organizations" play a crucial role in navigating and influencing global affairs, acting as both architects and reflections of geopolitical interactions.

Sports and National Identity: Champion organizations in international sports, such as the NFL, UEFA, and NBA, as well as national teams participating in the Olympics, have significant sway over geopolitical dynamics. Nations with exceptional teams or standout athletes often leverage their sports achievements to craft narratives of national pride and global influence. The successes of athletes and teams frequently symbolize a country's cultural identity and collective unity. A notable example is the legendary U.S. "Dream Team" in basketball during the 1992 Olympics, which not only showcased American excellence in sports but also became a powerful symbol of the U.S.'s status and superiority in the post-Cold War era, reinforcing its role as a global leader. Similarly, Russia's impressive performances in the Winter Olympics are closely linked to narratives of national resilience and power, often portraying the country as a formidable contender on the international stage.

Corporate Power and Economic Influence: In today's landscape, corporations—especially global giants like Apple, Google, and Amazon—hold substantial geopolitical influence. Their vast market capitalization and significant presence can reshape both economic and political spheres globally. Technology leaders such as Google and Facebook navigate complex issues, including privacy, freedom of expression, and government regulation. The geopolitical rivalries between the U.S. and China have been amplified by intense competition among tech companies. For instance, Huawei has become a focal point in trade disputes, facing allegations of espionage and contentious discussions surrounding digital sovereignty. The trade conflicts of the 2010s vividly illustrate this dynamic, with Huawei's role in developing the 5G global infrastructure raising national security concerns and highlighting the intricate layers of economic competition between major powers.

Global Institutions and Diplomacy: International organizations like the United Nations (UN), World Trade Organization (WTO), and International Monetary Fund (IMF) wield significant geopolitical authority as they create and implement the structures of global governance. Champion organizations in the diplomatic realm, such as the UN, play vital roles in mediating international conflicts, promoting human rights initiatives, and establishing the foundations of international law. They often provide platforms that reflect existing power imbalances and manage interactions among countries. However, they are frequently criticized for prioritizing the interests of dominant powers. A prominent example is the UN Security Council, where the permanent members—comprising the U.S., U.K., Russia, China, and France—hold considerable influence over global security issues, thus reflecting the prevailing geopolitical power structures and sometimes perpetuating inequalities.

Sustainability: The growing threat of sustainability has propelled champion organizations in the environmental and renewable energy sectors to the forefront, significantly enhancing their geopolitical influence. Nations and corporations leading the way towards sustainable technologies—such as Tesla with its electric vehicles and clean energy initiatives—as well as international agreements like the Paris Agreement play pivotal roles in shaping global environmental policies. These organizations promote initiatives while navigating the complex intersections of national interests and global sustainability goals. The Paris Agreement exemplifies how collective efforts—spanning governmental and non-governmental entities—forge platforms for geopolitical collaboration. Countries' commitments to reducing carbon emissions are driven not just by ethical considerations but also by economic motivations and geopolitical alliances, influencing national policies across the globe.

Cultural Influence and Soft Power: Champion organizations in entertainment, media, and fashion contribute significantly to establishing cultural norms that shape global geopolitical interactions. Hollywood, for example, has been instrumental in defining and disseminating American cultural values worldwide, often serving as a powerful tool for exercising soft power. In a similar vein, South Korea has effectively leveraged the rising global popularity of K-pop and its dynamic film industry to enhance its cultural outreach and soft power. The **Magnificent 7** refers to the seven largest publicly traded companies in the world by market capitalization, particularly in the context of the U.S. stock market. These companies have become some of the most influential entities globally due to their sheer size, innovation, and dominance in the tech and consumer sectors. As of recent data, Magnificent 7 usually includes Apple, Microsoft, Alphabet (Google), Amazon, Tesla, NVIDIA, Meta (formerly Facebook).

These companies collectively represent a huge portion of the global stock market value and have an outsized influence on the broader global economy. The performance of these companies is closely watched by investors globally, and their stock price movements can influence investor sentiment. Strong earnings reports or breakthroughs in products can boost confidence in other tech firms, while challenges faced by these companies (e.g., regulatory pressures or product failures) can lead to broader market share increases. These companies often control critical parts of global supply chains, particularly in electronics, semiconductors, and software. Their demand for raw materials, labor, and technology drives economic activity across multiple regions and industries. For instance, **Apple** and **Tesla** are major consumers of raw materials like lithium and cobalt for their products and electric vehicle batteries, directly influencing global commodity markets. As these companies grow, the flow of investment into the tech sector increases, influencing capital markets and global monetary policy. Central banks, particularly the U.S. Federal Reserve, monitor the performance of these companies as an indicator of broader economic conditions. The dominance of these companies can also impact interest rates and bond markets. When tech stocks surge, it can lead to a rise in asset prices and encourage higher levels of risk-taking in financial markets. Central banks may respond with different monetary policies to ensure that the economy doesn't overheat or experience bubbles. The massive size and market power of Magnificent 7 have raised regulatory concerns. Governments and regulators in the U.S., Europe, and

Asia are increasingly scrutinizing the practices of these companies related to antitrust, privacy, and data security. The regulatory decisions made by governments regarding these companies can have ripple effects on the global economy. For instance, **Meta (formerly Facebook)** and **Google** face ongoing scrutiny related to privacy laws and data collection, with the European Union leading the charge in enforcing regulations like the GDPR.

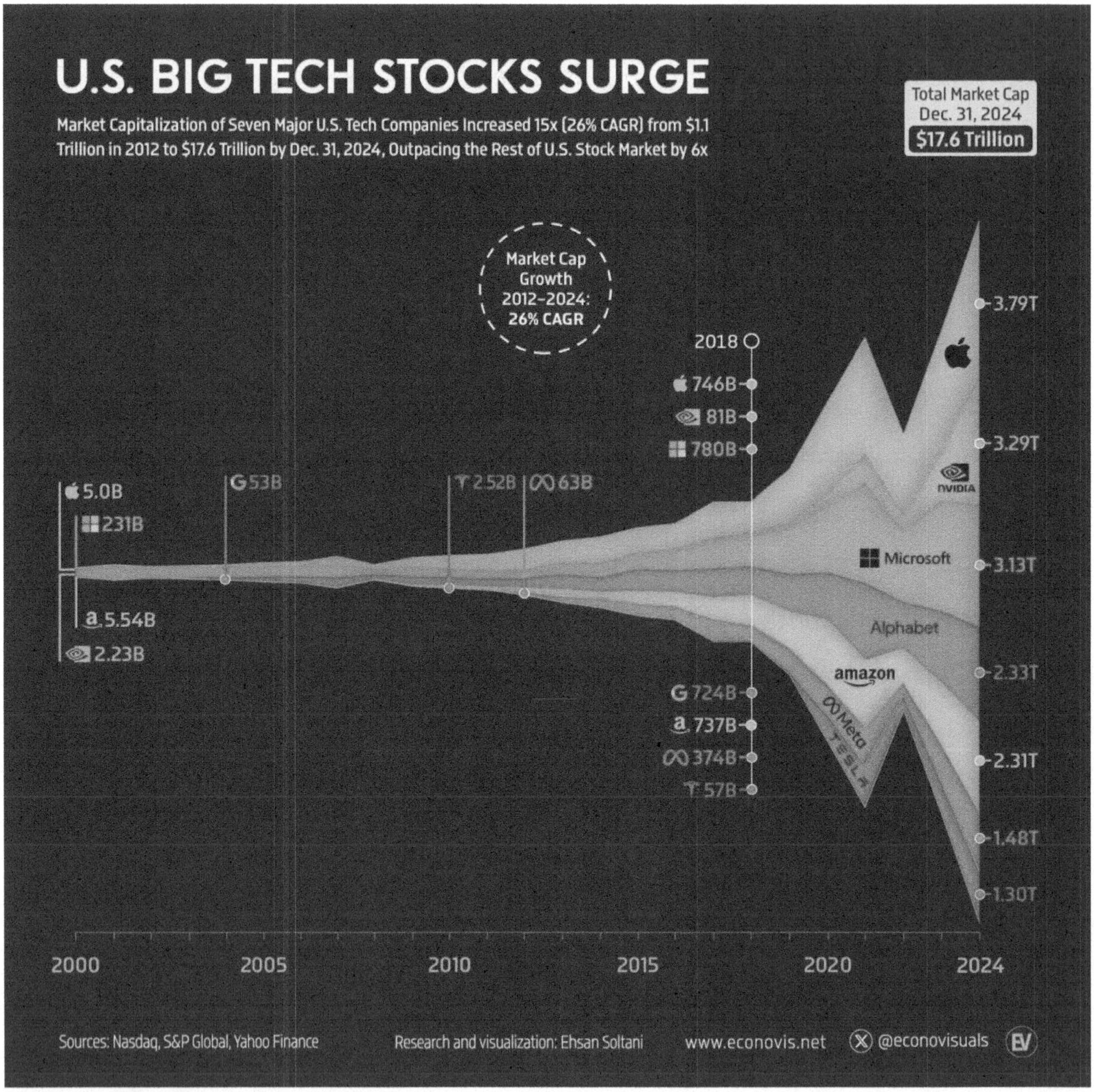

Figure 2: Magnificent 7 Chart

The geopolitical impact of these companies extends beyond regulation. For example, the U.S.-China tech rivalry has had significant economic consequences, with Chinese companies like Huawei and TikTok in direct competition with U.S. tech giants like Apple and Google. U.S. sanctions against Chinese companies or vice versa have created supply chain disruptions and influenced the global flow of technology and capital. These companies have a massive global footprint, with offices, manufacturing facilities, and data centers across multiple continents. They contribute to economic integration by facilitating trade in goods, services, and intellectual property. For instance, **Microsoft** and **Google** provide cloud services globally, influencing the development of digital infrastructure across countries. The global dominance of these companies gives their home countries significant soft power. The U.S. has used tech firms as an avenue for spreading its culture and influence globally, with **Apple** and **Microsoft** being ubiquitous in global markets. This, in turn, enhances the U.S.'s influence in international trade and economics. The market value of the Magnificent 7 contributes significantly to global wealth creation. Their valuation often exceeds the GDP of entire countries. The rise in stock prices of these companies has made them key players in wealth distribution, especially for institutional investors, pension funds, and individual investors who hold shares in these companies.

On the flip side, the vast size and valuation of these companies can also pose risks. The weight these companies carry in the market indices can lead to overvaluation, which in turn may cause significant market volatility if their stock prices fall sharply due to external factors like economic downturns or regulatory actions. In the space of winning the race of digital transformations, numerous factors determine their successful implementations and accomplishments. Though sharp insights raise the success rate, rapidly changing markets demand phenomenal efforts. No rule book could state how to go faster or what reengineering in enterprises should occur to hit the path of success. Recent changes in enterprises from the viewpoint of work cultures, remote working, marketing strategies, technologies stagnancy, and immense preference of one technology over others etc., are some of the reasons constantly impacting the minds of business transformation leaders. The main question remains whether the technology-driven innovations that induced enterprise transformations in the last few decades have lost their significance and if that were the case, what would support acceleration now? How could enterprises pick up the right momentum required for transformation now? What should be the primary set of considerations that the leaders should have in mind to put enterprises at sonic speed? If you want to surpass the barriers of sonic level digital transformation speed, you must go all out in removing the bottlenecks. By bottlenecks, I mean the Governance Models. In simpler terms, a Governance Model is an approach describing how the top-down management exercises control. The previous generation organizations had a tight grip of management controls where even a small change would seek massive efforts from all fronts. What impedes the expansion of big enterprises is the siloed nature of their processes. Too many siloed processes and strategies in the organizational culture pose the biggest bottlenecks. Governance models also include social aspects of governance which mean including people's participation-based type of Social Governance models. Social Governance doesn't believe in the rudimentary style of allocating responsibilities that used to happen in the earlier days like, "Hey, here you go. This is the role that you must play. Finish these duties first and then report to the pyramid-like hierarchy of command. Understand it this way - when people tend to introduce the chain of commands in governance models, they are giving birth to another bureaucratic organization within the organization leading to more bottlenecks. The new generation of Social Governance models must be introduced, and the focus should primarily be on the social and voluntary participation-based governance model. The second major thing to achieve in quick digital acceleration is building an Ecosystem. In the past, the key focus of enterprises looking for transformations was to further chisel their area of specialization. More specialization means narrowing down the scope of expansion which further means more limitations and constraints. On the other hand, the unicorns could outperform century-old companies valued at billion-dollar in just five years or less. The secret ingredient for this recipe of such rapid success rests in the concept of ecosystem. The old school saying, “don’t expand in the beginning, you first specialize and then look for expansion” have no place in the room of wisdom anymore. The new concept that enterprises must imbibe in their core pillars of foundation is developing and thriving in the functional ecosystem. Get into an ecosystem model. The third key point in the accelerating digital transformation is technology. A wise Businesses Architect of today would suggest that don’t just get stuck or carried away with one technology. Rather use technology to support business progress. If you are getting married to a specific technology, you will go down with it if it goes down. Repeatedly, every generation of CEO’s fail to learn this. They get attached to technology and innovation and when technology falls short, they take a plunge with it. The example is the virtual reality goggles that went down several years ago because there were not many takers for it. The solution is to create a technology ecosystem where you don't bank completely on a particular technology but use a specific aspect of it. For example, if someone wants to have a decentralized organization, don't fall completely in love with Blockchain or crypto assets. Just stick to the important aspect of it which is decentralization and voluntary participation. So, essentially it doesn't matter what technology the enterprise is using; it could be a set of multiple technologies like hundreds of technologies coming together.

6.6 Economic Intelligence than Innovation

As we briefly saw in chapter 4, Joseph Schumpeter popularized the term "creative destruction" to describe the process of new innovations replacing existing ones, leading to the destruction of existing economic structures. This destruction paves the way for new structures to emerge, which can create long-term economic growth and progress. So, innovation is an inevitable force, absolutely no doubt about it. But, more than that, the Economic intelligence should be the driving and governing force on top of it.

Most Nations around the world and the organizations that operate under their judiciary power struggle to make their geopolitical play as they have a poor understanding of how geoeconomics and its tools perform a crucial role in the geopolitics. To fully grasp the significance of geoeconomics, it is essential to understand the dynamics of power within geopolitical contexts. According to Susan Strange, the four pillars of international power include: 1) Financial Power—leveraging finance and the creation of money to gain an edge over competing nations; 2) Production—dominating global markets through superior means of production; 3) Security—safeguarding national and regional security, often through military might; and 4) Knowledge. But up until recently with the exorbitant development in the artificial intelligence, knowledge is being taken to the next level to the wisdom right that's where people like me come in with the Deep Tech and all and we've been talking I mean talking about it for the last few years I've been helping organizations startup ecosystems and all to how to use the Deep Tech not just only the artificial intelligence but anything that is deep Tech to take the knowledge to the next level which can help the Nations nation states economic regions and even the large organizations to dominate and basically of outpower the competitors.

As the global landscape continues to evolve amidst rapidly changing political, economic, and technological conditions, there emerges a compelling opportunity for new nations, nation-states, and various international organizations to actively engage in a profound transformation of how empowerment is interpreted on a global scale. This transformation marks a significant shift from the traditional focus on mere knowledge acquisition to a deeper and more profound pursuit of wisdom—a concept that extends beyond mere intelligence and encompasses understanding, insight, and thoughtful application in complex contexts. In this intricate tapestry of international relations, the notion of geo-economics is increasingly coming to the forefront. It is beginning to be recognized not just as a critical subset of geopolitics, but as a foundational element that significantly shapes the strategic dynamics of geopolitical maneuvering and international encounters. Despite its emerging importance, many analysts and policymakers continue to overlook the role of geo-economics as a fundamental catalyst for exerting global influence in these complex realms. Understanding this paradigm is essential for nations and organizations that seek to assert their place on the world stage.

Geo-economics involves the strategic deployment of a wide array of economic tools and instruments to secure advantageous results in both geopolitical and geostrategic arenas. This approach emphasizes the maximization of trade advantages, carefully balancing economic aspirations with the prudent utilization of capital resources—ranging from natural resources to human capital. Countries possess a rich palette of economic tools that have been refined over centuries through a combination of scholarly insights and practical applications. By strategically leveraging this diverse array of resources, nations can create positive geo-economic outcomes that not only enhance their economic gains but also align with their energy resources, fostering robust and sustainable trade relationships. The overarching focus of geo-economics should center on enhancing trade benefits and mutual prosperity, rather than pursuing economic or geopolitical supremacy over rival nations, regions, or economic blocs. It is critical to place special emphasis on the efficient use of capital resources—which includes not only financial assets but also human capital and intellectual resources. In this context, many nations, large corporations, and their leaders often falter, neglecting the potential rewards that come from wisely managing and deploying these vital assets.

At its core, geo-economics embodies a process-driven approach aimed at achieving shared objectives and fostering interdependence rather than fostering competition and conflict. This viewpoint does not elevate the pursuit of power or geopolitical ascendance to the forefront of national ambitions. While such victories may indeed materialize naturally over time, the primary aim should remain focused on maximizing trade outcomes and collaborative opportunities. History has shown that economic factors are often the root causes of numerous conflicts and tensions around the globe, reinforcing the necessity for a more thoughtful and strategic approach. So, how are nations currently strategizing to attain global dominance, and how can they arm themselves against those seeking to assert authority over them? The answer lies in placing geo-economics at the center of their geopolitical ambitions. By prioritizing geo-economic goals, nations will likely find that their broader geopolitical aspirations will follow suit in due course. This prioritization should similarly extend to organizations and institutions that aspire for market dominance; adopting geo-economic strategies as a foundational principle is imperative rather than relying solely on traditional and perhaps outdated methodologies.

The foundational elements of geo-economics should concentrate on the complexities involved in supply chains and the dynamics of market interactions. This entails advocating for a collaborative approach, one that fosters partnership and mutual benefit between nations, rather than a confrontational stance that could lead to escalation and conflict. These guiding principles should inform the development and execution of economic strategies, aimed at fostering long-term transformations that can adapt to evolving global realities. It is essential to recognize that geo-economics should not be predicated on isolated events; rather, it should revolve around ongoing processes of transformation that respond to the currents of change in international relations. The effectiveness of geo-economic strategies should be assessed based on the processes and mechanisms employed—such as interventions, collaborations, and tactical decisions—rather than solely on final outcomes or short-term gains.

Currently, a multitude of nations pursue geopolitical dominance while neglecting the integration of sound economic strategies. These countries often expend substantial financial and human resources to cultivate "champion" organizations, a practice that can lead to flawed decision-making when they blindly rely on outdated historical precedents. Some nations tend to over-invest in singular corporations based on this skewed philosophy, a move that can have adverse effects on the economy. Instead of nurturing sustainable economic growth and innovation, this tendency can artificially inflate the perceived value of these entities, setting them up for potential failure and jeopardizing the broader national economy.

Additionally, many countries strive to secure a competitive economic advantage over their rivals through innovation. However, a significant challenge arises innovation does not always scale effectively, and the leap from innovative concept to mass production is fraught with difficulties. While groundbreaking initiatives may hold substantial promise and theoretical value, they often require considerable time, investment, and market readiness for development, which may impede nations and the corporations they give rise to from achieving their aspirations for dominance. As they grapple with the intricate challenge of translating innovative ideas into widespread economic success, nations must recognize the importance of a strategic, inclusive approach that integrates geo-economic principles to thrive in the increasingly interconnected global economy.

The landscape of innovation is an ever-evolving tapestry, characterized by rapid advancements that frequently focus on markets or geographic regions. These innovations, while potentially successful within their localized contexts, often lack the broader capacity to function as geopolitical instruments that influence the global market or sway other world powers. This raises a critical question: Why does this phenomenon occur? The core challenges extend beyond the mechanical aspects of mass production and delve into the complex issues related to mass adoption. Many innovations result in products and solutions that struggle to achieve widespread integration into existing systems and frameworks. The way these innovations are promoted, marketed, and advocated for—essentially the strategies employed to secure mass acceptance—can play a pivotal role in determining their ultimate success or failure.

Throughout history, we can trace the development of transformative innovations such as railroads, aircraft technology, and the internet, each of which has catalyzed significant economic growth and enabled nations to assert their dominance on a global scale. A shared characteristic among these revolutionary innovations is their inherent scalability; they are designed to grow and adapt to various contexts. If an innovation fails to scale effectively, it inevitably encounters substantial hurdles, hindering its potential impact. Moreover, scientific breakthroughs often require a nurturing incubation period, necessitating time for these nascent ideas to mature into fully realized solutions. Even with attempts to safeguard innovations as trade secrets, it tends to be the case that, over time, these ideas will be emulated or replicated by others. Take, for example, the development of ChatGPT, which skillfully utilized resources made publicly available by Google back in 2014. Critics argue that Google's decision to share its framework constituted a strategic blunder, inadvertently paving the way for subsequent innovators to build upon it. Yet, the nature of many innovations often renders containment a nearly impossible endeavor. A personal example is my creation, the Karma Capsule Network, for which I applied for a patent in 2020. This invention is rooted in Geoffrey Hinton's groundbreaking work on CapsNet. Recognizing the necessity for rigorous scientific validation, I purposefully aligned my work with his research, positioning my innovation as an augmented version of CapsNet that seamlessly integrates the principles of reinforcement learning with the original framework.

Innovations of this nature hold the capacity to be adopted and adapted by others, enabling further development. Initially, I considered keeping my invention private, believing that maintaining confidentiality would protect my intellectual property. However, such a concept soon felt counterintuitive; I came to understand that withholding my creation could lead to someone else asserting ownership of it before I had the opportunity to claim authorship. By placing my work into the public domain, I effectively establish myself as the original creator, which serves as my safeguard against potential infringement. While many others are welcome to capitalize on its potential, I remain committed to sharing my vision for the benefit of the broader community.

In a parallel context, nations themselves can act as catalysts in advancing their innovations. A particularly striking example of this phenomenon is China's rapid ascent within the realm of artificial intelligence. This progress has been significantly bolstered by a wave of engineers returning to China after receiving their education and training in the West, particularly in the United States. Much of the deep technological expertise in artificial intelligence is now being channeled back to China, allowing it to reach unprecedented heights of capability and influence. This scenario underscores a critical aspect of innovation: the original inventor may hold a groundbreaking idea, but it is often those who imitate and enhance that idea who reap the most substantial rewards. This observation applies equally to both corporations and nations, highlighting the importance of geoeconomics in this dynamic landscape.

Moreover, it is vital to recognize that the focus should not solely be on innovation itself. Take, for instance, the ongoing discussions concerning the semiconductor market. While securing a foothold in this critical sector can yield tangible success, the mere act of investing substantial capital—as is currently being attempted by the U.S.—does not guarantee a favorable outcome. The effective and strategic application of that capital is crucial and will ultimately delineate geoeconomic triumph. By the time significant investments are realized, and production capabilities are established over the next few years, it is conceivable that China may have already developed entirely new technologies, potentially diminishing the necessity for factories in locations such as Arizona to produce these chipsets. In conclusion, this exploration elucidates the notion that China possesses a deep understanding of artificial intelligence, which distinctly positions them ahead in this domain. While I recognize that their application of this technology does not always align with ethical or beneficial standards, I maintain an optimistic perspective. It is my belief that artificial intelligence should be harnessed to enhance human experience while respecting individual liberties and freedoms, ensuring that advancements serve the greater good of society.

Across the globe, human beings embody a remarkable spectrum of perspectives, each uniquely shaped by their cultural, social, and historical contexts. As a Libertarian, I deeply appreciate ideologies that prioritize individual freedom and advocate for minimal government interference. Yet, it is crucial to acknowledge that many nations operate under frameworks that starkly contrast with these ideals. In such environments, the pursuit of dominance and progress often overshadows the principles of individual liberty, raising pressing questions about whether these actions truly serve humanity or encroach upon the rights of individuals. This situation underscores a significant concern: we must be vigilant against an overreliance on innovation, which can easily be suppressed or stifled by oppressive structures embedded within society.

Another vital consideration is market readiness—the critical stage at which a product has been sufficiently developed and tested, making it fit for consumer introduction. In the fast-paced arena of entrepreneurship, the pressure exerted by investors to launch products ahead of schedule can be overwhelming. This relentless urgency often disregards the vital incubation periods necessary for genuine innovation to take root and flourish. Entrepreneurs may find themselves caught in a frantic race against the clock, often overlooking the intricate complexities involved in ushering a product to market. Market conditions, consumer behaviors, and regulatory environments can vary dramatically across different geographical regions, complicating the replication of success from one area to another.

Moreover, the world of finance grapples with the phenomenon of speculative trading, where investor behavior is frequently influenced by speculation rather than solid fundamentals. This creates a volatile landscape characterized by unpredictable market fluctuations. This dynamic cultivates a demand for products that can be hurriedly developed and rapidly scaled to yield immediate profits. However, speculators tend to prioritize perceived value—what appears lucrative based on current trends and forecasts—over actual value, which is rooted in the substantial benefits and long-term sustainability of a product. Consequently, even if an organization is diligently crafting real, lasting value, the meddlesome presence of speculators can disrupt the market landscape, hindering the optimal realization of a product's potential.

Furthermore, even the most innovative technology may encounter formidable challenges posed by competitors entering the market armed with extensive financial backing and aggressive marketing tactics. These rivals often exploit superficial claims that overshadow the rigorous effort and creativity invested in meaningful innovation. This challenge extends beyond individual companies; it mirrors broader trends that stifle the overall innovation ecosystem. The frenetic pace of modern market competition can stymie the essence of creativity and originality, ultimately hampering progress for all stakeholders. In conclusion, while the opportunities for innovation are abundant, navigating the landscape is fraught with formidable challenges that require astute awareness and careful maneuvering. Employing proactive strategies is essential to safeguarding the conditions under which genuine innovation can thrive, ultimately benefiting not just businesses but the fabric of society itself.

I am delving into the complex and often intricate dynamics that lie at the intersection of corporations and nations—an exploration that may initially appear unconventional. However, there exists a compelling rationale for embarking on such an analysis. While nations are typically defined by distinct geographical boundaries and structured governance, they do not always function as cohesive and unified entities. This disjointed nature can frequently echo the operational characteristics of multinational and transnational corporations. In many respects, these corporations act in ways akin to sovereign nations, making it insightful to examine their interactions and relationships in tandem.

Political leaders worldwide are becoming increasingly cognizant of the vast potential that transnational organizations possess. Often, they strive to leverage the influence and resources of these corporations to further their national interests and political agendas. On the flip side, these organizations are equally driven by the pursuit of geopolitical and geostrategic advantages, seeking to fortify their own positions within competitive market landscapes. This mutual dependence weaves a complex web of interrelationships, highlighting the critical necessity of perceiving both nations and corporations as interconnected players on the intricate global stage.

One of the prominent challenges that both sectors confront is the scarcity of highly skilled labor. The interplay between innovation and specialized expertise is paramount; novel innovations often spawn job opportunities that demand unique skill sets, particularly in technology-centric industries. When corporations invest heavily in research and development yet face significant attrition rates among their highly skilled workforce, they run the risk of undermining their capacity to innovate effectively. This issue extends beyond the corporate sphere; nations that aspire to enhance their geopolitical standing through innovation must also focus on nurturing and retaining talent to secure their potential for progress. Consider the United States—a nation that, perhaps unintentionally, has been disseminating its vast reservoir of knowledge and expertise across the globe, particularly to countries such as China and India. China has adeptly absorbed this knowledge, amplifying it through its own innovations and achievements, thereby asserting its presence on the world stage. In stark contrast, India has often positioned itself as a global hub for knowledge services, subcontracting its capabilities instead of fully harnessing this wealth of knowledge to propel its own geopolitical ambitions. To my mind, this approach signifies a considerable strategic miscalculation for India; it would stand to gain immensely by striving for greater innovation and autonomy rather than merely settling into the role of a compliant service provider in the ever-evolving global marketplace.

The pressing issue of developing a skilled workforce serves as a double-edged sword, impacting both corporations and nations alike. Certain countries grapple with the formidable challenge of adequately training their workforce to adapt to the shifting tides of economic demands. A relevant example is the ongoing transition from traditional industries—such as coal mining—to more sustainable alternatives in energy production. This transformation is laden with obstacles, as retraining individuals who have devoted years to blue-collar roles to acquire entirely new skill sets can prove to be a daunting and protracted endeavor. Many workers possess deep-seated ties to their trades, making the shift to different skill sets or industries even more challenging.

Moreover, the realm of scientific inquiry and innovation is further complicated by Max Planck's insightful assertion that "science progresses one funeral at a time." This phrase encapsulates the reality that scientific theories are often contested and transformed by subsequent generations of scholars. Innovations typically build upon pre-existing scientific frameworks, and by the time new scientists emerge to challenge established concepts, the ongoing progression of knowledge can create significant barriers to breakthrough innovations. This continuous cycle of inquiry, skepticism, and reevaluation can render the path to transformative discoveries more arduous, as younger scientists endeavor to carve out their own understanding and interpretations that may stand at odds with their predecessors.

Let's explore the intricate and multifaceted relationship between innovation and economic dynamics in greater detail. At its core, innovation can be likened to state machines, operating through a series of seamless transitions between various stages—essentially referring to the conception, development, and implementation of groundbreaking ideas or technologies. However, when the primary motivation behind innovation is reduced to merely generating automatic profit and value, this machine-driven philosophy often fails to unlock the full spectrum of its potential. The crux of the matter lies in the very nature of economies, particularly those defined by free market principles, which necessitate rapid adaptability and transformation. Should the pace of innovation lag the ever-evolving demands of these dynamic markets, significant obstacles may arise, hindering growth and impeding progress.

Reflecting on the historical contexts of innovation, it becomes increasingly clear that many prominent ancient civilizations, especially the Chinese dynasties, displayed a significant reluctance to share their technological advancements with the broader world. This hesitation stemmed from a profound anxiety: these civilizations feared that once other nations acquired and fully understood these innovations, their own competitive advantages would inevitably wane. This pattern underscores a pivotal characteristic of innovation: it is intrinsically a double-edged sword. While the promise of innovation heralds unprecedented progress and advancement, it can also unleash unforeseen consequences that may inadvertently undermine its benefits.

Moreover, the journey from innovative ideas to mass commercialization is fraught with challenges that often inhibit success. A variety of factors come into play, including scalability and expandability. Many companies born from innovative ideas find themselves operating within confined clusters of similar businesses, which limits their market impact. Transitioning from small-scale operations to mass production necessitates thoughtful strategic planning that considers geoeconomic factors. When innovations are built upon technologies that are simple to replicate or reproduce, they run the risk of being easily duplicated by other regions or nations. Such duplication can sometimes lead to superior production outcomes, further complicating the original innovator's competitive standing. This dynamic provides some historical context for understanding why China chose to withhold the technology of the printing press from the world for more than five centuries following its invention.

Historical examples, like the enduring Sangam Age Tamil Kingdoms, which thrived for over 4,000 years, demonstrate the importance of embedding social, economic models based on collaborative but, independent decentralized systems within the governance using innovative approached. Following that foot path, the Roman Empire did master the integrated approach of Society, Governance and Trade through modern tools, technologies and innovations of that age. So, for a digitally transformed world, modern geoeconomic factors within advanced networks driven by technological advancements such as artificial intelligence becomes the necessary ingredient. In this context, the custodians of innovation would consist of independent gadgets or smart systems, creating a paradigm shift that could fundamentally alter our understanding and implementation of innovation. I firmly believe in its critical role as a cornerstone of both societal and economic evolution. However, it is imperative that we approach innovation with the necessary caution and foresight. I propose that innovation should be deeply grounded in the principles of geo-economics—a multidisciplinary field that examines the intricate interplay between geographical contexts and economic strategies.

Practically speaking, our efforts should focus on purposefully implementing geo-economic principles to guide our innovative pursuits. Instead of allowing innovation to be propelled solely by unregulated market ambitions or the self-serving geopolitical motives of individual nations, it is essential to align our endeavors with best practices and adhere to established ethical guidelines. By doing so, we can navigate the intricate landscape of innovation more effectively, ensuring that the outcomes are positive, sustainable, and beneficial for society, the economy, and our planet. Through a collective commitment to these principles, we can hope to harness the full potential of innovation while mitigating its risks.

Chapter 7. Transformational Union and Geoeconomics

A **transformational union** refers to collective organizations that aim to significantly reshape the dynamics of the Participants, economy, and society. Unlike traditional unions, which typically focus on defending the interests of participants, improving working conditions, and negotiating wages, transformational unions seek broader systemic changes, both within the participant's movement and in society at large. Transformation union is a broader societal transformation along the lines of socialism, progressive economic policies, or environmental justice. In the realm of geopolitics or economics, a transformational union could describe an alliance or merger of nations or states that results in significant structural changes. For example, the European Union (EU) represents an economic and political transformation from a collection of sovereign nations to a collective that aims for political integration, economic cooperation, and shared governance. For unions to drive measurable and sustainable success through their programs, it is imperative to establish a comprehensive and well-structured framework that enables effective decentralization to sub-national and municipal levels. This framework must empower local municipalities to make informed decisions and take targeted actions that directly address the specific challenges and opportunities within their communities. Moreover, it is essential that local initiatives align with a broader global framework to create a cohesive strategy that maximizes impact.

International organizations like the United Nations and the World Bank possess the expertise and resources necessary to design effective programs. However, these initiatives often fall short due to gaps in understanding market dynamics and business operations. Many professionals within these organizations lack firsthand experience in managing or operating a business, which can lead to a disconnect between proposed strategies and the realities on the ground.

Increasing the involvement of local entrepreneurs, especially those who are highly educated and equipped with relevant skills, is critical for advancing local economic development. These individuals are vital to economic projects through their capacity for innovation, job creation, and knowledge-sharing. Collaborating with non-profit organizations is key to developing a robust startup ecosystem, providing essential resources, mentorship, and networking opportunities for small businesses. Fostering cooperation among various small-scale industries, both regulated and unregulated, is crucial for cultivating a vibrant local economy. An integrated approach that engages local policymakers, mayors, district governors, and other relevant officials will facilitate collaborative efforts. This cooperation will yield shared goals and initiatives that more effectively address local economic needs. Establishing special purpose entities (SPE) is a necessary step in facilitating local economic initiatives. These entities can be specifically tailored to fit local frameworks, requirements, and contexts, while considering relevant legal, economic, and social aspects. SPEs serve as platforms for managing negotiations and executing programs, facilitating contributions and support from a diverse range of stakeholders, including local communities and international partners. By concentrating on specific industries or broader economic sectors, SPEs will promote a cohesive strategy that harmonizes people, processes, and physical resources, ultimately enhancing efficacy and driving successful economic outcomes for the community.

Transformational unions and Social Purpose Enterprises (SPEs) are emerging as pivotal entities in the ongoing struggle to address the entrenched systemic issues that pervade our economy and marketplace. These organizations are increasingly recognized for their potential to confront significant challenges, including economic inequality, power imbalances, and various forms of exploitation that persist across a wide range of industries. By vigorously advocating for economic justice and social welfare, transformational unions and SPEs aim to establish a more equitable distribution of resources that transcends the limitations of traditional market mechanisms and contractual frameworks. A particularly innovative approach employed by these unions involves the organization of production through cooperative models and decentralized decision-making processes. This methodology facilitates a more democratic allocation of power and resources among all participants, creating an alternative to the conventional hierarchical structures typically seen in corporate environments. By empowering members to actively participate in decision-making, these unions foster a sense of ownership and accountability within the community. Additionally, transformational unions may champion progressive policies such as universal basic income (UBI), which is designed to provide a safety net for individuals, thereby enhancing their agency and economic independence. The overarching vision guiding these efforts is to cultivate a societal framework where all participants not only gain access to reliable resources but also exert greater control over their economic systems and the outcomes that arise from them. This effectively challenges and seeks to reimagine the traditional capitalist paradigms that currently dominate the landscape. However, the implementation of these transformative models is not without its challenges. One notable concern is the risk that one segment of the union could inadvertently support or subsidize another segment. Such dynamics could lead to potential distortions in market integrity and perceptions of fairness among participants. As a result, the effectiveness of transformational unions hinges on their ability to function as hybrid frameworks that integrate elements of both capitalism and socialism. This balance is essential in ensuring that the benefits derived from collective endeavors are equitably disseminated among all stakeholders, thereby fostering a more inclusive economic environment.

The potential for success in establishing a transnational union is significantly enhanced when a geoeconomic framework is adopted. This innovative approach entails the creation of smaller sub-unions, each with their own governance structures, while adhering to overarching principles of good governance that promote transparency, accountability, and inclusivity. Within these sub-unions, the establishment of dedicated economic zones can facilitate tailored incentives and rewards, which can be substantially rooted in digital assets, such as cryptocurrencies and tokens. This decentralized financial infrastructure enables the movement of both fungible and non-fungible assets within and across these zones. Moreover, introducing specific credit syndications—dictated by the unique characteristics of each zone—can foster a climate of constructive interdependency among participants, encouraging collaboration and shared prosperity.

In today's increasingly multipolar global landscape, nations are increasingly leveraging geoeconomic tools as a strategic means of safeguarding their interests against sanctions and hegemonic pressures from more powerful countries. In this context, the primary challenge is ensuring that interdependence remains constructive rather than exploitative, both at the national and international levels. Designing dynamic governance structures that are adaptive and resilient at all levels emerges as a critical solution. To support these adaptive structures, the implementation of immutable algorithms can provide the necessary stability and accountability, ensuring that governance remains robust even in the face of evolving challenges.

Historical treaties, such as the Trans-Pacific Partnership (TPP), the Transatlantic Trade and Investment Partnership (TTIP), and the North American Free Trade Agreement (NAFTA), have frequently encountered substantial opposition from various special interest groups. These challenges have often led to significant disruptions or even the complete abandonment of these agreements. Considering these experiences, it is crucial that future treaties be designed with a robust framework that emphasizes immutable, cause-based agreements. This foundational approach would not only protect the integrity of the treaty but also allow for the integration of dynamic control mechanisms that are governed by unchangeable algorithms. Such a system could greatly enhance the accountability of the parties involved while providing the necessary adaptability to respond effectively to the complex and ever-evolving global challenges we face today.

Moreover, to further improve the efficacy of these treaties, it would be beneficial to implement digital asset-based economic transactions among the distinct zones and sub-zones of the union. This strategy entails the development of digital asset-swapping systems, which could replace traditional currency-swapping methods that are currently prevalent among nations. By adopting this innovative approach, we can streamline cross-border transactions and reduce reliance on legacy financial systems that can be slow and cumbersome. Additionally, the inherent fungibility of digital assets would play a vital role in facilitating capital mobility between the various economic zones. This mobility is essential for ensuring not only the economic success of the regions involved but also for promoting stability within the broader geo-economic landscape. By leveraging the advantages of digital assets, we can create a more integrated and responsive economic framework that is better equipped to handle the demands of the global economy in the 21st century. By adopting these approaches, transformational unions and SPEs have the potential to reshape their respective economic landscapes, promoting a more equitable and just society for all participants.

Chapter 8. Intrinsic Value of Assets and their Orientation

8.1 The Knowledge and Social Taxonomies

As Kenneth Bounding, a prominent economist, I contend that humanity has undergone a profound transformation through the integration of social evolution alongside the established physical and biological forms of evolution. This notion of social evolution can be further divided into two categories: primitive evolution and composite evolution. Primitive evolution refers to developmental processes that occur within the confines of a singular community, often characterized by localized cultural practices, social structures, and knowledge systems. In contrast, composite evolution transcends these boundaries, occurring across multiple, diverse communities that interact and exchange ideas, leading to a more complex and interconnected social fabric.

One of the most significant challenges we face today lies in effective mining, curating, extracting, and trading of knowledge. In an increasingly information-rich world, the ability to manage this vast ocean of data and turn it into actionable insights is crucial for economic growth and societal advancement. Humanity possesses what can be termed the noosphere, a collective sphere of knowledge, ideas, and know-how that facilitates learning, innovation, and the communication of insights. This realm results in what is referred to as noogenetic evolution, where the generation of real economic value is contingent upon the establishment of composite evolution models. These models thrive on perfect interconnection with a plethora of primitive knowledge hubs, allowing for a seamless exchange of information and resources that can drive development.

The KEM-AI, TOP-AI and TIE-AI Taxonomies

In Chapter 2, we discussed the Social Taxonomies KEM, TOP and TIE. For over two centuries, economists have recognized the intricate interconnectedness and interdependence among all economic variables. This foundational belief can be broadened, particularly in the later theories put forth by Vilfredo Pareto, to encompass the realm of social variables as well. Economist Kenneth Boulding aimed to provide a comprehensive framework to articulate this interconnectedness and has developed a complex and multifaceted paradigm that captures its essence. Boulding's paradigm is both vast and intricate, encompassing components that resemble a model while articulating specific hypotheses concerning structural organization, interactions among elements, and the nuanced relationships that exist between continuity and change within economic and social systems. The hallmark features of Boulding's paradigm include multicausality, where multiple factors contribute to outcomes; interaction, emphasizing the relationships among various elements; and cumulative causation, which highlights how earlier events or conditions can shape future outcomes in unpredictable ways.

Central to Boulding's grand paradigm are three primary elements, each illustrating a general interdependence and further subdivided into three subcategories. These elements are arranged into triads that correspond to the overarching triad of physical, biological, and social evolution. The first of these sub models is termed the TOP sub model, which differentiates among three fundamental categories: things, organizations, and people. While these terms might seem simple or even lacking in sophistication, they encapsulate a wide array of theories and concepts from economics, political science, and sociology that can be effectively categorized within these broad definitions.

The second element, known as the KEM taxonomy, categorizes the core factors of production into three distinct categories: knowledge, energy, and materials. This triad is crucial for understanding the foundations of economic activity and the dynamics of production systems. Lastly, the TIE sub model revolves around systems of threat, integration, and exchange, creating a space to analyze how these various systems interact and influence each other. Each of these triads consists of additional levels or sub-elements, highlighting the complexity of interactions at play. The internal relationships among these components are characterized by complexity, often described as kaleidoscopic and evolutionary, where interactions can sometimes be conflictual. Boulding interprets society as a vast and intricate system, and he has systematically sought to identify subsystems or subprocesses that operate within this larger framework. These subprocesses interact in ways that yield results that are open-ended and resistant to deterministic analysis, resulting in a model of cumulative multi-causation that leads to radical indeterminacy.

At the core of these interactions lies the dynamics of knowledge—often referred to as the noosphere—which is molded by various forms of human activism. This evolutionary process is distinctive to humankind, especially concerning values that individuals perceive as actual, possible, or desirable. Historically, conflicts stemming from social, political, and military rivalries have contributed to fluctuating values; however, Boulding suggests that the most significant driver of change is rooted in knowledge conflict. Within the noosphere, myriad interpretations of science, as well as competing paradigms and ideologies, coalesce to influence the formation of "images," which subsequently shape individual thoughts and behaviors. The mechanisms through which learned behaviors and belief systems are disseminated and enacted can be both deliberative—conscious and intentional—and nondeliberative—automatic and subconscious.

It is crucial to understand that knowledge does not exist in isolation or a social vacuum; comprehending any "thing" necessitates considering it in relation to the TOP, KEM, and TIE subprocesses and their interactions. In the context of the social sphere embedded within the ecological system, conflicts, and power dynamics emerge amongst the TOP, KEM, and TIE subprocesses. In certain respects, this ecological economic system behaves with a degree of autonomy, where forces such as freedom of choice and power often engage in opposition to one another. Individuals and smaller groups within this framework are continually striving to exert control and reshape social and institutional structures to serve their interests. Furthermore, the economy embodies more than just the mere static allocation of resources. The advent of artificial intelligence (AI), which both challenges and complements rational intelligence, possesses the ability to transcend mere instinctual responses and conventional perceptions of value. However, this evolution comes with significant concerns. Bias, which can play both beneficial and detrimental roles—though it mainly manifests negatively—poses profound challenges in the current landscape of AI, especially as it operates within private capitalist frameworks. This raises pressing concerns regarding the potential for a singular individual's or a collective group's intelligence to unduly shape the perspectives of the broader populace, ultimately influencing societal perceptions of value and worth. However, I believe all the three taxonomies are incomplete, as it neglects a critical contemporary force: machine intelligence. While de Chardin envisioned the Omega Point as a harmonious convergence of human unity, the rapid rise of artificial intelligence and machine cognition presents a significant challenge to this equilibrium. The increasing prevalence and influence of AI could overshadow human contributions to this collective consciousness, thus threatening the harmonious integration that de Chardin envisioned. To address this oversight, it is essential to incorporate "AI" into the existing frameworks, thereby evolving them into what I propose as the KEM-AI, TOP-AI and TIE-AI taxonomies. This reinterpretation not only acknowledges the transformative impact of machine intelligence on human evolution but also emphasizes the necessity of coalescing human and AI capabilities to foster a more balanced and inclusive future.

8.2 Currency Consumption

In discussing currency consumption and its implications for the intrinsic value of assets, it's important to recognize the significant increase in money printing over the past few decades. This trend has emerged from a complicity among political leaders, banking institutions, and legislative frameworks, resulting in an abundance of fiat currencies. Historically, the United States' detachment from the gold standard in the 1930s, followed by President Nixon's decision in 1971 to sever the U.S. dollar's link to gold, established the dollar as a fiat currency. This transition initiated a new economic dynamic that solidified the dollar's role as the primary global trading currency. However, recent years have witnessed a profound transformation in the market, signaling the emergence of a new world order. While the dollar continues to account for approximately 70 percent of global trade as of 2024, the major concern lies not solely in the act of printing dollars, but in the broader ramifications of this practice. Many people perceive that banks and central banks have exclusive authority to create money, leading to widespread economic challenges. However, the increasing involvement of national governments in the money printing process poses even greater risks on a larger scale. As a result, nations now prioritize the distribution of printed money to the public, cultivating consumer behavior among citizens. This phenomenon often occurs alongside a limited number of banks and large corporations that wield considerable control over individuals' lives, while citizens increasingly relinquish their liberties in favor of market engagement.

Regrettably, many citizens show indifference, desiring only the provision of necessities. Political leaders have effectively persuaded the populace that they will be supported, mainly through the distribution of printed money. This reliance on printed currency fundamentally contradicts economic principles and the inherent laws of nature. When banks create money, individuals are typically motivated to work for their earnings, fostering entrepreneurship and innovation. In contrast, the current environment, where governments take on the responsibility for substantial money printing, undermines the foundation of entrepreneurship and concentrates significant power in the hands of a few corporations closely aligned with governmental interests.

Historically, equities have served as a vital instrument, enabling equitable access to the intrinsic values of companies that were once closely held by wealthy families. These companies maintained their value within familial lines for generations, restricting broader access to intellectual properties and business innovations. The trading of equities has created opportunities for entrepreneurs to tap into previously inaccessible value. However, the current landscape reflects a troubling shift in which only large corporations exert control over these intellectual properties. As more printed money flows to these corporations, often with the approval of banks, the balance of power becomes disproportionately skewed. This imbalance manifests in various challenges, as the role of currency in trade has become increasingly distorted. The original intention of money was to serve as a medium for trading goods and services, facilitating exchanges on a global scale. Presently, however, we observe a concerning trend where trade is primarily centered on the exchange of money itself, fostering the perception that financial capital can purchase any asset disregarding the Intrinsic Value. This phenomenon is creating a bubble that threatens to disrupt global economic stability, leading to potential catastrophic consequences.

Many entrepreneurs today are grappling with significant challenges in securing the financial capital necessary to sustain and expand their businesses, particularly as the economic landscape continues to shift in unpredictable ways. The ongoing trend of people staying home due to various factors, be it health concerns, remote work policies, or economic uncertainty—has raised serious concerns about productivity levels across multiple sectors which in turn influences the creation of shallow assets with no intrinsic value. In this context, the stock market's traditional appeal may falter, as investors increasingly perceive cash to hold more immediate value. This perception is largely driven by rising interest rates, which enhance the returns on cash holdings relative to equities and assets with intrinsic value. So, as investors consider their options, there is a growing inclination to channel funds into bonds or government securities, operating under the assumption that these vehicles could potentially yield higher returns. However, this intense focus on short-term monetary gains risks overshadowing critical considerations related to the quality of products, services, and the overall quality of life. When the drive for profit inadvertently prioritizes financial returns over intrinsic value, the consequences can be detrimental to innovation, sustainability, and consumer satisfaction.

The ascendancy of the dollar as a global reserve currency is a phenomenon that can be traced back to the complex geopolitical landscape that emerged in the aftermath of World War II. Before the 1950s, the U.S. dollar was not the predominant currency in international trade; that title had historically shifted among various dominant powers. In ancient times, different kingdoms relied on coins crafted from precious metals such as gold and copper, establishing early forms of currency that facilitated trade and commerce. The Romans played a pivotal role in this evolving currency system, showcasing sophisticated methods of coinage that laid the groundwork for future monetary systems. This was followed by eras where the Portuguese and Dutch exerted considerable influence over global trade, dominating the flow of goods and currency in their respective times. As the centuries progressed, the British pound took the lead in the global currency arena, becoming synonymous with economic power during the height of the British Empire. However, following the devastation of World War II, Britain faced significant economic challenges and a gradual decline in its global hegemony. This weakened state created a unique opportunity for the United States to step into the role of the world's leading currency provider. In the wake of the war, the U.S. emerged as a beacon of economic stability, with the dollar embodying the essential characteristics required to assume the mantle of a global currency. The dollar was backed by a robust economy, a strong industrial base, and the trust of international markets that led to the dollar's emergence as the world's primary reserve currency. This pivotal transition occurred in the aftermath of World War II, a period when the global economy was in dire need of a stable and trustworthy currency to facilitate international trade and economic relations. The U.S. dollar stepped into this role, supported by the strength and resilience of the American economy.

A watershed moment came in 1971 when President Richard Nixon made the monumental decision to decouple the dollar from the gold standard, thereby transitioning the dollar into a fiat currency. This significant shift meant that the dollar was no longer backed by a physical commodity, allowing the government to print money without the constraints imposed by a gold reserve. While this change provided greater flexibility in monetary policy, it also introduced new complexities and risks, as the value of the dollar became more dependent on trust and confidence rather than tangible assets. The narrative stresses that the enduring strength of any currency, the U.S. dollar included, is fundamentally tied to the productivity of the economy it represents. Historically, the United States enjoyed high levels of productivity, particularly in the decades following the world wars, due to a unique culture that championed freedom, innovation, and entrepreneurship. However, contemporary concerns are surfacing about a potential decline in American productivity. Many citizens seem to lack the drive for innovation, opting instead for complacency within their professional roles. Education is presented as a pivotal factor in sustaining a robust currency. The discussion critiques the heavy focus on traditional educational paths, such as obtaining PhDs, pointing out that these credentials do not always equip individuals with the skills necessary to meet the evolving demands of the economy. Instead, there is a pressing need to develop a productive economic system that can effectively utilize a skilled workforce, rather than simply directing educated individuals towards large corporations or government positions that may not fully leverage their talents. Moreover, the theme of trust in governance emerges as a crucial element for a currency to achieve global acceptance. The American model of governance, which is deeply rooted in a strong constitutional framework, has historically fostered a high level of trust among its citizens and international partners. However, recent events that challenge this foundational trust call for a critical examination of how governance operates and is perceived by the public. This scrutiny emphasizes the dynamic interplay among productivity, education, and the confidence in governmental stability, all of which are essential for maintaining the integrity and value of the currency in an increasingly complex global economy. Over the past few decades, many countries have come to recognize that these broad agreements often disproportionately benefit the United States; similar concerns have also arisen in Europe. This realization has prompted nations to seek more tailored, individual treaties based on mutual interests, rather than relying on blanket agreements. As a result, trust in the U.S. dollar is diminishing, as countries increasingly engage in currency exchanges and swaps without the need for the dollar.

Historically, the United States led the world in infrastructure development throughout the 19th and 20th centuries, creating extensive projects. However, other regions, particularly in Asia and Africa, are now advancing in infrastructure development at a pace that challenges U.S. dominance. China has emerged as a significant player in the global economic landscape by leveraging its Belt and Road Initiative to establish a vast network of infrastructure projects across over 100 countries. This initiative enhances confidence in the Chinese currency, even though China's lack of a democratic governance structure raises trust issues. India also has the potential to become a significant player in global trade, benefiting from its democratic framework. However, it faces challenges that must be addressed to elevate its currency to a position of global significance. Essential characteristics for achieving this include strong governance, the will of the people, and a proactive approach to international relations. The experiences of past global leaders, such as England and the United States, serve as cautionary tales for nations navigating their paths toward becoming influential global currencies. Furthermore, the volume of money, the rate at which the currency circulates through the economy, is increasingly stalling. This stagnation, particularly pronounced in the shrinking middle class, creates obstacles for economic growth and cycles. As money becomes stagnant, it can lose its purchasing power, leading to broader implications for consumer confidence and economic stability.

8.3 Energy and Oil Economics

The dynamics of oil trading are experiencing profound changes, particularly intensified by the outbreak of the Ukraine war. Traditionally, oil has been traded predominantly in U.S. dollars, a practice firmly established by the Organization of the Petroleum Exporting Countries (OPEC). This dollar-centric model has long been viewed as an integral part of the global financial system, reinforcing the currency's status as the world's primary reserve currency. However, a noticeable shift is beginning to take place, as several countries are exploring and actively implementing the use of their own currencies for oil transactions. This emerging trend has the potential to significantly diminish the dollar's dominance in global markets and alter the landscape of international trade. Accompanying this transformation is a wave of increased diplomatic agreements and the formation of new economic alliances. Nations are forging partnerships that foster trade in local currencies, signaling a move away from U.S. economic hegemony. This trend not only reflects geopolitical realignment but also indicates a desire among various countries to assert greater control over their economic destinies and reduce their dependence on the dollar. Despite the continuing geopolitical and economic influence of the United States, there are rising concerns that the younger generation may struggle to maintain the nation's historical achievements. A key factor contributing to this anxiety is the declining traditional reliance on oil as a backing resource for the dollar. This reliance is weakening, as evidenced by the evolving energy landscape characterized by the growth of renewable energy sources and the fluctuating demand for fossil fuels. With hydrogen entering the race and winning substantially through more adoption, there is a clear change in the energy landscape especially when tokenization of these energy commodities as digital assets with intrinsic value.

8.4 Innovation driving Intrinsic Value

Throughout history, innovation has served as a pivotal catalyst in re-establishing and amplifying a nation's influence as a global leader. A striking illustration of this phenomenon is China's ascendance as a prominent global power, a transformation propelled by groundbreaking advancements in technology and communication. This journey began with the invention of the printing press, which drastically altered the landscape of information dissemination. The ability to reproduce texts efficiently opened pathways for literacy, education, and the spread of revolutionary ideas throughout the populace. In more recent historical contexts, Europe experienced a profound metamorphosis, driven by innovations such as radar technology and refined accounting practices. These advancements were instrumental in fostering economic expansion and enhancing military efficacy, allowing European nations to command significant power on the world stage. Moreover, innovation in shipping has been crucial in shaping the intricate dynamics of global trade. The ancient Tamil kingdoms, located in present-day India, were celebrated for their superior naval capabilities, which enabled them to dominate trade across Asia while establishing extensive commercial networks. During this era of maritime strength, Tamil merchants utilized their sophisticated shipping technologies—such as advanced shipbuilding techniques and navigational skills—to facilitate trade with far-flung markets, including Vietnam and China. The Chola dynasty, inheritors of this maritime legacy, further extended these trade connections, enriching the cultural tapestry along the routes they traversed and contributing to a vibrant, interconnected economy. The ability to innovate has thus emerged as a decisive factor impacting the rise and fall of civilizations throughout history. As we navigate today's rapidly evolving global landscape, a nation's aptitude for adaptation, innovation, and the forging of new economic pathways will undoubtedly shape its future standing in an increasingly competitive and interconnected world. This historical narrative underscores the vital role of innovation in trade, particularly exemplified by the dynamic interactions between the Romans and the Tamils. This relationship thrived on the pervasive acceptance of Roman currency, which the Tamils regarded as a reliable medium of exchange, thus facilitating their trade activities. The Romans celebrated for their groundbreaking contributions, particularly in shipping and cartography, leveraged their innovations to monopolize trade routes, further asserting their dominance.

Yet, the contemporary scene in the United States and Europe brings forth pressing challenges concerning innovation. Despite a notable surge in the number of startups and an influx of financial backing, significant questions linger regarding the real impact and value generated by these enterprises. While innovation flourishes globally, it often appears fragmented, underscoring the urgent need for strategic consolidation to effectively propel economic revitalization across various regions. Recognizing the vital role that intrinsic value plays in determining asset worth is imperative for anyone navigating today's financial landscape. The stability and strength of a nation's currency are intricately tied to the underlying value of its assets, which include tangible properties like real estate and financial instruments such as equities. In recent years, there has been a notable decline in the intrinsic value of the U.S. dollar, which has prompted a reassessment of its reliability as a premier asset. Consequently, gold, with its historical reputation as a stable store of value, is becoming increasingly sought after as an alternative backing for the currency.

It is important to acknowledge that although the U.S. dollar remains functional as a medium of exchange, its purchasing power is steadily declining. This erosion of value signals that individuals and investors would be prudent to leverage the current peak valuation of the dollar by diverting their assets into tangible investments. Strategically allocating funds towards global enterprises and real estate that possess intrinsic worth is advisable. One must remember that the dollar itself is, fundamentally, a construction upheld by debt rather than a physical asset, which diminishes its substantive value. The takeaway is clear: individuals should actively pursue the creation of a diversified investment portfolio that incorporates meaningful, value-driven assets. Moreover, to adeptly confront the multifaceted challenges presented in the current economic climate, a broad spectrum of stakeholders—including corporations, investors, entrepreneurs, and policymakers—must reinforce their dedication to fostering a culture of innovation. This aspiration can be realized through intentional strategic collaborations among leaders across various sectors, establishing robust institutions focused on developing assets characterized by intrinsic value. Organizations that prioritize cultivating intrinsic worth are positioned to thrive amidst an increasingly competitive global marketplace.

Fostering intrinsic value within companies is particularly vital against the backdrop of the significant economic transformations currently underway. This process entails a thorough reassessment of products, solutions, and intellectual properties to guarantee they are not only appealing in the marketplace but also resonate with cutting-edge practices that enhance their inherent worth. Such alignment has the potential to spark innovative breakthroughs that deeply connect with consumers and stakeholders alike. Ultimately, the onus falls upon organizational leaders to spearhead this essential transformation. While it is possible to impose regulations on capital flow in certain markets, there exists a pressing need to forge alternative value-generation frameworks—often referred to as "value printing" that can be optimized within both equities and assets. By concentrating on these innovative strategies, it becomes realistic to create stocks and organizations that truly embody substantial, tradable value on the global stage. This strategic pivot not only promises to fortify the economic landscape but also yields enduring benefits for all stakeholders involved. I have devoted numerous years to examining geo-economics through the lens of the Fourth Industrial Revolution, and I am eager to share insights that stem from both thorough research and invaluable firsthand experiences garnered from my travels across diverse global markets. My primary concern lies in the increasing speculation surrounding cryptocurrencies, particularly Bitcoin, which I perceive as a highly unstable and risky investment. I often liken Bitcoin to a "mountain goat," adept at scaling steep, rugged terrains only to inevitably lose its footing and tumble. This metaphor vividly captures the unpredictable nature of such speculative financial instruments. I urge potential investors to be cautious about the seductive appeal of quick profits, as I foresee that the landscape of global currencies is on the cusp of a significant transformation. Alternative currencies may rise to prominence, potentially challenging the longstanding dominance of the U.S. dollar. Drawing on my credentials as an entrepreneur, economist, and historian, I stress the critical importance of comprehending the shifting dynamics of global currency. I advocate for proactive financial planning, emphasizing the necessity for individuals to equip themselves with knowledge and strategies to stay ahead of these emerging trends. The culmination of my extensive research and analysis in economics and market behavior has led to the development of mayaNomics—a framework that offers a novel perspective on the intricate complexities of modern finance. This initiative encourages stakeholders to adapt and thrive within an ever-evolving economic environment. The seeds of my exploration into intrinsic values were planted in 2006 at a transformative seminar led by John Zachman, often regarded as the Father of Information Engineering on Enterprise Architecture. Over the years, I crafted several innovative Enterprise Architecture (EA) frameworks for prominent clients, with the most noteworthy being the Services Oriented Architecture (SOA) for U.S. Steel. After four months of meticulous analysis and design, I delivered a comprehensive blueprint and architecture guidelines, earning high praise from the U.S. Steel team for the clarity and depth of my work. Despite operating as a solitary force in architectural planning at the time and being ahead of my peers, I found validation years later when the information architect overseeing my project reached out to express how my contributions, made six years earlier, had gained newfound relevance. He admired my foresight and inquired how I had managed to envision such future trends. This experience underscores the original intention behind EA planning, which was to generate substantial value for enterprises. The concept of Services Oriented Architecture was crafted by practitioners like me to cultivate incremental yet sustainable value at the foundational level of components and services. Institutions that recognized the significance of comprehensive architectural planning and delved deep into their internal components, services, tools, and infrastructure were able to swiftly adapt their business models for enhanced value creation. Unfortunately, oligarchies within the business consulting and IT consulting sectors frequently disregarded or appropriated these valuable projects, favoring solutions that catered to their clients' immediate interests. Historically, technology and innovation have often been misused as mere rhetoric to redistribute dollar flows from the upper echelons of the economy to the middle classes without yielding tangible values, consequently failing to create any accumulation of capital. This unsettling pattern has resurfaced with the advent of AI and digital assets, as a select few companies, commonly known as the "magnificent seven," have channeled billions into generative AI, proclaiming their dominance in the AI market, and reaping the benefits from a resulting stock market rally. For over fifty years, the United States has maintained a leading position in technology, while various other nations have primarily acted as enablers and consumers not as good output or products but merely as partners in the dollar life cycle game. Despite having the opportunity to spearhead advancements, countries such as India have inexplicably opted to export their software talent in exchange for mere printed fiat dollars. Meanwhile, European nations have chosen to prioritize manufacturing, redistributing their earnings back into the U.S. through financial assets and real estate holdings. Similarly, Japan and South Korea have focused their efforts on enhancing their electronics sectors. However, a formidable challenger has emerged: China, which is unyielding in its ambition to dominate technology and prepared to confront the U.S. head-on. I believe this rivalry presents a substantial opportunity for the U.S. and the global community, as it will inevitably shift the spotlight toward genuine innovation and the creation of true value for investors.

Chapter 9. New Avatars of Assets driven by DeepTech AI

DeepTech refers to a category of advanced technologies that are built on significant scientific and engineering innovations, often involving breakthroughs in fields like artificial intelligence (AI), quantum computing, blockchain, robotics, biotechnology, and more. When applied to geoeconomics, these technologies have the potential to reshape global economies, influence geopolitical relationships, and drive new forms of economic competition, cooperation, and security.

Geoeconomics, a blend of geography and economics, involves using economic instruments (such as trade, investment, sanctions, and tariffs) to achieve geopolitical objectives. In an increasingly interconnected world, the fusion of DeepTech and AI is transforming how geoeconomic strategies are formulated and executed. AI-driven solutions can influence everything from economic policies and international trade to security and resource management.

Here's a deep dive into how AI-driven DeepTech is impacting geoeconomics:

9.1 AI-Driven Geoeconomics: Key Concepts

AI is increasingly integrated into geoeconomics by enabling faster decision-making, enhancing predictive capabilities, and automating various economic processes. Here are a few key areas where AI and DeepTech are intersected with geoeconomics:

Predictive Analytics for Economic Forecasting

- AI in Predictive Models: AI algorithms can analyze vast amounts of economic data (such as trade flows, financial markets, commodity prices, etc.) to predict trends and events that may affect global markets. This ability is crucial for governments and multinational corporations to anticipate economic shifts, policy changes, or crises that could reshape the geopolitical landscape.

- Geopolitical Risk Analysis: AI-driven models can analyze political stability, social unrest, or military conflict data and forecast potential impacts on trade routes, supply chains, and investment. This predictive capability can help decision-makers prepare for disruptions in global trade or the rise of new geopolitical power centers.

Trade and Investment Strategies

- Smart Trade Negotiations: AI-powered platforms can help governments and businesses optimize trade negotiations by analyzing large datasets related to market demands, political factors, and historical trade agreements. This improves the decision-making process by highlighting potential risks and opportunities in trade relations.
- Global Supply Chain Optimization: AI and machine learning (ML) can be used to enhance the efficiency and resilience of global supply chains. By predicting disruptions, AI systems can recommend actions to mitigate risks, helping businesses and governments manage geoeconomic shocks, such as trade wars or sanctions.

Economic Sanctions and Diplomatic Leverage

- Sanction Monitoring and Enforcement: AI tools can help monitor and enforce economic sanctions imposed on countries, organizations, or individuals. Machine learning models can analyze international financial transactions to detect violations of sanctions, ensuring compliance.

- Diplomatic Leverage: Countries can use AI-driven insights to better understand the economic vulnerabilities of their adversaries, allowing them to deploy sanctions more effectively or form targeted diplomatic alliances to apply economic pressure.

9.2 DeepTech in Geoeconomics

DeepTech, especially AI and blockchain, can enhance the effectiveness of economic policies and geopolitical strategies by enabling more precise, data-driven, and automated processes. Here are the prominent DeepTech sectors influencing geoeconomics:

Blockchain for Trust and Transparency

- Supply Chain Transparency: Blockchain technology, a critical part of DeepTech, enables secure, transparent, and immutable records of transactions. For geoeconomics, this is crucial in trade, where trust and transparency are essential for maintaining fair and efficient international trade systems.
- Digital Trade Agreements: Blockchain can facilitate the creation of smart contract-self-executing contracts with the terms directly written into code. This can automate trade agreements, reduce friction, and increase the speed of cross-border transactions.
- Financial Systems and CBDCs: Blockchain underpins the creation of Central Bank Digital Currencies (CBDCs). These digital currencies can enable faster, safer, and more efficient international transactions, potentially shifting power dynamics in the global financial system.

Quantum Computing for Economic Modeling

- Quantum AI in Financial Markets: Quantum computing has the potential to revolutionize economic forecasting, financial modeling, and market prediction. Quantum algorithms can analyze complex economic systems faster and more efficiently than traditional computing, enabling more accurate predictions about currency markets, trade negotiations, or global market trends.
- Cryptography and Security: Quantum computing also poses a challenge to traditional cryptographic systems used in financial transactions and digital assets. As a result, countries may need to develop new cryptographic strategies to safeguard their economic interests in the face of advanced quantum capabilities.

AI in Global Resource Management

- AI for Natural Resources: AI and DeepTech are increasingly used to manage global resources, from energy and water to rare earth minerals. These technologies enable more efficient and sustainable resource extraction, which is critical in the geoeconomic context of securing resources in international competition.
- Geospatial Data for Geopolitical Strategy: AI can be used to analyze satellite data, geographic information, and environmental factors to help countries make more informed decisions about resource management, border security, and climate-related issues, all of which are integral to geoeconomics.

9.3 AI-Driven Geoeconomics and Global Business

AI-driven geoeconomics is transforming how businesses operate on a global scale. DeepTech innovations provide companies with new tools for managing risk, optimizing resources, and enhancing decision-making:

Data-Driven Economic Strategies for Multinational Corporations (MNCs)

- Corporate Diplomacy: AI enables businesses to better understand the political and economic climates in different countries. By analyzing trends, policies, and data, corporations can navigate complex regulatory environments, predict market behavior, and optimize their international expansion strategies.
- Real-Time Risk Management: AI models can analyze real-time data to identify emerging risks, such as political instability or regulatory changes, that could impact multinational operations. Companies can use this data to adjust their strategies and avoid potential disruptions.

Investment and Economic Intelligence

- Predictive Investment Models: AI-powered investment tools analyze data from global markets, trade flows, and economic policies to make more informed investment decisions. These tools help investors and firms identify opportunities and risks across different regions, improving portfolio management in a geoeconomic context.
- Geoeconomic Trends and Investment Flows: AI can detect emerging geoeconomic trends (e.g., shifts in trade patterns, the rise of new economic blocks, or the impact of digital currencies on global finance), allowing investors to align their strategies with these evolving dynamics.

9.4 Geoeconomic Implications of DeepTech AI

The integration of AI and DeepTech into geoeconomics has far-reaching implications for global relations and economic competition. Here are the primary impacts:

Shifting Global Power Dynamics

- AI and Technological Dominance: Countries that lead in AI development and DeepTech research are poised to wield significant geopolitical influence. By leveraging these technologies, nations can enhance their economic power and shape global standards, making AI-driven geoeconomics a key aspect of future international competition.
- Resource Control: Nations that control critical digital infrastructure—such as data centers, quantum computing research, and AI talent—gain strategic advantages, further solidifying the central role of technology in geopolitics.

Trade Wars and Geoeconomic Rivalries

- AI-Enhanced Trade Wars: Geoeconomic rivalry could intensify as nations leverage AI for strategic advantages in trade wars. For instance, countries might use AI to anticipate and counteract tariffs, sanctions, or other economic measures, leading to a new kind of "trade warfare" driven by technological superiority.
- Currency Wars and Digital Sovereignty: The rise of digital currencies (both CBDCs and cryptocurrencies) introduces new forms of economic warfare. Countries could manipulate digital currency markets or blockchain systems to gain a competitive edge in global trade or to impose financial sanctions.

AI for National Security and Economic Protection

- AI-Driven National Security Policies: AI is not only reshaping the economy but also national security strategies. Governments may use AI for surveillance, cybersecurity, and to protect vital economic interests such as intellectual property and natural resources. These measures ensure that countries' geoeconomic strategies are secure from foreign interference.
- Cybersecurity and Economic Protection: As digital assets and transactions become more prevalent, the need for AI-driven cybersecurity solutions becomes paramount. Countries and businesses must protect their financial systems and economic infrastructure from cyberattacks, which could have devastating economic and geopolitical consequences.

Challenges and Considerations

Despite its potential, the application of AI and DeepTech in geoeconomics raises several challenges:

- Ethical and Privacy Concerns: AI systems, especially in surveillance and data-driven geoeconomics, raise significant privacy and ethical questions. The balance between economic security and individual freedom needs to be carefully managed.
- Technology Dependence: Over-reliance on AI and DeepTech could create vulnerabilities, as adversaries might exploit weaknesses in digital systems to disrupt economies or supply chains.
- Regulation and Control: There is a need for global cooperation in regulating AI and DeepTech to prevent monopolies, technological abuse, and economic imbalances. National sovereignty may also clash with the global nature of these technologies.

AI-driven DeepTech is revolutionizing geoeconomics, transforming how nations and businesses navigate global competition, trade, and economic influence. By leveraging predictive analytics, blockchain, quantum computing, and other advanced technologies, both governments and corporations can gain a significant edge in shaping the future of the global economy. However, to fully harness the potential of these technologies, global collaboration, ethical considerations, and proper regulation are essential to mitigate risks and ensure that technological advancements benefit all parties equitably.

9.5 Tech transfer as a capital injection

Technology Transfer (tech transfer) refers to the process of transferring new technologies, scientific research, or innovations from their original source—typically research institutions, universities, or businesses—into the marketplace where they can be commercialized, applied, and developed further. This can involve the licensing of patents, selling of intellectual property (IP), or partnerships for joint development and production.

Tech transfer as a capital injection involves leveraging knowledge, innovations, and technologies that are transferred from one entity (e.g., university, research lab, or corporation) to another, often with the objective of driving economic growth, fostering new businesses, and generating returns on investment. In this context, technology transfer can be viewed as a form of capital injection into the economy or a specific company, offering funding, resources, and opportunities for growth. This process is especially significant in driving the economic development of regions or industries, as it converts intangible assets—such as patents and innovations—into tangible capital. Here's how tech transfer functions as a capital injection. Tech transfer can take several forms, each offering a different level of capital injection into businesses or regions:

Licensing of Intellectual Property (IP): A university, research institution, or company licenses its patented technology to another organization, which then commercializes it. The organization receiving the license often pays an upfront fee, royalties, or a combination of both.

- Capital Injection: The license fee or royalties provide an immediate cash inflow to the research institution or the entity transferring the technology. The recipient organization gains access to valuable IP, which can lead to new product development and revenue generation.

Equity Investment and Joint Ventures: In cases where tech transfer involves a startup or an existing company, the transferring institution might take equity stake in the company or enter joint ventures to co-develop and market the technology.

- Capital Injection: By taking equity or entering joint ventures, the research institution or university receives a stake in the company's future success, providing a potential capital gain. The company receiving the technology infusion can use the capital investment to scale its operations, hire staff, and expand its production.

Research and Development (R&D) Partnerships: Companies or institutions may enter strategic partnerships where they collaborate on R&D efforts to commercialize a technology. These partnerships may involve funding from the corporate partner or public grants.

- Capital Injection: The capital infusion in this case often comes in the form of joint funding, infrastructure, or operational support to conduct R&D. These collaborations also allow the tech recipient to reduce research costs while gaining access to advanced technologies, which can lead to new products or services.

Spin-Off Companies: Universities or research institutions may create spin-off companies to commercialize new technology. This allows the institution to maintain ownership or licensing rights to technology while providing the necessary capital for the spin-off to develop and grow.

- Capital Injection: Spin-offs can attract venture capital or government grants, providing the financial resources needed to bring the technology to the market. This capital is injected directly into the economy, with the potential for job creation, economic growth, and long-term returns for the institution.

Benefits of Tech Transfer as a Capital Injection

1. **Economic Growth and Innovation:**

- Increased Productivity: By transferring new technologies into the commercial sector, tech transfer stimulates productivity in industries that adopt them. This can lead to the creation of new businesses, products, and services, all of which drive economic growth.
- Job Creation: Startups and businesses that benefit from new technologies often require additional workforce for research, development, and production, leading to the creation of jobs and boosting employment in high-tech sectors.
- Enhanced Competitiveness: Regions that effectively manage tech transfer create ecosystems where innovation thrives, which can make them more competitive globally. Access to cutting-edge technology can help businesses improve their operations, products, and services.

2. **Capital Formation:**
    - Venture Capital Attraction: Tech transfer often attracts private investors, including venture capitalists, who are interested in investing in high-

potential technologies that can generate significant returns. This private capital acts as a supplementary injection to the economy.

- Access to Funding: Research institutions, universities, and companies involved in tech transfer gain access to a range of funding sources, including grants, partnerships, and venture capital, which can be used for further innovation and scaling of businesses.
- Return on Investment: In cases where equity is involved (such as in spin-offs or joint ventures), tech transfer acts as a capital injection with the added benefit of a long-term return on investment, as the business grows and becomes profitable.

3. Market Expansion

- New Product Development: Tech transfer enables companies to develop new products or improve existing ones by incorporating cutting-edge research and innovations. These new products can create new markets or disrupt existing ones, driving economic activity and business growth.
- Global Trade: Technologies that are transferred across borders can stimulate international trade, with businesses seeking to export new products or technologies to different markets. This global reach enhances the economic footprint of the transferring institution or business.

4. Strengthening Regional Economies

- University and Industry Collaboration: In regions where universities and research institutions play a significant role, tech transfer can become a cornerstone for local economic development. By facilitating collaboration between academia and industry, regions can foster high-tech industries, create new businesses, and improve local economies.

- Tech Hubs and Innovation Districts: Successful tech transfer initiatives can contribute to the growth of innovation districts, tech hubs, or clusters, which further fuel regional economic development. These areas become magnets for talent, investment, and entrepreneurial activity.

Challenges in Tech Transfer as a Capital Injection

Intellectual Property (IP) Protection and Valuation

- Challenges: Properly valuing and protecting intellectual property can be difficult. Universities and research institutions must balance the potential for commercialization with the desire to maintain control over their innovations. Without strong IP protection and a clear pathway for commercialization, tech transfer efforts may fail to generate significant capital.
- Solution: Ensuring clear IP agreements, obtaining patents, and maintaining strong legal protections are essential steps to guarantee that tech transfer efforts are successful and can lead to substantial financial returns.

Risk of Failure and Market Acceptance

- Challenges: Not all technologies successfully transition from the lab to the marketplace. Even if technology is promising, there may be challenges in adoption, scalability, or market demand. This risk of failure can be a barrier to attracting investment.
- Solution: To mitigate this risk, companies and institutions need to carefully assess the commercial potential of technologies before pursuing tech transfer. Building strong partnerships with experienced investors or firms can also increase the chances of success.

Alignment of Incentives

- Challenges: Ensuring that all parties involved in the tech transfer process—such as research institutions, companies, investors, and government agencies—are aligned in their goals can be difficult. Disagreements over ownership, revenue sharing, or project direction can derail the transfer process.
- Solution: Clear agreements and negotiations up front can help resolve potential conflicts. Using intermediaries such as tech transfer offices or business incubators can also help align incentives and streamline the process.

Institutional Support and Infrastructure

- Challenges: Tech transfer requires a supportive ecosystem, including knowledgeable personnel, infrastructure, and access to capital. Without adequate resources, research institutions may struggle to effectively transfer technology to the commercial sector.
- Solution: Governments, universities, and research institutions must invest in tech transfer offices, incubators, accelerators, and other resources that support innovation and commercialization.

Tech transfer as a capital injection represents a powerful way to convert scientific knowledge and innovation into tangible economic benefits. It not only provides immediate capital to research institutions, universities, and businesses but also stimulates long-term economic growth, job creation, and technological advancement. However, for tech transfer to be successful, it requires careful management of intellectual property, strategic partnerships, and robust infrastructure. When done effectively, tech transfer can fuel innovation, create new markets, and foster economic prosperity both locally and globally.

9.6 AI as an Asset Creator

Artificial Intelligence (AI) has rapidly evolved from a conceptual technology to a tangible tool with vast potential to generate value across various sectors. As an asset creator, AI doesn't just improve existing processes or optimize business functions but also creates entirely new assets that can drive economic growth, business innovation, and global competitiveness. Assets are typically defined as anything of value or usefulness, and in the context of AI, this can refer to both tangible and intangible assets. AI as an asset creator refers to the way AI can contribute to the creation, development, and enhancement of assets, whether through the development of new technologies, intellectual property, data-driven insights, or even new business models. AI is increasingly becoming an essential driver of asset creation across industries ranging from technology and finance to healthcare, entertainment, and manufacturing.

9.7 AI-Driven Intellectual Property (IP) Creation

One of the primary ways AI acts as an asset creator is by generating intellectual property (IP) that can be owned, licensed, and monetized. This can include patents, trade secrets, and proprietary algorithms.

Generating New Patents and Inventions

- AI in Research and Development (R&D): AI systems can process vast amounts of scientific data, identify patterns, and generate innovative solutions. By automating or assisting in the R&D process, AI can create novel inventions or improvements to existing products that can be patented. This intellectual property becomes an asset that can be licensed or sold.

- AI-Generated Content: AI models, especially generative models (like OpenAI's GPT models or deep learning systems), can create art, music, literature, and even software code. This type of content is considered intellectual property, and businesses can use it as a revenue stream or sell/license it.

9.8 AI Algorithms and Data Models

- Proprietary Algorithms: AI algorithms, particularly those that improve over time, can become valuable assets for companies. For example, machine learning models developed for predictive analytics, natural language processing (NLP), or computer vision can be patented and licensed to other companies.
- Data-Driven Assets: AI creates valuable insights by analyzing large sets of data, which can be transformed into marketable products. The ability to collect and process proprietary data through AI systems generates unique insights that can be turned into data-driven products or services.

9.9 AI-Enhanced Physical and Digital Products

AI not only drives the creation of intangible assets like intellectual property but also contributes to the development of both physical and digital products, transforming existing industries.

Smart Products:

- Consumer Electronics: AI is integrated into consumer electronics, such as smartphones, smart home devices, wearables, and autonomous vehicles.

These AI-enhanced products have become valuable assets in the marketplace, attracting significant consumer interest.

- IoT and AI Integration: AI-powered Internet of Things (IoT) devices, such as smart thermostats, wearables, and industrial machines, are creating valuable physical products that are increasingly integrated with AI algorithms to offer greater functionality and efficiency.

Digital Services and Platforms

- SaaS and AI as a Service: Companies like Amazon, Microsoft, and Google are leveraging AI to offer AI-as-a-Service (AIaaS), allowing businesses to access AI tools without having to develop their own systems. These AI-driven platforms represent valuable digital assets that generate recurring revenue through subscriptions or pay-per-use models.
- AI-Driven Platforms: Platforms that leverage AI, such as recommendation systems in streaming services (Netflix, Spotify) or e-commerce (Amazon, eBay), create significant economic value through customer engagement, ad revenue, and marketplace optimization.

9.10 AI-Powered Data as an Asset

In the modern digital economy, data is considered one of the most valuable assets. AI plays a pivotal role in transforming raw data into actionable insights and marketable assets.

Data-Driven Insights:

- Predictive Analytics: AI models can be trained in vast amounts of historical and real-time data to create predictive models. Businesses can use these insights to improve decision-making, optimize supply chains, and better understand consumer behavior, ultimately creating value from data.

- Behavioral Analytics: AI-powered behavioral analytics can uncover insights about customer preferences, product use patterns, and even market trends. This data can then be packaged and sold, creating an asset for companies involved in marketing, retail, or customer service.

Data Monetization

- Data Marketplaces: As AI systems generate and process data, businesses can monetize this data through data marketplaces where third parties can purchase or access this valuable information. For instance, businesses in sectors like finance, healthcare, and retail may use AI to analyze consumer data, which can then be sold to other businesses or investors.
- Personalized Experiences: AI can help create highly personalized products or services for consumers, which increases demand and loyalty. For example, personalized advertising or tailored product recommendations based on user data can create additional economic value for businesses and enhance customer retention.

9.11 AI-Driven Automation and Process Optimization

AI also acts as an asset creator by transforming business processes and operations, turning efficiency improvements into valuable assets.

Automation of Labor-Intensive Tasks

- Cost Reduction and Productivity: AI can automate repetitive tasks, reduce labor costs and increase operational efficiency. The resulting efficiency savings are valuable assets for businesses, improving profitability and freeing up human capital for more creative or high-value tasks.

- Scaling Operations: AI-powered systems allow businesses to scale their operations more quickly and cost-effectively, creating an asset in the form of an automated infrastructure that can handle increasing volumes of work without proportional increases in costs.

Supply Chain Optimization:

- AI in Logistics: By integrating AI with supply chain management, companies can create smarter, more efficient logistics operations. AI tools predict demand, optimize routes, reduce inventory costs, and manage supplier relationships, all of which enhance the overall value of the company.
- Just-in-Time Manufacturing: AI-driven predictive analytics and real-time monitoring systems allow businesses to reduce waste and optimize inventory levels, transforming manufacturing systems into a more valuable, efficient asset.

9.12 AI as an Asset Generator for New Business Models

AI enables the development of entirely new business models, where AI technology itself becomes a core asset for creating new revenue streams and markets.

AI-Driven Startups

- AI Startups: Many new startups are emerging specifically around AI technology, creating innovative products or services that leverage AI as a core differentiator. These startups can quickly become valuable assets due to their unique AI-based solutions.
- AI Platforms and Ecosystems: Some companies, like Google and Amazon, have developed entire ecosystems around AI technology. These platforms provide tools, resources, and services that enable other companies or

developers to build on top of them, creating an expanding network of businesses reliant on AI. This results in new revenue streams and growth potential for the parent company.

Monetization of AI-Driven Innovation

- AI in Finance: AI technologies like machine learning (ML) models are creating value in the financial sector by enabling better predictions for stock markets, risk management, and automated trading. These technologies themselves become significant assets, driving new products such as AI-driven investment funds or robot-advisors.
- AI in Healthcare: In healthcare, AI is used for everything from diagnostics (AI reading medical images) to personalized medicine (genomics and treatments based on AI models). These AI innovations are valuable assets in improving healthcare outcomes and creating revenue-generating products.

9.13 AI as an Asset in Sustainability

AI is increasingly being leveraged to address global challenges such as sustainability, climate change, and resource efficiency, transforming environmental efforts into economic assets.

AI in Renewable Energy

- Optimizing Energy Grids: AI systems can optimize energy distribution networks, improving energy efficiency and integrating renewable energy sources more effectively. These AI-enhanced systems create assets in the form of smarter, more reliable infrastructure.
- Energy Efficiency Technologies: AI-driven innovations in energy efficiency (such as smart thermostats, AI-powered building management systems,

and energy consumption forecasting) provide businesses and consumers with the ability to reduce costs and contribute to sustainability efforts, creating both economic and environmental value.

AI for Resource Management

- AI in Agriculture: AI-powered technologies for precision farming create valuable assets by improving crop yields, reducing water usage, and optimizing the use of fertilizers and pesticides.
- Circular Economy Models: AI can play a role in creating sustainable business models by enabling better recycling, waste management, and resource allocation, creating valuable assets in the process.

AI is undeniably one of the most transformative technologies of our time and is increasingly viewed as an asset creator. Whether through generating intellectual property, creating new digital products and services, enhancing operational efficiency, or enabling new business models, AI is unlocking value across industries and sectors. The ability of AI to create both tangible and intangible assets makes it a core driver of economic growth, technological innovation, and long-term business success.

As AI continues to evolve, its role as an asset creator will only expand, offering businesses and economies new opportunities for growth, investment, and competitive advantage. However, to fully harness its potential, careful management, ethical considerations, and regulatory frameworks will be necessary to ensure that AI-driven assets are developed responsibly and equitably.

9.14 AI as a DNA trigger

AI as a DNA trigger that can transfer the wisdom to the next generation humans regardless of the "Doctrine of Bias". Almost every successful society got destroyed within a period and the primary reason for it is that the People Died and so the wisdom of the society. Before the invention of Printing press there were a limited and odd ways of transferring the wisdom to the others through stone carving and other forms like palm leaves writing (Sanga Tamil). Most of the writings were destroyed either by natural calamities or by human oppression and aggression. So, most of the wisdom and knowledge within the society was transferred through word-of-mouth education that went from one generation to the next. When such a chain of education system was hijacked by the invaders who introduced bias and wrong feeding of information, then they failed to catch up. Research shows that the information embedded inside human DNA stays there over 2000 years and gets transferred from one generation to the other. Along the way, it transforms through a series of biases. When AI is used as a DNA trigger, many of the previously held or lost knowledge can be brough back magically.

In recent years, the concept of a New World Order has garnered significant attention from experts, particularly regarding its implications for global trade and the dynamics of currency exchange. This evolving paradigm has the potential to dramatically reshape the landscape of intellectual property (IP) and the associated accounting practices. As we witness a gradual but marked decline in the dominance of the U.S. dollar, alternative currencies are beginning to emerge, signaling a shift in economic power that could redefine international financial relations. Historically, the wealth of nations has been intricately linked to their accounting methodologies concerning assets, with a particular emphasis on intellectual property. Predominantly, the major holders of patents, copyrights, and trademarks have been the United States, Japan, and various Western European countries. This substantial accumulation of intellectual property has not only provided these nations with a competitive edge but has also established formidable barriers for other countries attempting to bridge the gap. The ability to generate, protect, and monetize intellectual property has become a critical determinant of national wealth and global influence.

Currently, we find ourselves during an emerging economic war between nations, which focuses increasingly on intellectual property rather than solely on traditional manufacturing capabilities. While manufacturing prowess and market dynamics remain essential contributors to economic power, the focal point of this conflict lies in how nations account for and leverage their intellectual properties. This intensifies the stakes in the competition, as nations that effectively capitalize on their IP can significantly influence economic flows and market valuations.

For emerging economies, the challenge is multifaceted. It is not enough for these nations to simply increase the quantity of intellectual properties they produce; they must also enhance the tradable value of these assets in a global marketplace that is largely dominated by a handful of established countries. This disparity poses a critical obstacle, as many emerging nations struggle to penetrate markets where competition is stiff, and the existing powers have already established strongholds through refined accounting practices and sophisticated financial systems. Nevertheless, there is potential for positive change. A proposed global patent initiative could serve as a meaningful opportunity for nations to more effectively capture and capitalize on their intellectual properties. For this initiative to succeed, however, it will necessitate the adoption of coherent frameworks and methodologies that support innovation and protection of intellectual assets.

Ultimately, while developing nations may make strides in increasing the volume of their intellectual properties, they must also prioritize enhancing the quality and tradable value of these assets. This strategic focus is essential for navigating a global economic landscape increasingly dominated by a few powerful players. By fostering environments that encourage creativity and innovation, and by creating systems that adequately value and protect IP, these nations can begin to level the playing field and foster more equitable global competition. Artificial intelligence (AI) rapidly emerges as a transformative force in the realm of intellectual property (IP), fundamentally reshaping the ways in which assets are valued, created, and traded. Unlike traditional software, which operates on predefined codes and fixed programming paradigms, AI harnesses complex mathematical algorithms and principles from various fields of science to generate innovative forms of IP. This leads to a multidimensional approach to asset creation and management that stands in stark contrast to conventional methods.

As AI technology matures, it transcends the limitations of rigid programming structures, employing dynamic algorithms that learn and adapt based on interactions with their environments. This continuous learning process not only augments the system's inherent intelligence but also facilitates the large-scale generation of new IP. For instance, advanced AI systems can analyze vast datasets from both public and proprietary sources, extracting insights that transcend simple information retrieval. This profound capability enables AI to identify intricate patterns and relationships within diverse data sets, making it applicable across a multitude of industries such as finance, healthcare, and creative arts. The potential applications for AI-driven algorithms are extensive and increasingly sophisticated. In the financial sector, for instance, AI can analyze extensive historical data related to public company stocks, providing investors with innovative strategies that leverage predictive analytics. These strategies can extend into specialized fields such as precision agriculture, where AI models can interpret climate data, soil conditions, and crop yields to optimize farming techniques, ultimately leading to increased productivity and sustainability. Similarly, in biotechnology, AI can aid in drug discovery by analyzing biological data to identify promising compounds more efficiently than traditional methods. As these technological advancements continue to progress, the role of AI in not only developing but also managing and commercializing IP expands significantly. This evolution paves the way for new opportunities in understanding and utilizing intellectual property within a rapidly changing market environment. Companies and individuals alike are beginning to recognize the potential of AI to enhance asset management practices and unlock previously unattainable value within their IP portfolios. In this dynamic landscape, the intersection of AI and intellectual property continues to drive innovation, leading to profound changes in how we perceive and engage with the world of intellectual assets.

The Karma Capsule Network represents a groundbreaking advancement in the realm of Neural Deep Tech Networks, specifically engineered to analyze, create, and manage intellectual property assets. This network is uniquely founded on the principle of nominalism, a philosophical concept that traces its roots to Aristotle, which posits that categories and concepts are mere names, not reflective of intrinsic realities. By harnessing nine distinct factors, the Karma Capsule Network operates under the premise that intelligence is fundamentally derived from continuous interactions with its environment. This interaction enables the network to gather a wealth of intellectual property, transforming it into a dynamic and evolving asset.

In stark contrast to traditional digital assets, which tend to be static and unchanging, the Karma Capsule Network fosters an environment where the value of intellectual property can undergo perpetual evolution through what is known as recursive intelligence creation. Each individual capsule within the network is equipped with its own form of intelligence, generating new insights and knowledge that contribute to the overall intelligence of the network. This self-reinforcing mechanism allows the network to adapt and grow, amplifying its capacity to learn and innovate based on ongoing environmental stimulus. A particularly noteworthy application of this pioneering technology is its integration with smart contracts. These smart contracts serve as immutable electronic agreements, which streamline and facilitate transactions in the modern digital economy. Unlike traditional contracts that are often subject to modifications and renegotiations, smart contracts leverage the embedded intelligence inherent within them, granting them a robust resilience against fluctuations and disputes. This inherent intelligence allows for automatic execution of agreements, ensuring trust and efficiency in transactions.

Furthermore, the Karma Capsule Network shifts the paradigm by promoting the creation and management of intellectual property assets at the network level rather than relegating this responsibility to the application layer. This innovative structure diminishes the previous centralized control exerted by a handful of dominant entities in the digital landscape, thereby democratizing access to intellectual property creation and ownership. In summation, the proliferation of advanced deep tech networks, epitomized by the Karma Capsule Network, signifies a profound evolution in the processes of intellectual property creation, valuation, and exchange. By enabling a more fluid and dynamic growth of asset value, this network not only transforms the landscape of digital assets but also fosters a more equitable and participatory economy on a global scale. It delves deeply into the transformative capacity of technology and innovation in reshaping the economic landscape of a nation. It posits that even the smallest and seemingly less significant countries can wield considerable influence over the global economic equilibrium through the strategic and effective utilization of technological advancements. These advancements can lead to the creation of national assets and play a pivotal role in stimulating GDP growth, thereby enhancing a nation's financial standing and global competitiveness.

Economic output, fundamentally understood through the lens of the aggregate production function, is contingent upon three essential factors: technology, financial capital, labor, and natural resources. Each of these factors plays a critical role in shaping the economic output of a country. However, it is important to note that overexploiting these resources, especially financial capital—can precipitate a decline in economic stability and prosperity. The discussion emphasizes the need for nations to adopt a more introspective approach, closely examining their local economies to uncover unique opportunities for innovation, even when confronted with challenges such as currency instability or limited natural resources. A significant concern is pertaining to the treatment of labor. Historically, when a labor force faces deprivation, necessity often drives innovation as workers seek to improve their circumstances. However, with the current era marked by rising inflation and stagnating wages, this proactive motivation has been severely diminished. Consequently, the middle class finds itself under considerable strain, grappling with the repercussions of unsustainable debt practices propagated by financial institutions that have prioritized profit over the welfare of the labor market. This dynamic has led to an environment where the potential for innovation is stifled.

Furthermore, while natural resources have consistently been viewed as a historical source of national wealth, the contemporary economic landscape necessitates a paradigm shift toward the generation and cultivation of digital intelligence assets. As economies transition to this derivative economy, it becomes increasingly crucial for nations to develop and implement sound policies and incentives that effectively leverage technology and foster innovation. This approach not only promotes sustainable economic growth but also enables countries to remain adaptable in the face of rapid technological advancements. Ultimately, it is not merely the quantity of the labor force that determines a nation's economic success; rather, it is the quality of motivation and capacity to innovate within that workforce that will prove decisive. Nations must create an environment where labor is encouraged and empowered to engage in innovative practices, which will be the key to unlocking future economic potential and ensuring long-term prosperity.

Throughout history, Western nations have relied on asset accounting practices as a fundamental strategy to enhance and solidify their national wealth. These methods traditionally involved the meticulous tracking of tangible and intangible assets, with the aim of maximizing economic stability and growth. However, this approach is increasingly facing challenges as nations across the globe adopt innovative financial instruments and leverage advancements in both natural and artificial intelligence. As these innovations proliferate, we can observe a notable shift: traditional methods of accounting, as well as control over trade routes, are beginning to wane in their effectiveness. This decline is particularly pronounced as intelligence and innovation increasingly emerge from decentralized networks—like blockchain and peer-to-peer systems—rather than from centralized institutions or corporations.

As we look to the future, it is clear that the concepts of asset definition and management are on the verge of significant transformation, with the potential to reshape the foundations of the global economic order. Historically, the focus has primarily been on monetary currencies; however, we are now encountering emerging challenges that suggest a need for a paradigm shift. For example, fiat currencies are increasingly being employed to tackle social issues—such as healthcare, education, and housing—rather than being predominantly utilized to build substantial reserves of assets. Furthermore, immigration trends are shifting dramatically, moving away from the traditional goal of attracting highly skilled talent, which had previously been a priority for many nations. At the same time, the landscape of commodity trading is becoming congested with new participants, leading to increased competition and pressure on established players. In this rapidly evolving economic environment, the core of trade will rely heavily on the concept of "trust." The integration of artificial intelligence alongside blockchain technologies offers a pioneering opportunity for transactions to occur within trustless networks, where genuine value exchanges can take place without the need for traditional intermediaries or outdated accounting practices. As currencies that do not adapt might become obsolete, the paradigm of trade is shifting towards fostering relationships founded on trust and transparency.

The future success of nations will hinge on their ability to effectively navigate this complex and shifting landscape. Even smaller nations, often overlooked in the global economic arena, could experience exponential growth in their Gross Domestic Product (GDP) and could significantly elevate their influence on the world stage if they strategically implement innovative approaches. By prioritizing the generation and protection of artificial intelligence-driven intellectual property assets, these nations could position themselves as leaders in the new world order, capitalizing on the opportunities presented by this transformative era. Through embracing technology and adapting to the new norms of value exchange, the potential for growth is vast, and the geopolitical landscape could witness a dramatic realignment of power and influence. The discourse examines the heightened global competition for technological supremacy, particularly within the rapidly developing field of artificial intelligence (AI). It highlights that not all nations are adopting a judicious approach toward the advancement of AI and deep technology. In fact, several countries may succumb to the allure of swift technological progress, potentially allocating substantial national resources in an incautious or uninformed manner. While China is often regarded as possessing a more nuanced understanding of the complexities inherent in deep technology, it nevertheless faces significant challenges in establishing itself as a preeminent leader in this arena. A pivotal factor impeding its progress is China's propensity to disregard and infringe upon established global intellectual property norms, which may obstruct its advancement and acceptance on the international stage. Furthermore, the discourse emphasizes that the benefits derived from deep technology extend well beyond mere intellectual property rights; they encompass a broader array of tangible assets and commodities. As AI continues to evolve, traditional accounting and valuation methodologies may become obsolete. This obsolescence can be attributed to AI's distinctive ability to capture, analyze, and transfer value in manners that conventional frameworks fail to recognize. This evolution serves as a cautionary advisory for Western nations, which may be underestimating the extensive potential and ramifications of accurately deployed AI technologies. Many AI applications currently in operation are relatively basic and simplistic. Significant challenges persist regarding the effective application of AI in domains such as asset trading and comprehensive value capture. This dynamic landscape possesses the capacity to redefine global power structures. For example, smaller nations such as Singapore, which strategically invest in military capabilities alongside technological evolution, may ascend to prominence as they skillfully leverage deep technology networks to enhance their economic positions. Ultimately, success in this new technological paradigm will not be dictated by the size or population of a country, but rather by its ability to harness emerging technologies effectively for trade, innovation, and economic advancement. Nations that can successfully navigate this terrain will be exceptionally positioned to reshape the future of global commerce and exert influence.

9.15 Digital Assets and Tokenization of Funds

Digital assets and the tokenization of funds are transforming the global financial ecosystem, enabling more efficient, transparent, and accessible financial transactions. These concepts are reshaping the way assets are represented, stored, and exchanged in both traditional and emerging markets.

Understanding Digital Assets

A digital asset refers to any asset that exists in a digital form and is typically represented using blockchain or other decentralized technologies. Digital assets can include cryptocurrencies, digital securities, tokens, and digital representations of traditional assets. Unlike physical assets, digital assets exist in the digital realm, and their value is derived from their underlying technology, usage, or market demand.

Types of Digital Assets:

- Cryptocurrencies: Digital currencies like Bitcoin (BTC), Ethereum (ETH), and others, built on blockchain technology, are the most well-known form of digital assets. They offer decentralized, peer-to-peer value transfer systems, without the need for intermediaries such as banks.
- Digital Tokens: These are representations of assets on a blockchain. Tokens can represent a variety of things, including ownership in a company, access to a service, or a claim to a future cash flow (security tokens). They can be categorized into utility tokens, security tokens, and asset-backed tokens.
- Non-Fungible Tokens (NFTs): A specific type of token that represents ownership of a unique item, typically digital art, collectibles, or intellectual

property rights. NFTs are part of the broader digital asset space but have a focus on uniqueness and scarcity.

- Stablecoins: A category of digital assets pegged to the value of traditional assets, such as the US dollar. They are designed to provide stability and minimize the price volatility associated with cryptocurrencies, making them ideal for transactions and storing value.
- Digital Commodities: This category includes tokenized versions of traditional commodities such as gold, oil, or real estate, where ownership or interest in the commodity is represented on the blockchain.

Tokenization of Funds

Tokenization refers to the process of converting rights to an asset into a digital token on a blockchain. The token acts as a digital representation of ownership or interest in the asset, whether that's a physical or financial asset. Tokenization can be applied to a wide range of asset types, including real estate, stocks, bonds, and even collectibles.

How Tokenization Works:

- Asset Digitization: An asset is represented as a token on a blockchain. For example, a piece of real estate might be represented by a token that can be traded or sold. This token might represent a share in the property or a fractionalized portion of ownership.
- Smart Contracts: Tokenization is often facilitated through smart contracts—self-executing contracts with the terms of the agreement directly written into code. These smart contracts automate transactions and ensure that tokens are exchanged or transferred according to predefined conditions.
- Decentralization: Tokenization on a blockchain allows assets to be represented in a decentralized manner, meaning no central authority or

intermediary controls the asset. This decentralization reduces transaction costs and increases transparency.

Key Benefits of Tokenization:

- Fractional Ownership: Tokenization allows for fractional ownership of an asset. For example, with tokenized real estate, investors can own a fraction of a property rather than the entire asset, making high-value investments more accessible to a larger pool of investors.
- Liquidity: Tokenized assets can be traded on blockchain-based exchanges, which can increase liquidity. Assets that were once illiquid, such as real estate, fine art, or private equity, can now be more easily bought, sold, or traded, providing greater flexibility and market access.
- Global Access: Tokenization allows assets to be made available to a global pool of investors. This expands the potential market and enables cross-border investment without the need for intermediaries or complex regulatory procedures.
- Transparency and Security: The use of blockchain technology for tokenization ensures transparency, as all transactions are recorded on a public ledger. Additionally, blockchain's inherent security features reduce the risks of fraud, manipulation, or unauthorized access.

Digital Assets and Tokenization in Finance

In the financial sector, digital assets and tokenization are revolutionizing how capital is raised, managed, and invested. These changes are leading to more efficient, lower-cost financial markets, with the potential to democratize access to investment opportunities.

Tokenized Securities and Funds

- Security Tokens: Security tokens are digital tokens that represent ownership of an underlying asset, such as equity or debt. They are governed by regulatory frameworks (such as securities laws) and can be bought, sold, and traded just like traditional securities. By tokenizing securities, investors can have easier access to a wider range of investment products.

- Tokenized Funds: Traditional investment funds (such as hedge funds, private equity funds, or mutual funds) can be tokenized, allowing investors to buy and sell shares of the fund digitally. Tokenized funds are managed by smart contracts, which automate the processes of asset management, fund allocation, and dividend distribution.

Investment and Crowdfunding

- Tokenized Crowdfunding: Tokenization allows companies to raise capital through Initial Coin Offerings (ICOs), Security Token Offerings (STOs), or Tokenized Asset Offerings (TAOs), where investors purchase tokens instead of traditional shares. This provides an alternative to traditional methods of raising funds (like IPOs or venture capital) and opens the door for smaller investors to participate.
- Real Estate Investment: One of the most prominent uses of tokenization is in real estate. Tokenizing a real estate asset allows investors to own a fraction of the property, which can provide higher liquidity than traditional property investment. Fractional ownership also makes it more affordable for individual investors to participate in high-value properties.

DeFi (Decentralized Finance)

- Decentralized Finance (DeFi): DeFi is a movement that leverages blockchain and cryptocurrency technologies to provide decentralized financial services such as lending, borrowing, trading, and asset management. In the DeFi ecosystem, tokenized assets, including cryptocurrencies and tokenized representations of traditional assets (stocks, bonds, etc.), are used to create decentralized financial markets.
- Yield Farming and Liquidity Pools: In DeFi, investors can participate in yield farming or liquidity pools, where they contribute digital assets (such as

stablecoins or tokenized assets) in exchange for rewards or interest. The tokenization of assets plays a significant role in enabling these decentralized financial products by allowing assets to be traded and transferred without intermediaries.

Benefits and Challenges of Tokenization

Benefits:

- Increased Liquidity: Tokenizing assets can unlock liquidity in traditionally illiquid markets (real estate, fine art, etc.). Tokens can be bought and sold on blockchain exchanges 24/7, increasing the ease of transaction and market access.
- Broader Investment Access: Tokenization allows for fractional ownership, meaning that even small investors can invest in high-value assets. This opens opportunities for retail investors to participate in markets that were previously out of reach.
- Cost Efficiency: Tokenizing assets reduces the need for intermediaries, such as brokers or clearing houses, which can lower transaction costs. Additionally, the process of token issuance and transfer is often faster and more efficient than traditional asset transfers.
- Transparency: Blockchain provides transparency, as all token transactions are recorded on a public ledger, allowing investors to track the ownership and transfer of tokens in real-time.

Challenges:

- Regulatory Uncertainty: The regulatory environment for digital assets and tokenization remains unclear in many jurisdictions. The classification of tokens (whether they are securities, commodities, or something else) is still evolving, and businesses involved in tokenization must navigate complex legal and regulatory hurdles.

- Security Risks: Although blockchain technology is considered secure, the overall security of tokenized assets depends on the protocols and platforms used. Smart contracts and decentralized exchanges may be vulnerable to hacking or technical failures, which could lead to financial losses.
- Market Volatility: While tokenized assets may provide easier access to new investment opportunities, they can also introduce volatility, particularly in markets like cryptocurrency. Investors must be aware of the potential for rapid price fluctuations.
- Technology Adoption: Despite growing interest, there is still a barrier to adoption for many traditional institutions. Some financial players may be hesitant to embrace blockchain-based systems due to technological complexity or lack of familiarity.

9.16 Future Outlook

The future of digital assets and tokenization looks promising, as the technology behind them continues to evolve and gain adoption. As regulatory clarity increases, more financial institutions, corporations, and investors will likely embrace tokenization to enhance efficiency, accessibility, and liquidity. Additionally, the rise of decentralized finance (DeFi) platforms and blockchain-based applications will continue to push the boundaries of what can be tokenized and traded. Ultimately, digital assets and tokenization of funds will play a central role in the future of finance by democratizing access to investment opportunities, streamlining financial transactions, and creating more efficient and transparent markets. As technology and regulatory frameworks mature, these innovations will likely become integral to the global financial system, offering new ways for individuals and institutions to create, trade, and manage assets.

Chapter 10. Cumulative Cause-Effect and Cause Level Agreement

Cumulative causation is an economic theory that was first articulated by the Swedish economist Gunnar Myrdal in the mid-20th century and later expanded upon by Kenneth Boulding and other scholars. This concept posits that small initial changes in an economic or social system can set off a series of interrelated events that not only sustain but also amplify those changes over time. The theory highlights the dynamic and often self-reinforcing nature of various processes, suggesting that these initial changes can lead to a cascading effect that reinforces the original trends. For instance, a minor economic investment in a region can lead to job creation, which in turn increases consumer spending and attracts further investments. This, however, can result in uneven development as certain areas or social groups benefit disproportionately from these cycles, leading to widening inequalities. Cumulative causation is often employed to analyze and understand the complexities of economic growth, social stratification, and even environmental changes. It sheds light on how factors such as technology, capital flow, and policy decisions can interact in ways that perpetuate disparities within and between regions, making it a critical framework for examining issues related to economic development and social justice. Through this lens, one can analyze how these intertwined processes affect long-term trajectories, reinforcing systemic patterns of advantage and disadvantage.

The concept of liberation from the traditional "Cause and Effect" framework holds vital significance for the prosperity of businesses and institutions operating within an economic ecosystem. This transformation in perspective allows us to reconsider the roles of Cause, Effects, Karma, the Karta (the initiator of action), and the Seyalpadu (the executor of action). By doing so, we can shift our understanding of "Cause and Effect" from a potentially detrimental blueprint to a strategic roadmap for success across all areas of life, including personal development, business growth, social dynamics, political strategies, and career trajectories.

At the heart of this concept is Karma, which denotes action. Every action inevitably leads to specific outcomes, which we classify as effects. It is crucial to realize that every effect originates from a precursor—its cause. This understanding compels us to delve deeper into the nature of these causes and the various forces that drive them, enabling us to unveil underlying truths and address challenges with greater efficacy. Importantly, we must recognize that a cause is not simply an action taken; rather, it is an action that possesses direction—essentially functioning as a vector. Thus, we can better define a cause as a combination of deliberate action coupled with a clear, defined goal. A critical differentiation must be made between the Karta, the individual or entity that initiates an action, and the Seyalpadu, who carry out that action. Many systems and strategies tend to overlook the pivotal influence of Karta along with their intended objectives. This oversight can often lead to ineffective or misguided responses. For example, during the COVID-19 pandemic, scientists and public health officials did not foresee the second wave of infections because they failed to account for the virus's inherent capability for mutation, ultimately ignoring its role as the Karta in this unfolding situation. This highlights the necessity for systems thinking that genuinely integrates the complexities involved in causative relationships.

To build robust and successful systems, it is imperative to conduct a thorough analysis that distinguishes between the Karta and the subsequent actions taken. A frequent pitfall occurs due to indecisiveness in the establishment of these systems, leading them to falter. The optimal path forward exists in detaching oneself from the immediate cause-effect relationship. This detachment grants individuals and organizations the ability to gain a more profound understanding of the intricacies inherent in both concepts. Furthermore, in the pursuit of wisdom and improvement, it is essential first to acquire the relevant knowledge needed to navigate these complexities. Contemporary systems should intelligently incorporate an element of skepticism alongside the analysis of data. This approach enhances predictive analytics and equips stakeholders with the tools necessary to better foresee future events and outcomes. By adopting such a multifaceted perspective on causality, we can aspire to design and implement effective, resilient systems capable of adapting to the dynamic and often unpredictable nature of the world around us.

Predictive Analytics Using Cause-Effect is a sophisticated approach that emphasizes the importance of understanding how specific variables influence one another. This methodology involves predicting future outcomes by analyzing historical data while focusing on cause-and-effect relationships instead of simply identifying correlations. By uncovering these relationships, analysts can gain deeper insight into the dynamics between different factors and improve accuracy in forecasting. The implementation of this analytical framework begins with comprehensive data collection. It is crucial to gather data that includes potential causal variables alongside their corresponding effects. Sources for this data can be diverse, encompassing transactional records, survey responses, experimental data, and information from various sensor technologies. For example, in a healthcare context, researchers might collect data on patient demographics (such as age, gender, and socioeconomic status) and medical history (including previous diagnoses and treatment regimens) as potential causes, while tracking health outcomes (like recovery rates or the incidence of complications) serves as the effects.

Once the data has been amassed, the next critical step involves identifying the causal relationships that exist within it. There are several techniques available for this identification process, each with its advantages and suited applications. Statistical methods, such as regression analysis, enable analysts to determine the extent to which one variable can reliably predict another. Granger causality tests offer another layer of sophistication by assessing whether changes in one variable consistently precede changes in another, indicating a directional influence. Additionally, domain expertise plays a vital role in recognizing and validating causal relationships; practitioners with deep knowledge in a specific field can offer invaluable insights that may not be immediately evident from the data itself. For more complex scenarios, advanced machine learning techniques, particularly causal inference methods, can help disentangle intricate relationships and assess the impact of interventions or changes in conditions. A practical illustration of this approach can be found in the field of economics, where researchers may analyze how fluctuations in interest rates lead to variations in consumer spending behavior. By focusing on these cause-and-effect links, predictive analytics not only aids in forecasting economic trends but also enhances understanding of the fundamental factors that drive those trends. This comprehensive understanding can inform policy decisions, business strategies, and various interventions aimed at achieving desired outcomes. In summary, predictive analytics that utilize cause-effect frameworks offer a powerful tool for stakeholders across various domains, allowing for more accurate predictions and a deeper understanding of the mechanisms at play within complex systems. Building a predictive model is a multifaceted process that involves meticulously identifying and analyzing the relationships between various causes and their corresponding effects. This requires a thoughtful examination of how adjustments in one variable can subsequently influence another, with the objective of creating a robust framework to predict future events.

To facilitate this, a variety of analytical techniques can be employed. One of the most prevalent approaches is regression analysis, which encompasses both linear and multiple regression methods. Linear regression focuses on establishing a straight-line relationship between a single independent variable and a dependent variable, making it ideal for simpler models. On the other hand, multiple regression allows for the analysis of multiple predictors simultaneously, providing a more comprehensive understanding of how various factors contribute to the outcome. When the nature of the relationships being modeled changes over time, time series analysis becomes a critical tool. Techniques such as Autoregressive Integrated Moving Average (ARIMA) and Vector Autoregression (VAR) are especially useful in forecasting trends by leveraging historical data to identify patterns and make informed predictions about future occurrences. In cases where relationships are intricate or the data is high-dimensional, machine learning algorithms provide powerful alternatives. Techniques such as Random Forests, which harness the power of ensemble learning to improve accuracy, Support Vector Machines (SVM), known for their effectiveness in classification tasks, and Neural Networks, which excel in modeling complex, non-linear relationships, can all be utilized to derive insights from the data. Once a predictive model is constructed, testing its foundational assumptions becomes paramount to confirm the presence of causality—after all, correlation does not imply causation. Various rigorous methodologies, such as A/B testing, randomized control trials (RCTs), and the use of instrumental variables, can be employed to evaluate the impact of specific causes on outcomes in real-world scenarios. These methods help isolate the effect of an intervention or variable, thus providing a clearer understanding of causal relationships.

After the model has been validated, it can then be used to make predictions about future events. The effectiveness of the model rests on its ability to accurately forecast how alterations in independent variables will translate into changes in dependent variables. To ensure the reliability of these predictions, it's essential to compare them against actual real-world data, validating the model's performance and adjusting as necessary. The iterative nature of predictive modeling cannot be overstated; models must undergo continuous refinement as new data becomes available. This iterative process is crucial in accommodating any changes in causal relationships and in integrating new factors that may emerge as influential. Regular updates not only enhance the accuracy of predictions but also keep the model relevant in a dynamic environment. Within the realm of cause-and-effect predictive analytics, several specialized model types exist. Causal inference models are designed specifically to estimate the relationships between variables. These models utilize sophisticated techniques such as propensity score matching to mitigate bias, employing instrumental variables to infer causality and advanced statistical methods like path analysis and structural equation modeling (SEM) to capture and elucidate complex interrelationships. Furthermore, in industrial contexts, predictive maintenance models have been developed to foresee equipment failures by identifying specific predictive causes. These models analyze factors such as vibration levels, temperature variations, and other operational metrics that correlate with potential breakdowns, thereby enabling preemptive repairs and reducing downtime. In conclusion, the development and application of predictive models are essential in various fields, offering valuable insights and enabling proactive decision-making through a methodical examination of cause-and-effect relationships. Constant evaluation and adaptation of these models are vital to ensure their effectiveness in an ever-changing world.

Predictive analytics that leverage cause-effect relationships offer numerous advantageous applications across a broad spectrum of industries. Within the healthcare sector, for example, grasping the various determinants that affect medication adherence is essential. This comprehension is crucial for mitigating hospital readmissions by identifying patients who are at an elevated risk of non-compliance with their prescribed treatment regimens. By employing predictive models, healthcare providers can customize interventions and support mechanisms for these patients, ultimately fostering improved health outcomes and reducing healthcare costs associated with preventable hospital visits. Similarly, the retail industry derives substantial benefits from predictive analytics through a meticulous examination of customer interactions with promotional content. By analyzing how customers engage with different marketing materials—such as emails, advertisements, or in-store display retailers can more accurately forecast customer purchasing behaviors. This data-driven insight enables organizations to refine their marketing strategies, ensuring that promotions resonate with their target audience, thereby enhancing overall marketing efficacy and boosting sales.

In the financial services sector, institutions apply predictive analytics by integrating credit scores with comprehensive payment history data to evaluate the likelihood of loan defaults. This methodology supports advanced risk management practices by allowing lenders to make informed determinations regarding borrower eligibility. By accurately predicting potential defaults, financial institutions can adjust their lending strategies accordingly, which may yield reduced losses and contribute to healthier financial portfolios. Despite the advantages presented by cause-effect predictive analytics, the implementation of such models is fraught with significant challenges. One of the primary hurdles is ensuring high data quality; reliable and accurate data is vital for constructing predictive models that produce valid outcomes. Poor data quality may lead to misleading conclusions and ineffective interventions. Moreover, distinguishing between causality and correlation represents another considerable challenge.

The failure to recognize this distinction can result in erroneous predictions and misguided strategies. The complexity of real-world systems further exacerbates these issues, as such systems typically involve numerous interacting variables that can obscure clear cause-effect relationships.

Additionally, the availability of data presents a significant constraint. Comprehensive datasets that encompass all pertinent variables are often difficult to procure, which creates gaps in analysis and forecasting. The pandemic response to COVID-19 exemplifies these challenges. The experience underscored how simplistic cause-effect analyses could overlook vital elements, such as intrinsic viral characteristics and their mutation capacity, leading to incomplete understanding of the pandemic's dynamics. This reality highlights the risks associated with focusing solely on superficial relationships, which can result in the omission of critical underlying factors that drive complex phenomena. Within the framework of mayaNomics, an exploration of the nuanced dimensions of causality is further enriched by the concept of "Karta." This principle underscores the significance of context in understanding cause-effect relationships. By acknowledging that value generation should not solely concentrate on raw data but also consider how such data is framed and its directional meaning, more profound insights can be obtained. Many organizations currently grapple with indecision stemming from chaotic data interpretations. While a degree of uncertainty can stimulate constructive dialogue and promote innovative thinking, chronic indecisiveness may inhibit effective decision-making processes. To effectively confront these challenges and enhance the capabilities of predictive analytics, it is essential to transcend traditional cause-effect reasoning. This necessitates an expansion of perspectives beyond established paradigms. By adopting a broader outlook—like approaching problem-solving by constructing an external framework rather than being constrained by internal limitations, one can cultivate a more holistic understanding of complex systems. This approach may facilitate innovative designs and strategies, ultimately leading to more effective solutions in addressing the intricacies of contemporary challenges across various sectors.

The principle of karma yoga provides a nuanced and multifaceted framework for understanding the complexities of cause and effect, a concept that has resonated within various philosophical and spiritual traditions for millennia. A prevalent misconception regarding karma is its simplistic equation with fate or destiny; however, such an interpretation overlooks the fundamental essence of karma, which fundamentally refers to "action." Karma should not be perceived merely as a predetermined sequence of events that individuals are destined to experience in life. This misunderstanding often leads to a negative perception of karma, prompting some to dismiss it as mere superstition or fallacy. Despite this skepticism, it is crucial to recognize that karma is inherently linked to the intricate relationship between cause and effect, emphasizing the active role individuals play in shaping their own destinies. To explore this relationship more deeply, it is important to appreciate that cause and effect manifest through actions and their subsequent outcomes. The interplay between these elements can be categorized into various relationships: one-to-one, one-to-many, or many-to-many. Each action generates an outcome, which may also be interpreted as a reaction. The complexity inherent in the concept of action resides not only in the action itself but also in its vector or directionality, the specific path that the action takes. In this context, the "cause" extends beyond the action itself; it encompasses the directional component that influences nature and the consequences of that action. To illustrate this point, one may consider the scenario of shooting an arrow at an apple suspended from a tree branch. The act of shooting involves several steps: drawing the bow, aiming, and ultimately releasing the arrow. However, the true cause—the vector—exists in the intended direction towards the apple. Thus, the cause is delineated not only by the action taken but also by its intended trajectory. This example underscores that the execution of an action can significantly affects its resultant effects, thereby demonstrating how directionality can alter outcomes.

Recognizing this distinction is vital, as it is a common pitfall to equate the notion of cause solely with the action undertaken. The resultant effects may diverge dramatically depending on various factors of directionality, including the angle and force of the action. While this concept may appear intuitive to mathematicians and scientists who routinely engage with vectors, it applies universally across a diverse array of fields, including business management and organizational behavior. In organizational contexts, particularly during transformational initiatives, many leaders implement new systems or changes without a comprehensive understanding of the intricate interplay between their actions, the intended direction of those actions, and the contextual factors involved. There is often a tendency to apply a homogenized or one-size-fits-all approach, which can result in suboptimal outcomes and hinder the achievement of desired objectives. This oversight highlights the necessity for leaders and decision-makers to adopt a more strategic perspective, considering both the actions they undertake and the specific context in which these actions manifest.

Karma can be effectively understood as a deliberate action executed within a defined temporal and spatial framework, with the intention of achieving a particular goal. Consequently, the relationship between action and outcome can be succinctly encapsulated in the equation: action plus goal equals cause. This formulation emphasizes that the directionality of the action—when intertwined with its temporal and spatial dimensions—creates a vector that delineates specific outcomes. Each action conceivably yields multiple effects; for instance, when the arrow strikes the apple, it not only results in the apple's descent but also influences where it ultimately lands. The final position of the apple is contingent upon the vector through which it was impacted. Many individuals underestimate the extent to which varied actions, influenced by their specific directional attributes, can lead to significantly disparate outcomes. Achieving a comprehensive understanding of this principle can mitigate errors in interpreting causes and effects across diverse contexts, enhancing decision-making and fostering a deeper awareness of the interconnectedness of actions and their repercussions. This understanding empowers individuals to navigate life's complexities with greater discernment and responsibility, thereby cultivating a more meaningful engagement with the world around them. Lets delves deeply into the complex interplay of cause and effect across a multitude of contexts, emphasizing the pivotal role of individual agency in carrying out actions. In specific fields such as web design or logo creation, we can delineate two main components involved in the process: the action itself—designing—and the objectives that the design is intended to fulfill. Yet, a crucial element often overlooked is the designer's skill set, their prior experiences, and their innate abilities and creativity. This oversight underscores the vital human dimension that must be acknowledged to construct a thorough and holistic understanding of any cause-and-effect framework. Understanding the quality of the individual undertaking the action is essential for comprehending the outcomes produced; neglecting this aspect results in explanations that may be overly simplistic or insufficiently nuanced. To effectively predict or clarify the consequences of specific actions, it is imperative to assess not only the actions performed and their intended goals but also the personal attributes, training, and decision-making abilities of the individual executing them. This perspective illustrates the interconnectedness of these various factors, which ultimately shape the results we observe in different scenarios. The breadth of cause-and-effect relationships is vast and can be seen in everyday phenomena, such as meteorological forecasting or traffic management systems. For instance, consider the synchronization of traffic light patterns, which can significantly influence vehicular flow on city streets. The outcomes arising from these patterns can vary widely, resulting in situations that range from severe congestion, where traffic comes to a standstill, to conditions allowing for smooth and efficient transit. In such instances, it becomes imperative to factor in the behaviors, habits, and decision-making processes of the drivers involved, as these human elements critically impact the overall effectiveness of traffic control measures. A contemporary and poignant illustration of this principle can be found in the predictive modeling related to the COVID-19 pandemic. Epidemiologists diligently identified specific behaviors exhibited by the virus as causal factors influencing its spread and developed complex models aimed at forecasting potential outcomes based on historical data and trends. However, the predictive accuracy of these epidemiological models is heavily reliant on a nuanced understanding of human behavior and the various response mechanisms that individuals exhibit during a public health crisis. This highlights the essential truth: when we overlook the quality, expertise, and decision-making capabilities of individuals within any analytical framework, we jeopardize the reliability and validity of our predictions. Therefore, the integration of the human element into cause-and-effect analyses proves to be an indispensable requirement for cultivating a comprehensive understanding of diverse phenomena and their underlying complexities. This examines the intricate and multifaceted dynamics associated with viral mutations, particularly within the context of the COVID-19 pandemic. It is important to underscore the essential need for a comprehensive understanding of a virus's intrinsic characteristics and capabilities determined as "Karta"—to effectively manage outbreaks. While public health authorities commonly designate the virus as the primary agent of infection, people like me advocate for an in-depth analysis of the virus's genetic material alongside its unique properties. This absence of thorough investigation has led to a significant underappreciation of the virus's potential for mutation and adaptation. Health authorities recognized the virus's dynamic nature, specifically its capacity for rapid replication and genetic variation, more robust and effective control measures might have been implemented. They emphasize the importance of distinguishing the actions typically attributed to the virus from its biological nature. This perspective calls for a reevaluation of the understanding of the virus: not merely as a singular pathogen but as a complex biological organism with distinct characteristics and behaviors, analogous to the variability observed in human biology and other living systems. Moreover, the issue expands to include the application of these insights across various sectors, particularly in healthcare and economics. There is a need for a holistic model that integrates the unique attributes of different systems, fostering an understanding informed by the principles of "kari" (action) and "karma" (causality) in societal management. Advocates of the issue proposed that adopting a more nuanced approach to these concepts could lead to significant improvements in outcomes across multiple sectors. This strategy would necessitate preparedness for a diverse range of effects triggered by specific causes, rather than relying on broad, uniform responses that may neglect critical variables inherent to various situations. I conclude that such a comprehensive perspective could enhance resilience and adaptability in the face of future health crises and other societal challenges. Let’s explore the intricacies of the framework of MayaNomics and the Karma Capsule Network, providing a thorough examination of the interplay between causality and economic principles in today’s complex landscape. Central to the Karma Capsule Network is a fundamental proposition: the necessity of fully contextualizing the value generation process. This framework emphasizes that mere data analysis is inadequate; rather, it is essential to consider a range of temporal and situational variables that influence economic activities. The network highlights that value extraction is a multifaceted process, necessitating a nuanced understanding that transcends superficial data examination to encompass the underlying contexts and intentions shaping data collection and its applications. Numerous contemporary economic models are compromised by inherent ambiguities and a fundamental misinterpretation of the true nature of data. This indecisiveness can lead to disorder across various sectors, resulting in inefficient and suboptimal business practices that hinder innovation and growth. Contrarily, the Karma Capsule Network introduces a transformative paradigm whereby uncertainties and doubts are not merely regarded as obstacles but are elevated to the status of essential assets. Embracing these uncertainties encourages deeper inquiry and critique, enabling organizations to more clearly define the boundaries within which potential outcomes may unfold. This shift in perspective ultimately enhances decisiveness and effectiveness within systems, thereby creating a more solid foundation for decision-making. By meticulously capturing a wide array of elements, including actions, states of affairs, objectives, and inherent uncertainties, organizations can construct a sophisticated predictive framework that significantly enhances their decision-making capabilities. The principal argument advocates for liberation from the rigid constraints of traditional cause-and-effect relationships, underscoring the importance of attaining a clear understanding of one's present situation. Such clarity promotes a sense of freedom within the decision-making process, facilitating more informed and strategic choices. To fully comprehend the foundational principles of the Karma Capsule Network, an extensive and in-depth exploration of these concepts is strongly advised, paving the way for insights that could revolutionize economic practices and enhance overall efficacy.

Chapter 11. mayaNomics Framework Blueprint and guidelines

I sincerely hope that the previous ten chapters have provided you with a robust foundation upon which to build. As I embarked on the journey of writing this book in 2022, I chose to frame my insights through the lens of mayaNomics, all while assuming the role of a Business Architect. In the initial stages of this project, my primary focus was to create a comprehensive framework and blueprint that would guide the reader towards a deeper understanding of the subject matter. Having spent over twenty years as a deep tech entrepreneur and systems architect, I possessed the skills to craft this blueprint as a prescriptive guide filled with straightforward solutions. However, upon reflection, I came to recognize that an essential ethical principle governs the work of architects: **"Prescription before diagnosis is malpractice."** This realization was a pivotal moment for me. It became clear that the diagnoses I had at my disposal were inadequate. This limitation propelled me on an unexpected journey into the depths of economic history. The timeline of this book's publication mirrors the evolution of my thoughts and research throughout these three years. I delved extensively into various contexts—economic, historical, technological, and trade perspectives—to align my findings into a coherent narrative. By the year 2024, I reached a point where I felt confident in my ability to finalize the manuscript. Throughout this extensive process, I transformed the original blueprint into what now stands as the eleventh chapter of this book. I take great pride in knowing that this work transcends mere prescription—it is a comprehensive exploration that interweaves subjective and objective insights. It embraces the intricate evolution of economics alongside crucial elements such as geopolitics, history, finance, business, and technology. With that context in mind, I invite you to delve into the blueprint that I have meticulously crafted, as it serves as the foundation for understanding the complexities we face in today's world.

mayaNomics represents an innovative geo-economic framework that fosters collaboration and engagement among individuals, institutions, organizations, and governments across international boundaries. This dynamic framework emphasizes trustless interactions, voluntary participation, and cooperative methodologies, all grounded in robust consensus-driven decision-making processes. Central to mayaNomics is an ambitious vision for a transnational economic digital corridor, which is specifically designed to enhance cross-border exchanges while adhering to the highest standards of morality, ethics, and legality. By establishing an ecosystem conducive to flourishing economic activities, mayaNomics empowers individuals and collectivities to pursue wealth, liberty, and dignity through meaningful social engagements. In advocating for the realization of these objectives, mayaNomics affirms essential rights, including the freedom of contracting, expression, choice, and trade. It encourages individuals to proactively seek wealth and engage in consensual practices that respect their autonomy and values, while simultaneously promoting self-regulation and emphasizing social responsibility and accountability. This methodology fosters a sustainable and equitable economic environment. Through these foundational principles, mayaNomics is positioned to cultivate a harmonious and prosperous society wherein all members can thrive collaboratively, while simultaneously upholding individual freedoms and shared ethical standards.

11.1 Guiding Principles of mayaNomics

1. Trade Liberty: mayaNomics advocates for comprehensive trade liberty, emphasizing the importance of supporting individual and collective rights to engage freely in business, investment, and trade. This framework is intended to encourage economic growth and innovation.

2. Right to Private Property: The recognition of private property rights is defined as a fundamental human right. This principle includes the ownership of physical assets, such as land and real estate, as well as intangible assets like language, culture, religion, intellectual property, digital assets, creative works, and royalties. Protecting these rights is viewed as vital for maintaining dignity and autonomy.

3. Freedom of Knowledge: The importance of safeguarding the freedom of education and access to information is central to mayaNomics. By promoting the dissemination of knowledge related to trade, investment, and business practices, this principle aims to facilitate informed decision-making within economic activities.

4. Freedom of Communication: The principle of freedom of communication encompasses the right to express ideas freely and the need to protect the privacy and security of individuals and groups. Encouraging respectful discourse is intended to foster trust and collaboration among market participants.

5. Freedom of Trade and the Market: mayaNomics emphasizes the effectiveness of free trade and free markets. This principle advocates against monopolistic or oligopolistic practices and seeks to eliminate coercive behaviors that restrict competition. A free-market environment is believed to drive innovation and benefit consumers through improved products and services.

6. Freedom of Outcomes and the Virtue of Production: This principle supports diverse outcomes in economic engagement and recognizes the value of productive efforts. mayaNomics calls for the removal of constraints on various systems—social, political, technological, business, and legal—that may limit trade liberty, potentially leading to enhanced economic prosperity.

7. Freedom of Supply: The principle of freedom of supply underlines the necessity of unobstructed supply chains for essential goods, including food.

Ensuring freedom of supply is aimed at fostering a resilient economy capable of meeting the needs of its populace.

8. Empowering Unrepresented Groups: This principle commits to providing platforms and resources to empower unrepresented or marginalized groups. It encourages inclusive participation in the economy and aims to ensure that diverse perspectives are included in decision-making processes.

9. Trade Responsibility System: The promotion of social responsibility, both individually and collectively, is acknowledged as vital for an effective economy. mayaNomics supports decentralized scoring systems, enabling communities to evaluate and promote responsible trade practices without central governance, thereby encouraging accountability and ethical behavior.

10. Right to Self-Regulation: The advocacy for the self-regulation of private enterprises, societies, and communities is presented as essential for a functioning society. This principle asserts that individuals should possess autonomy in governing themselves within legal frameworks, fostering a sense of ownership and accountability.

11. Eliminating Central Governance: This principle underscores the importance of minimizing the influence of centralized power structures to cultivate a free economic environment. There is a concurrent emphasis on protecting individual privacy and maintaining secrecy, when necessary, provided these do not compromise the freedoms of others.

12. Near Stateless Market: mayaNomics promotes the concept of localism, envisioning a near-stateless market that empowers communities beyond national borders. The intent is to develop economic systems that allow for local decision-making while encouraging international cooperation.

13. Freedom of Association: The principle of freedom of association is fundamental to a free society, and mayaNomics advocates for this freedom across all social and economic interactions. This includes societal dynamics and international relations, affirming the right of individuals to choose their associations freely.

14. Non-Intervention: The principle of non-intervention posits that individuals, governments, societies, or organizations should not interfere in the voluntary actions and affairs of others within the market system. This approach aims to reinforce autonomy, self-determination, and respect for personal and collective decisions.

15. Voluntarism: Voluntarism underscores the importance of voluntary participation in all economic and social interactions, promoting a system where consent is paramount. This principle supports the notion that individuals should engage in trade and relationships freely, without coercion.

16. Non-Coercion and Non-Aggression: This principle emphasizes a rejection of coercion and aggression in all forms. mayaNomics posits that such tactics conflict with the respect for individual liberties and aim to create an environment where power dynamics do not undermine freedom.

17. Decentralized Systems: The vision of mayaNomics includes the promotion of decentralized systems, processes, and institutions globally. By distributing power away from centralized authorities, communities may enhance resilience, adaptability, and innovation within their economic frameworks.

18. Spontaneous Order: mayaNomics supports the concept of spontaneous order that arises organically within communities, institutions, and trade associations. This principle illustrates that complex systems can self-organize and achieve effective outcomes without extensive top-down control.

19. Fiat Currency: mayaNomics opposes the manipulation and flexibility of fiat currencies, advocating instead for the promotion of digital assets with intrinsic value, which are viewed as legitimate mediums for trading and exchange.

20. Natural Resource Allocation: This principle advocates for minimizing monopolistic and governmental control over natural resources, including energy and minerals. mayaNomics endorses a consensus-driven approach to resource allocation that considers the needs of local communities and encourages sustainable practices.

21. Natural Resource Pricing Control: Ensuring that the pricing of natural resources is determined by community consensus is seen as a way to promote equitable valuation and access. This approach aims to enhance transparency and fairness, allowing local stakeholders to participate in economic decisions affecting them.

22. Privacy and Surveillance: mayaNomics emphasizes the advocacy for privacy rights while opposing intrusive surveillance, profiling, and tracking practices. This principle focuses on protecting individual privacy as a fundamental liberty, ensuring respect for personal information.

23. Consensus and Referendum: Mechanisms such as referendums, repeals, and recalls are supported as important checks and balances against governmental or institutional negligence. Exercise of this principle requires caution to avoid infringing upon the rights of individuals holding dissenting views.

24. Non-Nationalization of Outputs: A policy opposing the nationalization of natural resources, agricultural products, land, forests, industrial outputs, and energy is central to mayaNomics. The emphasis is on local solutions and collaborative sharing through trade instead of state control, which could inhibit innovation and individual rights.

25. Automated and Immutable Governance: The promotion of automated and immutable governance systems is considered essential for modern governance structures. This principle advocates the use of technologies that enhance transparency, reduce corruption, and improve efficiency in the operations of governments, cooperatives, and public-private entities.

26. Freedom of Human Resources and Outcomes: The principle that governments should not claim ownership of human resources or labor is supported, allowing the workforce to engage in unrestricted trading of their time, outcomes, and products through binding contracts.

27. Promote True Federations: An encouragement for nations to adopt federated, liberty-oriented republican constitutions that align with constitutional principles is presented.

28. Intellectual Property Protection & Monetization: Advocacy for the protection of intellectual property rights and the secure management of royalties on creations is emphasized while recognizing these properties as digital assets.

29. Division of Labor: The promotion of the concept of division of labor and advocacy for the development of contemporary jobs and professions are highlighted.

30. Fungibility: Fungibility of Assets shall be promoted as the mechanism within the Financial and Economic processes.

11.2 The Things Model of mayaNomics

My first encounter of Aristotle's nominalism was in 2018 when I was doing my scientific research for releasing karma Capsule Network (the scientific name-reinforced CapsNet) a unique AI network for decentralized digital entities(things). You shall fine the white paper at https://github.com/karmaCapsuleNetwork/KCN1.0/blob/master/KarmaCapsuleNetworkV1.1.pdf

Aristotle's conception of nominalism represents the fundamental platform for karma Capsule Network which eventually laid the baseline canvas for mayaNomics, essential for elucidating economic concepts as well as the relationships among entities and their characteristics. Nominalism asserts that abstract universals, such as "humanity" or "beauty," do not exist independently; rather, they serve merely as labels for collections of individual objects that share certain traits. For instance, the term "human" denotes a group of individuals who exhibit common qualities, rather than signifying an independent entity. From this perspective, individual objects, or "things," are regarded as the only true realities. General terms such as "humanity" or "dog" function as linguistic tools employed to categorize these instances based on their similarities. A nominalist would argue that only individual entities truly exist, while the terms we utilize act as convenient descriptors. This is the reason why I hate it when generative AI is promoted as the real AI. The genAI and the platforms that enable them shall never come closer in finding and working with the real-world assets and their values. Only a deep-tech AI with the mechanism embedded inside of it to capture the true characteristics of a thing beyond description, can be a true AI that can solve not just the economic problem, but also many social, civic, health, food, energy, and infrastructure problems.

Aristotle made a significant distinction between substances and their attributes. Substances refer to concrete, independent entities, such as a specific tree or person, whereas accidents pertain to the properties or qualities—such as color, shape, and size—that describe these substances but cannot exist independently. This differentiation emphasizes that a substance is distinct from the modifications it undergoes, underscoring the importance of recognizing both the essential nature of "things" and the characteristics that define them. So, essentially the very first step in Thing modeling is to identify and define Things within the ecosystem framework that you are trying to design. In our case, the Economics at global political scale, the geoeconomics. So, the collection of things shall be comprehensive from various domains and aspects of economics, finance, technology, business, legal, history, evolution etc.,

Things of Geoeconomics

Money	Credits	Value of Assets	Units of Society	Culture
Digital Assets	Supply Chain	Moat	Community	Civilization
Digital Commodities	Inflation	Fiscal Policies	Media	Motivation
Doubts	Geopolitics	Monetary Policies	Education	Natural Capital
Commodities	Policies	Central Banks	Human Capital	Sovereign Wealth
Events	Treaties	National Banks	Military	Financial Vehicles
Trade	Capital Creations	Private Banks	Stock Market	Bonds
Small Businesses	Market Access	Data	Tariffs	Risk Appetite
Big Businesses	Velocity of Money	AI	Taxes	Moat
Micro Businesses	Assets Creation	Bias	Real Estate	Automation
Market Demand	ETF	Family Wealth	Energy	Free Market
Intrinsic Value	Tokenized Funds	Consumer	Liberty	Fair Market

Attributes (Manners, Modes): Strategic Use of Economic Power, Sanctions, trade wards, Investment leverage, currency manipulation, Interdependence and Vulnerability, Competition and Rivalry, Asymmetry of Economic Power.

In Aristotle's philosophy, the idea of individual substances is intricately connected to the forms they embody. He emphasizes that every substance—be it a living being, an inanimate object, or any entity—possesses a unique form that defines its essence, encompassing its nature and characteristics. These forms are not external or independent; rather, they exist within the objects themselves, shaping and informing their identities and properties. The phrase "things modified" effectively illustrates the dynamic relationship between substances and their forms, demonstrating how substances acquire their attributes through the specific forms they exhibit. Aristotle identifies two fundamental components that make up all entities: matter, representing the tangible essence of an object, and form, which signifies the defining nature of that object. This duality is crucial, as the identity of a substance is intrinsically linked to its form, expressed through its material composition. To better understand this philosophical concept, consider a block of marble. Initially, the block is simply unrefined stone, representing mere matter with basic physical properties. However, when a sculptor envisions a statue of an angel and begins to carve the marble, a transformative process begins. The sculptor's artistic intention embodies the ideal form of the angel, guiding the modification of the marble into a new identity. As the sculptor carves away the rough surface, the block evolves, gradually adopting distinct features and characteristics that resonate with the envisioned form of the angel. This illustrates that the marble is not merely altered; it is fundamentally redefined as it gains the properties associated with the sculpted form. Thus, this process beautifully demonstrates how essence and existence coalesce in individual substances, showcasing Aristotle's insightful perspective on form and matter as a meaningful commentary on the nature of reality.

11.3 Systemic Approach to geoeconomics

The modeling of various dimensions has established a foundational architectural framework for mayaNomics; however, the design phase necessitates a systematic and structured methodology. An extensive exploration of the fundamental state machine and continuum elements within the field of geoeconomics has revealed that the design process for mayaNomics must adopt a dynamic systemic approach. This approach requires meticulous consideration of the diverse range of elements involved, their varying states, and the intricate dynamics that govern their interactions. Additionally, a rigorous analysis of tensor characteristics is essential to comprehending the complex relationships within the system.

Embracing a holistic systemic perspective on geoeconomics is crucial for understanding the intricate interplay of multiple factors that shape global economic and political landscapes. This comprehensive viewpoint highlights the essential interconnectedness of various components, including, but not limited to, economic policies, financial architecture, trade mechanisms, technological advancements, and regional rivalries. By engaging in a thorough and collaborative analysis of these interrelated elements, one can conduct a complete assessment of how economic decisions reverberate through and significantly influence geopolitical dynamics. Such analysis not only enhances our understanding of the current situation but also informs strategic decision-making within an increasingly complex global environment. At the core of this approach is a holistic understanding that recognizes the interdependence between economic and geopolitical factors. It demands a thorough exploration of the intricate interactions and feedback loops among markets, government policies, and state behaviors. The geoeconomic landscape is in constant flux, propelled by rapid technological advancements, global crises, and the evolving strategies of states. This ongoing evolution highlights the critical need to acknowledge the dynamic relationships within the geoeconomic framework.

Strategic calculations are essential as states wield economic instruments—such as sanctions, trade agreements, or investments—aligned with broader geopolitical objectives. This maneuvering is further complicated by the rise of emerging powers and the growing interdependencies among nations, which dramatically reshape the geoeconomic landscape. As these shifts unfold, traditional notions of power dynamics are fundamentally redefined, resulting in a multipolar global environment. Furthermore, this systemic perspective equips us with a deeper understanding of the potential consequences of economic decisions. It enhances our predictive capacity concerning how these decisions can reverberate across international relations, influencing alliances, conflicts, and economic partnerships. By adopting a systemic approach to geoeconomics, analysts and policymakers can achieve more accurate forecasts of how intertwined economic actions impact the broader geopolitical context, enabling them to navigate the complexities of modern international relations with increased effectiveness.

11.4 The Architectural Blueprint of mayaNomics

The Art, Science, and Discipline of MayaNomics Geoeconomic Architecture represent a comprehensive framework grounded in a rich blend of principles, design methodologies, and construction techniques. This framework is uniquely designed to cultivate a global economic system composed of diverse sub-systems and processes. Each of these components is deeply entrenched in their own distinct local context, operating independently, yet not necessarily aligning with the overarching narrative of the larger system. Over the span of my 25-year career as a Tech Architect and my 15 years as an Enterprise/Business Architect, I have immersed myself in the intricate world of architectural blueprinting. My journey has been enriched by the teachings and insights of some of the finest minds—academicians, philosophers, scientists, and engineers—spanning a multitude of domains and industries. Colleagues and clients who have collaborated with me have often commended my exceptional ability to transform abstract ideas into compelling visual representations. For the past thirty years, I have had the honor of serving a diverse clientele that includes Fortune 50 and Fortune 500 companies, government entities, and non-profit organizations globally. Utilizing a wealth of architectural principles, models, frameworks, and foundational implementation strategies, I have crafted tailored solutions that resonate with this wealth of experience. My fervent exploration of economics and politics over the past decade has fueled my ambition in developing a comprehensive blueprint for geoeconomics. At the heart of the MayaNomics geoeconomic framework lie three indispensable components: 1. The Structure, which provides the foundational backbone, 2. The Mechanism, which facilitates the interactions and transactions within the system, and 3. The Architectural Parameters/Agreements, which govern the relationships and ensure coherence among these elements.

While these three components are crucial for the creation of a global economic architecture, there is another critical dimension that architects must incorporate" Relativity." When designing a system that exists within a broader ecological framework, which itself is part of an even larger ecosystem, it becomes evident that the components crafted for the current system risk becoming outdated if we neglect the transformative shifts occurring within the larger ecosystem. It is essential to propel your system forward in dynamic relation to competing or complementary systems, recognizing that change is constant. In particular, the political landscape is marked by a rich tapestry of competing ideologies, including Capitalism, Marxism, Socialism, Liberalism, Social Democracy, and Libertarianism. I personally identify as an old-school Free Market Libertarian, though I often find myself at odds with various contemporary Libertarian practices. These ideologies are fervently championed by diverse groups within different economic zones, wielding significant influence over market behaviors and, consequently, the economy at large. The formidable challenge we face is to devise a blueprint that acknowledges these competing forces while striving to unify them through shared principles and understandings.

This evolution, both social and political, cannot be sufficiently understood within the short span of a few centuries; rather, it requires a long-term perspective, spanning thousands of years. The insights derived from the preceding chapters should have underscored this fundamental truth.

11.5 Evolution of Things at various levels in an Ecosystem

As we have seen in chapter 1, throughout the annals of human history, the pursuit of wealth has been an enduring endeavor. Wealth, inherently a relative and subjective concept, encapsulates the perceived value of various assets in relation to one another. This "value" can encompass a wide array of tangible items, such as precious metals like gold and silver, gemstones like diamonds, and vehicles, alongside intangible assets including stocks, bonds, and other financial instruments. Furthermore, it extends to utility services and products specifically designed to resolve problems for individuals or businesses.

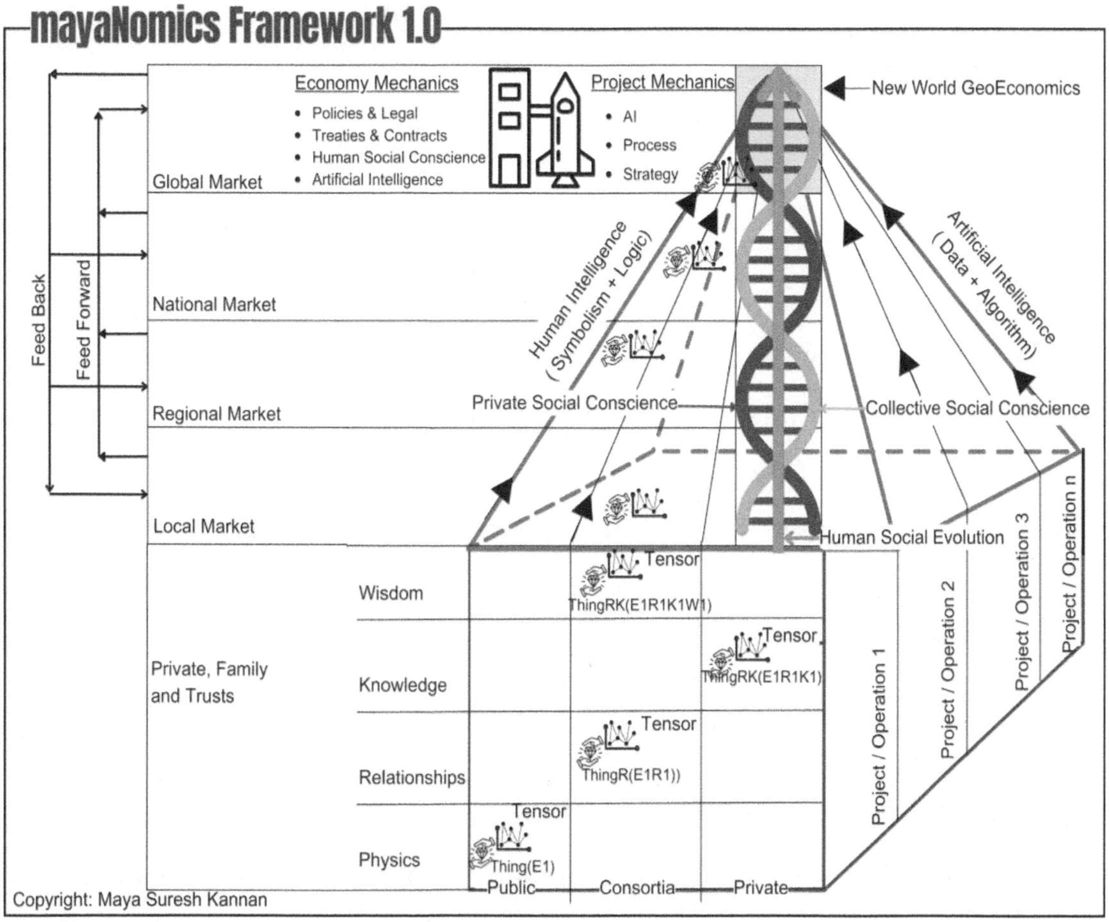

Figure 3: mayaNomics Framework 1.0

It is crucial to understand that while not all items qualify as assets, every asset fundamentally arises from the perceived valuation of one or multiple "things." These "things," regardless of their perceived tangibility or ideal form, are ultimately defined by the names and labels we assign to them, echoing Aristotle's principle of nominalism, which posits that classification is grounded in naming rather than inherent ideal qualities. To gain insight into individual entities, it is essential to analyze them in relation to one another, thereby identifying and categorizing groups that exhibit similarities based on their characteristics. This methodical approach forms the bedrock of mayaNomics, a philosophical framework that synthesizes symbolic, sub symbolic, and logical elements in a cohesive hybrid system. The life cycle of transient things, from their inception to the realization of a finalized version, adheres to a systematic process that unfolds through four distinct steps: 1. Conceive (Idea), 2. Judge, 3. Reason, and 4. Create.

The initial step, “Conceive,” involves the formation of a rudimentary perception of the entities in question, creating a form of tensor value that represents the inaugural evolutionary state. The subsequent phase, “Judge,” is characterized by the integration of disparate ideas or conceptions, where we either affirm or deny the validity of these representations. It is noteworthy that the brain executes judgments by contrasting these ideas against each other, rather than evaluating them independently in isolation. Following judgment, the process progresses to “Reasoning,” which involves establishing a new judgment derived from a prior collection of judgments concerning the same entity but approached from various vantage points. This reflective practice signifies the emergence of what can be termed the Level 3 Asset. The concluding step, “Create,” encapsulates the process of developing an extended iteration of a specific entity—the definitive product imbued with value. This creation is facilitated through diverse operations, or “Methods,” which function as agent algorithms. These algorithms leverage the vectorial associations among different entities, drawing insights from the surrounding environment and using feedback mechanisms to cultivate intuitive understandings.

It is crucial to highlight that even a fully matured asset, viewed as a valuable object within this framework, exists in a state of transience amid a cosmic system. Here, the relationships among entities, represented by various tensors across the dimensions of space and time, are in a state of perpetual evolution. This notion of potentiality signifies a future state characterized by limits (denoted as $a \rightarrow p$), illustrating that even the most developed asset will persist in its transient nature, continuously accumulating new value as time progresses. This is depicted in the framework deeply with the dynamics of various layers of markets, where the valuation of a specific share—considered a fully realized asset—experiences fluctuations that are influenced by an array of ecosystem parameters and the performance metrics of other equity shares within the market. Moreover, the methods and operations associated with these processes must conform to the overarching principles proposed by Arnold Antoine, ensuring they operate within a framework of higher rules and regulations.

The central axis of the framework illustrates Social Evolution, flanked by Collectivism and Individualism as two spiraling elements. The inverted cone's two sides represent Human Intelligence, driven by symbolism and logic, and Artificial Intelligence, driven by data and algorithms. As discussed in detail in Chapter 5, we currently face an elevated conflict between collectivism and individualism, highlighting the need for an integrated and collaborative approach between these two ideologies. MayaNomics advocates for this collaboration through the framework, leveraging both artificial and human intelligence to advance societal evolution alongside these competing perspectives. The apex point represents the proposed geoeconomic playing field where these two schools of thought align, achieving a harmonious level of social evolution that is ultimately reinforced by both human and artificial intelligence.

11.6 Economy Oriented Architecture

The economic system functions as a complex continuum, influenced by various interrelated forces, including social evolution, human emotions, environmental considerations, logical reasoning, and behavioral psychology. A significant challenge exists in directing these forces toward a unified objective, transitioning from current conditions to a desired future state. This ideal state, frequently viewed as difficult to attain, complicates efforts to facilitate a harmonious transition and establish a viable future scenario. With the emergence of artificial intelligence and the process of digitalization, navigating this transformation has become increasingly complicated. Traditional metrics that measure economic growth may no longer suffice. There is an imperative to adopt dynamic transformational metrics that account for changes—denoted as Delta ($\Delta\delta$)—across various characteristics, including social factors, logical reasoning, emotional intelligence, financial capital, labor dynamics, resource distribution, as well as traditional economic indicators like real GDP, GDP per capita, the Consumer Price Index (CPI), inflation rates, and the Human Development Index (HDI). Translating these variables into tensor values may require a reevaluation of existing mathematical and statistical methodologies to create indicators of economic health and progress. Furthermore, asset valuation should be based on contemporary criteria that emphasize qualitative aspects and tradable value, indicating a need to reassess current asset accounting practices. Developing independent practices at both regional and national levels that align with global standards is essential. Establishing new global geoeconomic institutions and forums would facilitate the creation and endorsement of these standards and practices.

MayaNomics proposes the development of specialized semantics, languages, modeling standards, and algorithmic patterns aimed at harmonizing new geoeconomic practices on a global scale. To support this, various architectures could be conceptualized, including Government Economy Architecture, Business Economy Architecture, Technology Architecture focused on economic goals, Social Evolution Architecture, Distributed and Decentralized Market Architecture,

Digital Assets Architecture, and Currency-Oriented Architecture. These frameworks could be implemented across governmental, private, public, and non-profit sectors as well as within different societal contexts. Additionally, MayaNomics suggests the introduction of stakeholder economic models—such as societies or consortiums—that would replace conventional equity assets with digital equity assets. Creating an alternative private trading system for the trade of these digital assets may facilitate their integration into traditional public markets. A relevant issue in the global economy pertains to inflated valuations within speculative asset markets, such as stock markets, which may exceed actual economic output by significant margins. This discrepancy often results in considerable private debts, indicating the need for a strategic reevaluation of economic practices and structures.

The current architecture of central banking systems, in collaboration with treasury departments, exerts significant control over financial markets through various sophisticated instruments, including bonds, Treasury Bills (T-Bills), interest rate adjustments, and numerous monetary policies. However, this existing framework is in urgent need of a comprehensive overhaul. To create a more resilient economic environment, it is essential to establish collaborative consortia comprised of experts from diverse fields—finance, economics, technology, and social sciences. These interdisciplinary groups should focus on developing innovative mechanisms that effectively bridge the gap between the tangible economy and speculative asset markets. At the same time, the fiscal policies implemented by governments must be radically reimagined to align with today's digital advancements and evolving geoeconomic contexts. Globally, governments must acknowledge that discontinuing their money-printing operations is not a viable option, regardless of the political party in power. This situation arises from self-interest and a pervasive inability to change established practices. Currently, nations are engaged in designing and rolling out Central

Bank Digital Currencies (CBDCs), which clearly indicates their intent to tighten control over the monetary supply and enhance regulatory oversight. A robust mechanism must be established to strike a balance in managing the money supply, ensuring that newly created financial capital is strategically allocated to initiatives and projects that promise sustainable growth and development. This strategy should allow for the creation of capital-generating engines within the economy, whether they are privately owned, publicly funded, or formed as consortia. The prevailing trend of directing low-cost capital primarily to large corporations and financial institutions must be expanded to include small and medium-sized enterprises (SMEs), decentralized communities, and collaborative economic entities.

On February 10, 2024, I produced a podcast titled "Eating Your Seed Corn," which explores the consequences of mismanaging or inadequately utilizing financial resources. The financial upheavals of 2001, 2008, and 2020 catalyzed numerous opportunities for various interest groups, some motivated by altruism and others by greed—to inject substantial amounts of inexpensive fiat currency into the economy. Over the last decade, the rise of fiat cryptocurrencies has contributed to the unprecedented proliferation of monetary forms, many of which are inexpensive yet lack genuine capital creation or intrinsic value. Historically, every cycle characterized by the expansion of cheap money leads to the inevitable bursting of economic bubbles. The collapse of 2001, rooted in the dot-com boom, differs significantly from the crises that followed in 2008 and 2020. The dot-com era saw a substantial flow of cheap money into productive ventures, resulting in significant advancements in digital assets such as websites, technological systems, infrastructure, and network development. In contrast, the 2008 financial crisis revolved around inflated asset values in equities, troubled secondary real estate mortgages, and complex derivatives. The resulting collapse failed to stimulate economic activity and exposed a fragile financial system precariously maintained by an influx of uncapitalized money.

The financial turmoil of 2020, ignited by the global coronavirus pandemic, triggered an extensive wave of money printing alongside unprecedented fiscal handouts. These measures aimed to facilitate immediate consumption across various sectors, benefiting banks, large corporations, and individual citizens alike. Thus, the 2001 crisis marked a pivotal moment in capitalistic dynamics—a significant buildup and subsequent contraction cycle that plunged us into uncharted economic territories. As Milton Friedman poignantly articulated, we reached a significant crossroads: to choose the path that aligns with liberty and prosperity, or to veer toward societal decay marked by diminishing creativity and productivity. Regrettably, we have largely chosen the latter path, straying further down this road with diminishing prospects for turnaround. In recent years, much of the money printed has remained trapped within financial markets, with limited infusion into the actual economy. Yet, within these challenges lies an opportunity to conceive a new, constructive trajectory if we can unite to establish innovative economic systems and frameworks. One such promising framework is termed MayaNomics. In revisiting the concept of "Eating Your Seed Corn," it is essential to emphasize that much of the money generated should serve as a catalyst for growth and innovation. Money, in its essence, is not synonymous with capital; rather, it functions as a significant catalyst residing outside conventional economic paradigms, thereby influencing economic dynamics in profound ways.

11.7 Reinforcement Feedback Feedforward Mechanisms

In the landscape of the economic state machine, it is becoming increasingly clear that a multifaceted approach is essential for building a robust portfolio of projects that can drive meaningful value, and the capital needed for sustainable growth. While the free market possesses great potential to stimulate development, it is important to recognize and address the risks of stagnation – scenarios in which economic progress may slow or stall due to various external and internal challenges. To proactively address these risks, the geoeconomic state machine should implement comprehensive feedback and feed-forward mechanisms. These strategies empower the system to learn from past experiences while anticipating future trends, thereby creating a dynamic and responsive economic atmosphere. The Captive economic structure that is prevalent around the world by a smaller circulation of products and goods from big businesses to consumers through a configured supply chain should go through a change to create circular economic supply chain models through consortia blockchain (distributed & decentralized) and AI enablement. Additionally, it is crucial to design economic systems and subsystems that can recognize and adapt to local, global, and even cosmic conditions. This nuanced understanding enables the implementation of differentiated strategies tailored to the unique characteristics and needs of diverse markets. By enhancing market knowledge and instincts through continuous observation and evaluation, these valuable insights can be reintegrated into the systems, fostering greater adaptability, in other words, true nominalism can be achieved. This holistic approach encourages collective progress across the entire economic state machine. It aligns strategies with the specific dynamics and transformational conditions faced by each market, ultimately enhancing resilience and competitiveness. By adopting an adaptive framework, economies will be better equipped to navigate challenges and seize opportunities, paving the way for more effective and sustainable growth.

11.8 Cause Level Agreement

The trajectory of an economy, whether toward success or failure, is fundamentally influenced by the intricacies of the market, its underlying dynamics, and the operational frameworks in place. As explored in the previous chapter, the functioning of the economy is deeply entrenched in a cause-and-effect relationship. This implies that the market itself necessitates the implementation of cause-level agreements, which act as regulatory mechanisms designed to ensure its orderly functioning. Mere reliance on free market ideologies does not inherently lead to economic prosperity; numerous countries that have hastily liberalized their economies have encountered substantial challenges. These challenges often manifest such as soaring inflation rates and a gradual erosion of the middle class, highlighting the risks associated with premature economic openness. On the other hand, an overly protective market, encumbered by excessive regulations and restrictions, can trigger adverse consequences that hinder economic growth and push vulnerable populations into deeper poverty. Such scenarios emphasize the delicate balance that must be struck in shaping effective economic policies. To attain targeted economic outcomes within specific zones, while simultaneously aligning with the broader global economic landscape, it is imperative to establish robust mechanisms for controlling economic parameters. Additionally, international treaties between varying economic zones and sovereign nations must be designed to be highly adaptable, fluid, and responsive to shifts in geopolitical and geostrategic realities. This adaptability is crucial for fostering cooperation and ensuring economic resilience in an ever-changing global context.

A key aspect of economic stability lies in safeguarding markets against extreme government interventions, particularly the nationalization of assets, a phenomenon observed in numerous instances throughout history. For instance, in 1938, Lazaro Cardenas, then president of Mexico, orchestrated the nationalization of the oil industry, a move that had profound implications for foreign investment. Similarly, in 1945, the French government took control of the car manufacturer Renault, while India followed suit in 1973 by nationalizing its coal and oil industries. In the United States, the nationalization of Amtrak in 1971, alongside the bailouts of financial entities like AIG and GM during the 2008 financial crisis, can be interpreted as a form of state intervention in private enterprise, often blurring the lines between private and public ownership. More recently, Vladimir Putin's government has taken steps to nationalize assets belonging to foreign companies that curtailed operations in Russia in response to international sanctions. Such governmental actions, whether in the form of nationalization or other drastic measures, can significantly undermine the security and ownership rights of global private investors, thus impacting their willingness to engage in specific markets.

To foster long-term stability, particularly amidst potential political volatility, it is essential for property rights to be intricately woven into the fabric of the market and its attendant assets. The concept of asset fungibility can play a pivotal role in this context, serving as a built-in mechanism that provides an automatic hedge against extreme fluctuations and adverse conditions. In this way, a well-designed economic environment can better withstand the pressures of both internal and external challenges, promoting a more stable pathway for growth and development.

11.9 Artificial Intelligence as the fourth leg of Social Economic Triad

By the year 2025, we find ourselves entrenched in an era characterized by fierce geoeconomic competition among global powers, where each nation is striving to secure its position on the world stage. At the heart of this rivalry is Artificial Intelligence (AI), a transformative technology that is being strategically harnessed by various countries as a critical asset in their efforts to outperform one another. The United States, with its wealth of resources, advanced educational institutions, and a dynamic tech ecosystem, possesses the potential to emerge as a leader in AI innovation and application. However, it is currently grappling with a series of significant challenges that undermine its competitive edge. Among these challenges is the rapid advancement of China's AI capabilities, which have been bolstered by substantial government investments and a strategic focus on developing a comprehensive AI framework. China's approach encompasses not just technological development, but also the integration of AI into various sectors, including manufacturing, healthcare, and surveillance, thereby generating greater data sets and enhancing its AI systems. This multifaceted strategy has provided the country with certain strategic advantages in various domains, including economic growth and geopolitical influence. As the landscape of geoeconomic competition evolves, the interplay of AI development and international relations will be crucial, with each nation seeking not only technological superiority but also the ability to shape global norms and standards surrounding AI usage.

In December 2024 and extending into mid-January 2025, the atmosphere was charged with enthusiasm for AI, largely propelled by the U.S. government's efforts and leading tech companies such as OpenAI, which had recently announced a pivotal collaboration with major players like SoftBank and Oracle. Nvidia also seeing a remarkable surge in its market value. To an observer, it may have appeared that the U.S. was on the brink of a new geoeconomic era dominated by AI. However, drawing from my experience in both market dynamics and technological innovation, I recognized that this optimism was precariously balanced, with an estimated 90% of it stemming from speculative behavior and only 10% rooted in tangible reality. I anticipated that the bubble around this speculative growth would soon burst, reminiscent of the volatile trends seen in cryptocurrencies, particularly those led by Bitcoin.

Reflecting on my research from 2018, during the initial design phase of the Karma Capsule Network, I analyzed a vast array of white papers and articles relating to AI and networking technologies. What struck me was the overwhelming dominance of research emanating from the United States and China, often bolstered by collaborations between American researchers and Chinese entities. These groups were notably ahead regarding advancements in Web Operating Systems and neural networks, illustrating a strategic focus on practical applications and use cases for AI technologies.

However, I was keenly aware of a troubling trend: much of this innovative research was quietly being financed by Chinese hedge funds and private investors, with tacit support from the Chinese government. While the tech giants Microsoft and Google were locked in a fierce battle over generative AI—often naively labeling it as a vehicle for market consolidation—they failed to learn from the significant lessons imparted by IBM's Watson AI failure. Their main objective appeared to be inflating their stock values through traditional stock market strategies, rather than genuinely investing in sustainable technological advancements. I had a foreboding sense that this speculative frenzy would inevitably lead to a downturn, dragging numerous investors and potentially several economies down with it. To my astonishment, the unforeseen reckoning arrived in the fourth week of January 2025 when Chinese tech developed a groundbreaking solution known as Deep Seek, which was produced for a remarkably low development cost of only $6 million. This stood in stark contrast to the staggering cumulative investments exceeding USD200B that had been poured into OpenAI and other major competitors like Google and Meta. This indicated a clear trend: the U.S. had once again pursued an extravagant valuation of AI assets early in the race through excessive capital investment.

Historically, such an approach may have yielded positive results within American and Western markets, but the landscape has fundamentally changed. The onset of a new player, represented by China, is challenging this traditional dynamic by not only competing effectively but also outpacing the U.S. in crucial areas. From my perspective as a specialist in AI and market dynamics, I believe that the true potential of AI will only be unlocked when Quantum Computing matures. This is another arena where the U.S. may find itself at a disadvantage unless it shifts away from speculative games and begins focusing on concrete market applications, directing funds toward projects that have genuine potential.

Net National Savings cannot be effectively bolstered merely through the expedient of printing money and injecting it into corporate consumption at minimal capital costs. The sustainability of such economic strategies hinges on capital that is both relevant and sensible. However, in the context of the previous two economic cycles, the so-called "magnificent seven" tech companies thrived in an environment of cheap money and inflated asset valuations yet devoted relatively little of their resources to creating the capital machines necessary for generating real products and solutions that stimulate the economy. Even when financial capital is allocated toward building tangible capital with sufficient resources and labor, the law of diminishing returns inevitably comes into play, undermining further output increases. Consequently, I argue that the economy must be structured as a state machine with well-analyzed transformational phases. Periodic and dynamic market studies, coupled with robust feedback mechanisms, should guide the process of recapitalization, ensuring the continuous development of newer products and effective solutions for the marketplace.

In May 2017, I embarked on a significant journey by publishing a comprehensive set of guidelines that addressed the intersection of the Internet of Things (IoT) and Artificial Intelligence (AI). This initiative was influenced by an in-depth discussion with a libertarian friend, which highlighted the ideological tension between my progressive perspectives on AI and the libertarian principles that prioritize individual autonomy and freedom. This conversation prompted me to delve deeper into the implications of AI in our lives and how we can navigate its integration into society responsibly.

My research underscored a compelling notion: we should empower individuals to condition and educate robots. This paradigm shift would enable machines to undertake monotonous and mundane tasks that often consume our time and energy. By delegating these responsibilities to AI, we could reclaim our humanity, allowing for more meaningful engagement in social activities, spending time in nature, and fostering connections with family. The objective is not just to eliminate drudgery but to encourage a lifestyle that prioritizes genuine human interactions over the overwhelming demands imposed by contemporary life. One of the critical observations I made during my exploration is that our excessive reliance on computers and digital technology has severely undermined our capacity for effective communication. The incessant stream of unfiltered information saturates our daily experiences, leading to constant crises and distractions. To counter this, I argued about the necessity of enabling robots to communicate among themselves. By doing so, we could liberate humans from trivial exchanges, allowing us to focus on deeper, more meaningful conversations and relationships. Creating a supportive social environment is essential for the progress of our society, especially in an era where social media often leads to isolation rather than connection.

I believe it's crucial to recognize that many innovations designed to improve our lives have, paradoxically, complicated our existence. Therefore, there's an urgent need to impose discipline and structure on our technological systems before we relinquish control to undisciplined robots. We stand at a pivotal crossroads; by establishing robust frameworks, we can create order and prevent potential chaos in our interaction with technology. AI has the potential to play several vital roles within our society. Firstly, as an asset creator, it can significantly contribute to wealth generation, reshaping industries and enhancing productivity. Secondly, AI can effectively manage labor division across various sectors, optimizing workflows and ensuring that human talents are utilized where they can add the most value. Moreover, it can serve as a catalyst for insights and knowledge, driving innovation and refining processes. Additionally, AI possesses the capability to counteract biases present in decision-making, thereby promoting fairness and accountability. By revealing truths and dismantling economic deceptions that have persisted, AI can illuminate paths toward transparency and informed choices. Furthermore, it can track innovation across diverse fields, serving as a barometer for societal progress. In the realm of finance, AI can facilitate intelligent financing solutions, evaluating potential beyond conventional credit assessments and offering access to opportunities for those who may be overlooked. Lastly, through its supercomputing abilities, AI can enhance the efficiency of transactions and supply chains, ultimately reducing waste and improving service delivery. By realizing and harnessing the multifaceted potential of AI in these critical roles, we can fundamentally transform our societal structures and interactions. This evolution has the power to pave the way for a more organized, connected, and equitable future, where technology enhances rather than detracts from human experience.

11.10 Assets, Projects and Programs under mayaNomics

The core philosophy of mayaNomics is intricately rooted in the concept of nominalism, which emphasizes the inherent qualities and characteristics of tangible 'things.' In this framework, an asset is defined as a "thing" that exhibits tensor characteristics; this means that assets are not merely static entities but dynamic constructs that possess measurable dimensions and attributes. These assets are initially formed within private sectors, undergoing a multifaceted journey of growth and transformation as they navigate through local, regional, and global markets. Throughout this journey, assets encounter a variety of states and market conditions, leading to shifts in their tensor characteristics that reflect the complex interplay of economic and social forces at work.

In prior chapters, we have delved deeply into the social evolutions that have taken place over time, examining their profound effects on economic systems. Notably, in recent decades, nations such as Korea, Japan, and Germany—countries that historically exhibited limited engagement with economic theories and social science—have experienced remarkable economic resurgence. This resurgence can be attributed not only to the influences of an artificially structured market dominated by the United States but also to the relentless dedication and hard work of their citizens. Productivity, engineering prowess, and availability of natural resources in these nations have led to a unique manifestation of excellence. However, it is vital to acknowledge that the most valuable insights often stem from grassroots initiatives, which serve as a foundation for sustainable growth. To cultivate a robust system of learning that promotes both horizontal and vertical evolution, it is essential to implement a structured framework through mayaNomics. This framework aims to bridge the historical divide between business practices and the social realities that shape them, along with the socioeconomic theories that underlie these interactions. During the 16th and 17th centuries, there existed a vital linkage between economics and politics, one that has become obscured by the 19th and 20th centuries when economics began to overwhelmingly eclipse political considerations, culminating in a convoluted relationship where the two became almost indistinguishable.

The significant issue that emerged in the previous century was the pronounced disconnect between the business sector and the political arena. Economics was often relegated to being viewed as a mere adjunct to political agendas, overlooking the critical truth that every political decision has tangible economic consequences, and economic realities in turn shape political landscapes. Regrettably, many national leaders today seem more preoccupied with the machinations of geopolitics and geostrategic maneuvering, often at the expense of understanding the economic dimensions that play a crucial role in these decisions. Nevertheless, there are signs that some nations and their leaders are beginning to recognize the paramount importance of economic considerations, leading to the integration of geoeconomics into their strategic frameworks. With the tenets of mayaNomics, these leaders can find a more coherent and effective methodology for developing successful and sustainable strategies. Moreover, in recent times, countries have come to the realization that globalization has skewed the balance of economic power in favor of a select few nations. A significant factor contributing to this imbalance is the West-driven idealism imposed on the global stage, which permeates social, political, and civil spheres. This idealism often operates as a façade for domination, fostering an obedient and compliant workforce, consolidating authority among a small elite within business and political systems, and creating barriers that keep other economies at arm's length through manipulation and deception. As we observe the shifting geopolitical landscape, particularly the transition of emerging powers from the information age to the intelligence age, it is evident that the idealism-based socioeconomic frameworks of these dominant countries are beginning to falter. MayaNomics posits that the forthcoming era of geoeconomics will be distinctly marked by nominalism, which deliberately rejects deceptive idealism in favor of practices that are tangible, and regeneration focused. This transition will be facilitated through nominal parameters that are informed by tensor characteristics and will leverage intelligence derived from grassroots projects and initiatives aimed at fostering genuine development and growth.

One of the most prevalent mistakes made by businesses and government entities across the globe is their decision-making processes regarding projects and programs that possess the potential to generate profit or deliver significant value. This misstep is often exacerbated in various industries, which display early warning signs of negative characteristics that can severely impede the development of effective products and innovative solutions. Some of these detrimental traits include a low consumption ceiling—indicating limited market demand—lack of elasticity in pricing or supply, an absence of accompanying consumption services that enhance user experience, difficulties in efficiently absorbing and integrating new technologies, the presence of rapid innovation cycles that outpace organizational adaptation, a labor force that cannot be effectively capitalized upon—essentially rendering skilled workers into undervalued commodities or burdens—and minimal incentives for reinvestment in emerging opportunities. To counter these challenges, leaders must prioritize a rigorous analysis and evaluation of the industries within which their products and solutions will operate. It is crucial to identify sectors where initiatives can not only create valuable assets but also enable the growth of those assets throughout the entire lifecycle of the industry. This approach requires a keen understanding of industry segments as well as the sweeping transformations taking place in the global market that influence these sectors. The cube model of MayaNomics offers a foundational framework that highlights the necessity for products and services to be designed and managed across four distinct yet interconnected layers: Physics (the tangible aspects of products), Relationship (the interactions between consumers and products), Knowledge (the expertise and information that underpins the industry), and Wisdom (the insights that guide decision-making). Adopting the right approach to product and project development necessitates engaging in an iterative process that effectively balances the initial phases of product development with ongoing innovation. This means that organizations cannot afford to innovate at the outset and then merely rely on the same product for ongoing sales; such a strategy will inevitably lead to stagnation. Whether an industry is flourishing or facing challenges, sustained sales can only be achieved by actively pursuing further innovations and enhancements. Moreover, as highlighted in the Value-Oriented Architecture chapter, it is vital to establish robust mechanisms that will allow organizations and institutions to identify, analyze, and enhance values right from the inception of a project. This process must continue throughout the growth trajectory of the project as it evolves across various markets, beginning at the local level and extending into the private sector. Additionally, nations should exercise caution and foresight to prevent hasty developments that could result in the establishment of flawed industries. Such industries might deplete national resources without yielding any genuine value or competitive advantage. The trade balance should be viewed through a more nuanced lens than simply comparing the merits of diamond versus copper; rather, it should involve a strategic balancing of trades between entities—denoted as (Xn vs. A)—that triggers desirable outcomes (B). Ultimately, this process can lead to a strengthened position of influence for the initiating entity (Xn power m), fostering a more sustainable economic environment.

11.11 Economic Contagion

Economic contagion is a critical phenomenon in today's interconnected global economy, where financial turmoil in one nation can have extensive repercussions for others. This transmission of economic distress occurs through multiple channels, including financial markets, trade relations, currency fluctuations, and shifts in investor behavior. When a substantial economy experiences a financial crisis—illustrated by events such as a stock market crash or a failure within the banking sector, the resulting panic can rapidly ripple through international markets. This immediate fallout often results in investors withdrawing their capital from regions perceived as risky, leading to dramatic declines in stock prices and tighter credit conditions, which can further escalate the crisis. Countries that are heavily reliant on exports to the stricken economy may encounter a significant drop in demand for their goods and services. This decline can threaten national growth rates and potentially plunge these economies into recession. A notable historical example of this is the 1997 Asian Financial Crisis, which was precipitated by the collapse of the Thai baht. This event sparked a chain reaction of financial instability throughout East Asia, adversely affecting nations such as Indonesia, South Korea, and Malaysia, all of which faced severe economic challenges due to diminished trade and investment. Moreover, a currency crisis in one nation often triggers a broader loss of confidence across other currencies, particularly impacting emerging markets. Such a scenario can lead to capital flight—where investors pull their money out to protect assets—causing significant currency depreciation and creating a vicious cycle of economic instability. Investor psychology plays a crucial role in amplifying these effects; fears of contagion may lead to irrational, excessive selloffs in seemingly unrelated markets, thus establishing a self-fulfilling prophecy of worsening economic conditions. Historically, examples of economic contagion include the Eurozone Debt Crisis, which spread through countries like Greece and Portugal, the Chinese Stock Market Crash of 2015 that affected global markets, the economic ramifications of the COVID-19 Pandemic, the Turkish Currency Crisis of 2018, and the ongoing Energy Crisis exacerbated by geopolitical tensions stemming from the Russia-Ukraine War. In today's economic landscape, various factors such as technological advancements, financial capital mobility, labor dynamics, and the availability of natural resources significantly influence economic output. The rise of digital assets and advancements in artificial intelligence challenge established practices for containing economic contagion, as they facilitate unprecedented speed in economic interactions and globalization. New divisions of labor and innovative digital resources further amplify the risk of rapid contagion spreading across the global economy. To effectively manage the complexities of economic contagion, innovative frameworks such as mayaNomics—focused on geoeconomics—can provide strategic insights. This approach includes monitoring potential contagion events and employing methods to channel their effects toward constructive outcomes within a sustainable circular economic model. By emphasizing resilience and adaptability, such frameworks aim to mitigate the adverse impacts of economic contagion while capitalizing on opportunities for growth and recovery in an interconnected world.

11.12 Some Geoeconomic Tools and Solutions for the Digitally Transformed World

1. Creation of Digital Assets, Currencies, and Commodities:

- Develop digital currencies that facilitate seamless peer-to-peer transactions across borders, reducing reliance on traditional banking systems.
- Establish digital assets that represent ownership of physical or virtual goods, such as real estate, art, or intellectual property, enhancing liquidity and accessibility.
- Introduce digital commodities that can be traded instantaneously on global markets, allowing for real-time price adjustments and efficient resource allocation.

2. Socio-Economic Models Reconciling Individualism and Collectivism:

- Explore hybrid economic models that embrace individual initiative while promoting community welfare, ensuring equitable wealth distribution.
- Implement community-driven economic programs that empower local enterprises and provide incentives for collective success, thereby balancing personal and societal interests.

3. Introduction of Oil-Backed Digital Assets:

- Develop blockchain-based tokens representing ownership of oil reserves, allowing investors to engage with energy markets without physical oil trading.

- Set up sovereign wealth funds that leverage oil-backed digital assets, enabling countries to stabilize their economies through more predictable revenue streams.

4. Establishment of Real-World Asset-Backed Digital Assets:

- Create frameworks for tokenizing real estate and other tangible assets, facilitating fractional ownership and increasing market liquidity.
- Launch exchange-traded funds (ETFs) and tokenized funds that provide easy access to diversified portfolios of real-world assets, appealing to a broader range of investors.

5. Mineral and Rare-Earth Element-Backed Digital Assets:

- Implement digital tokens linked to specific quantities of rare minerals, ensuring transparency and traceability in supply chains while attracting investment into sustainable mining practices.
- Utilize these tokens in sovereign wealth funds, providing nations with a stable financial foundation tied to their natural resource wealth.

6. Natural Capital-Backed Digital Assets:

- Develop digital assets that reflect the value of ecosystems, such as forests or wetlands, incentivizing conservation efforts and promoting sustainable economic practices.
- Create lean ETF structures that support natural capital investments, reconciling environmental stewardship with economic growth.

7. Promotion of Free and Fair Market Practices:

- Advocate for transparent pricing and fair competition across industries, ensuring that consumers benefit from favorable market conditions and innovation.
- Create regulatory environments that prevent monopolistic practices, allowing smaller enterprises to thrive alongside larger corporations.

8. Removal of Trade Barriers for Local Businesses:

- Develop policies that facilitate easier access to international markets for local startups, including reduced tariffs and simplified export procedures.
- Foster collaboration between governments and local businesses to identify and dismantle unnecessary bureaucratic hurdles.

9. Resilient Legal Enforcement and Contracting Systems:

- Establish a robust legal framework that supports dynamic contracting processes, ensuring that agreements are enforceable and adaptable in a rapidly changing digital economy.
- Integrate blockchain technology for transparent record-keeping and dispute resolution, enhancing trust among stakeholders.

10. Sufficient Capitalization for Local Businesses:

- Create incentives for investment in local private and consortium businesses that elevate their competitiveness on a global scale, such as grants or low-interest loans.
- Develop partnerships between financial institutions and local firms to facilitate access to capital, enhancing innovation and market responsiveness.

11. Encouragement of Consortiums and Stakeholder Collaborations:

- Promote the formation of industry consortiums that bring together various stakeholders, including businesses, governments, and civil society, to address common challenges and drive shared objectives.
- Foster public-private partnerships to leverage diverse expertise and resources, enhancing the effectiveness of initiatives.

12. Consensus-Driven Policies at National and International Levels:

- Emphasize the importance of inclusive policymaking processes that engage a wide array of stakeholders, utilizing decentralized methods to ensure broad representation.
- Establish immutable contracts that hold parties accountable while allowing for flexible adaptations in response to changing circumstances.

13. Promotion of Innovative Technologies:

- Invest in research and development initiatives focused on transformative technologies such as AI, quantum computing, and deep-tech networks.
- Create educational programs that integrate these innovations into business and governmental operations, enhancing overall productivity and efficiency.

14. Dynamic Tax and Tariff Structures:

- Develop adaptive tax systems that incentivize innovation and investment while addressing the complexities of a digital economy, including considerations for virtual goods and services.
- Implement tariff structures that promote fair trade while protecting domestic industries from unfair competition.

15. "Cause-Level Agreements" for Cooperation:

- Foster multilateral agreements that outline common economic or environmental goals, supported by mechanisms for transparent implementation.
- Utilize digital technologies to ensure compliance and adaptability, reinforcing cooperative commitments amongst nations.

16. Innovative Military Technologies Development:

- Invest in R&D for next-generation military technologies that enhance national security and position countries competitively on the global stage.
- Encourage collaboration between the private sector and defense agencies to leverage emerging technologies in military applications.

17. Leveraging Artificial Intelligence and Machine Capabilities:

- Empower businesses and governments to harness AI for decision-making processes, improving efficiency and responsiveness to market dynamics.
- Develop AI-driven platforms that can analyze vast data sets for strategic insights across various sectors.

18. Citizen Education on Tools and Technologies:

- Launch comprehensive educational initiatives aimed at informing citizens about digital tools, technologies, and new economic methodologies, fostering a savvy and skilled workforce.

- Promote lifelong learning opportunities that adapt to rapid technological changes, ensuring that citizens remain competitive in the job market.

19. Dynamic Resource Cooperation:

- Create frameworks for synergistic collaboration among nations in resource management, enabling shared access and sustainable practices.
- Develop international standards for resource utilization to promote fairness and efficiency across borders.

20. Basket of Currencies Management System:

- Establish a multi-currency framework that accommodates both traditional and digital currencies, supporting international trade and investment.
- Ensure the alignment of monetary policy among participating countries to stabilize exchange rates and manage inflation.

21. Market and Governance Environment for Digital Assets:

- Create a regulatory landscape that promotes the growth of digital assets, ensuring proper valuation and protective measures are in place to foster investor confidence.
- Design mechanisms that integrate digital assets into mainstream financial systems, enhancing legitimacy and usability.

22. Multiple Sovereign Wealth Funds:

- Establish a diverse array of sovereign wealth funds focused on various sectors, ensuring that nations can build resilience and leverage their assets strategically.
- Promote transparency and accountability within these funds to increase public trust and attractive investment.

23. Transformation of Institutional Systems:

- Upgrade public and private institutions to utilize blockchain or equivalent technologies, ensuring efficient, transparent operations that enhance trust.
- Implement integrated systems for data management, decision-making, and service delivery that align with evolving digital landscapes.

24. Creation of an Ecosystem of Investment Funds:

- Cultivate an ecosystem that supports the establishment and proliferation of various investment funds catering to different sectors and asset classes.
- Foster collaboration among fund managers to share best practices and drive innovation in investment strategies.

25. Deregulation of Exchanges and Markets:

- Encourage the deregulation of financial markets to welcome a diverse range of asset classes and foster competition, innovation, and investor participation.
- Implement proper oversight mechanisms that ensure market integrity while minimizing unnecessary regulatory burdens.

26. Tax Incentives for Entrepreneurship:

- Formulate attractive tax incentives that encourage investments in high-risk startups and support entrepreneurs, addressing their unique challenges.
- Create an ecosystem that rewards innovation and risk-taking, fostering a culture of entrepreneurship.

27. Alternative Systems of Trust and Scoring:

- Develop alternative credit scoring systems that are digitally enforceable, focusing on positive behaviors and rewards rather than punitive measures.
- Enhance trust in lending and financial interactions through transparent systems that account for diverse economic contributions.

28. Revamping the Division of Labor:

- Assess and realign labor structures to address the unique demands of digital and AI-driven roles, ensuring that workforce development meets both local and global market needs.
- Promote vocational training and education that equips individuals with the skills necessary for emerging industries.

29. Management of Asset Fungibility:

- Ensure effective fungibility of assets through appropriate market mechanisms, enhancing liquidity and accessibility for all market participants.

- Create a conducive regulatory environment that supports diverse asset classes and encourages investment through alternate trading systems.

30. Decentralized Market Structure Enforcement:

- Advocate for the establishment of a truly federal and decentralized market structure, enhancing autonomy at local levels through AI-driven algorithms.
- Implement regulations that empower local markets and encourage innovation while maintaining a cohesive national economic strategy.

11.13 Value Oriented Economic Architecture

My exploration of intrinsic value began long before 2006, during a time when I was an ardent proponent of Enterprise Services Architecture. I believed that this framework could unveil hidden "Hot Spot Values" embedded deep within an organization's infrastructure, network, and technology components. While the IT community was primarily fixated on a narrow objective—transforming internal services into external offerings via technologies such as Web Services, I aspired to achieve a more ambitious vision: to unlock and amplify the value derived from the enterprise's existing assets, thereby fostering a sustainable competitive advantage. Unfortunately, this goal was often misinterpreted by technology-focused groups who frequently dismissed broader concepts as extraneous or irrelevant to their immediate work. This constructed a barrier to meaningful dialogue. Simultaneously, the business community, predominantly composed of individuals with MBA degrees, tended to overlook the significance of expanding the enterprise's value proposition. Many of these managers expressed a lack of responsibility regarding these discussions, suggesting that they were too concentrated on traditional management tasks. On another point, high-level executives often disregarded these conversations altogether, citing relentless schedules filled with meetings and strategic planning sessions as a reason for their disengagement. Fast forward to 2025, and the landscape remains largely unchanged in the corporate sphere. Numerous professionals still cling to established routines, finding solace in elaborate reports, meticulously crafted presentations, and extensive documentation, all of which further entrench them in their roles. This tendency is magnified as organizations scale, leading to bureaucratic inertia rather than innovation. It's no surprise, then, that countless corporations grapple with the challenge of generating intrinsic value from within. Many hesitate to invest in transformative initiatives or pursue acquisitions that have the potential to genuinely enhance their value metrics. Curiously, a significant portion of individuals within the investment and capital markets lack a profound understanding of how to discern assets with intrinsic value, whether they exist in the private sector or are publicly traded. Instead, they tend to adhere to conventional trading practices that favor speculation in public markets, largely overlooking the nuanced analysis that could lead to more informed investment decisions and ultimately more substantial returns. Identifying, implementing, and nurturing intrinsic value within diverse entities presents a formidable challenge that requires an intricate understanding of both fundamental and market dynamics. Drawing on over two decades of experience in enhancing enterprise value and refining deep tech framework development, coupled with a solid ten-year background in capital markets, I have crafted the comprehensive Value-Oriented Architecture blueprint. The intrinsic value of any entity is in a constant state of flux, influenced by myriad factors in both local and cosmic environments. The local environment imposes a cross-entropy cost function—an essential mechanism to measure the level of disorder or uncertainty in predictions—and employs sophisticated methods like stochastic gradient descent alongside backpropagation to optimize decision-making processes.

Typically, an entity receives predictions represented as multi-dimensional tensors from preceding layers in its architecture and endeavors to form tighter clusters around these predictions to enhance meaningfulness and accuracy. When a tighter cluster is successfully identified, the entity can output two critical pieces of information: a) a high probability indicating that a specific entity, referred to as a "Thing," exists within its operational domain, and b) the entity's general relativity, allowing it to contextualize itself in relation to the identified cluster.

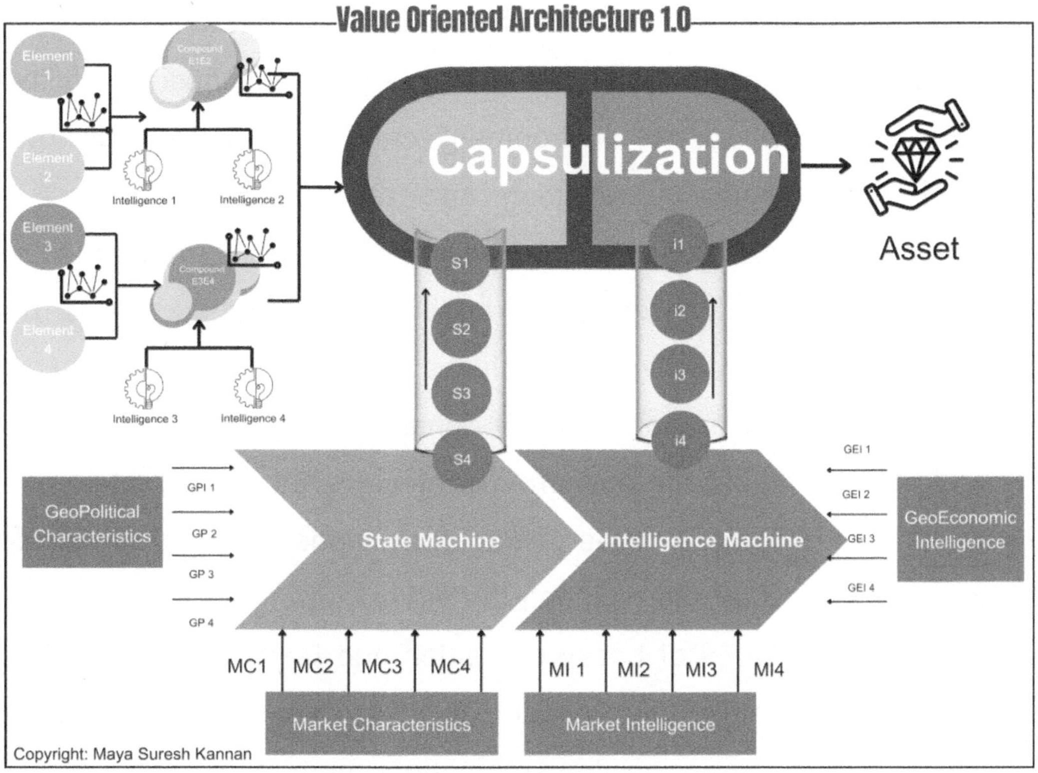

Figure 4: Value Oriented Architecture

This mechanism acts as a powerful proof of value, effectively filtering out noise and potential fraudulent claims, since the coincidental occurrence of high-dimensional similarities is statistically unlikely. Essentially, a collective of low-level entities effectively votes for the recognition and valuation of a higher entity within the system. At the foundational level, if a "Thing" shifts to a different perspective or undergoes changes in its tensor attributes, it may be represented by an alternative capsule. This phenomenon, known as place-coded equivariance, signifies that the higher-level capsule encapsulates the entirety, while the lower-level entities serving as its constituents provide the necessary inputs. Even if a component experiences minuscule variations in its tensor values, it will still be represented by the same capsule; however, the outputs corresponding to that capsule will vary. For instance, consider the entity "Gold"—a slight alteration in its characteristics, such as karat (purity level), continues to define it as Gold, albeit with a differentiated quality assessment based on the ratio of gold present to other metals, such as copper. This is best illustrated through the concept of rate-coded equivariance. Higher-level capsules possess enhanced visibility and acceptability within the cosmic environment, creating conditions for low-level place-coded equivariance to transition into rate-coded equivariance. This intricate interplay is facilitated by two critical mechanisms: 1) the State Machine, which is dynamically influenced by a multitude of geopolitical and market characteristics, and 2) Intelligent Machines, which harness insights from geoeconomic intelligence and market analytics to enhance contextual understanding. Throughout the economic continuum, these characteristics and intelligence inputs undergo a series of transformations, which are meticulously fed back into the capsule—representing the entity in its most developed form—through iterative processes of backpropagation and feedback loops. The high-level Value-Oriented Architecture conceptualized by mayaNomics is positioned to provide a diverse array of implementation methodologies and specific derivatives, thoughtfully tailored to meet the nuanced needs of various market segments and economic zones. This approach aims not only to enhance the valuation processes but also to foster a deeper understanding of the interplay between entities within complex environments.

Chapter 12. Transitioning into the digitally Transformed World

Society operates as both an ongoing continuum and a complex state machine, illustrating the intricacies involved in social dynamics and transitions. Attempting to enact rapid changes through forceful regulations, rigid frameworks, or strict methodologies often leads to resistance and ineffectiveness. Therefore, it is essential to consider the mayaNomics Framework as a viable transitional strategy for navigating the challenges of a digitally transformed world. Transitioning into this newly inherited environment is a multifaceted endeavor that demands careful planning and execution. Rather than envisioning a straightforward switch from System A to System B, it is crucial to recognize that a gradual transitional period is necessary. This period involves the intricate integration of diverse components, including individuals, subsystems, and various groups within society. It is imperative to bring together these disparate elements while also acknowledging the need to segregate certain social and economic units for a more effective collaboration. The process should emphasize fostering cooperation and coordination among an array of stakeholders, operating within local, national, and international contexts. This transitional journey is not limited to logistical considerations; it also encompasses several critical domains. Legal frameworks must adapt to new realities, which require rethinking regulations and policies that have governed traditional practices. Business models, too, must transform to align with the evolving economic landscape, presenting new opportunities and challenges for entrepreneurs and businesses alike. The political terrain will inevitably shift, necessitating an awareness of changing dynamics and power structures.

Educational systems will play a pivotal role in this transition, requiring significant shifts to prepare future generations for the new economic realities. Infrastructure upgrades are necessary to support emerging technologies and business needs, while cultural evolution will be vital to reshape societal values and norms in response to the changing world. Achieving a successful transition involves the implementation of numerous programs and projects tailored to the demands of the new environment. Many existing state components and processes remain incompatible with the ambitious goal of realizing substantial economic impacts at local, national, and international levels.

In the winter of 2022, I had the opportunity to participate in a conference in Warsaw, Poland, organized by the World Bank. The event showcased comprehensive findings derived from two years of focused work on initiatives aimed at just-in-coal transition. Throughout the conference, I encountered numerous thought-provoking insights; however, one overarching theme emerged, resonating strongly not only from the presentations but also through conversations with local residents and my own research, which was supported by my team's diligent efforts. The focus of the conference was on the post-mining era and the necessary transitions that are required to facilitate this shift. Key topics included land reclamation, which seeks to restore and revitalize areas previously dominated by mining activities. Additionally, discussions centered on rebuilding local economies, transforming impacted regions into new economic zones that can thrive independent of their historical ties to the mining industry. Ultimately, the goal is to create sustainable opportunities for local communities and businesses, ensuring that those who have traditionally relied on mining find viable avenues for future growth and prosperity. During my formative years in Tamil Nadu, I had the unique opportunity to observe my father as he managed a local stone quarry. This experience was more than just a childhood memory; it profoundly shaped my understanding of the myriad challenges faced by workers in the mining industry. I witnessed firsthand the physical demands of quarrying, the safety concerns that permeate the workplace, and the pressing environmental issues that arise from extracting resources. These insights fostered a deep empathy for the laborers who toiled in these conditions, and I became acutely aware of the regulatory hurdles they navigated daily. After relocating to the United States and settling in the coal-rich region of West Virginia, I found myself drawn to the local coal mining communities. My frequent visits to these areas opened my eyes to a different set of challenges that mirrored those I observed in Tamil Nadu. The struggles of the local populace, heavily reliant on a dying industry, tugged at my heartstrings. I engaged in conversations with miners and their families, who shared stories of uncertainty, sacrifice, and resilience as they navigated the complexities of an industry in decline. Over the past 10 to 15 years, many of my connections on LinkedIn and Facebook have witnessed my unwavering advocacy for individuals and communities affected by the abrupt transitions within the mining sector. I have taken a Libertarian stance, firmly believing in the market's ability to correct itself naturally, without the need for government intervention or coercive measures from private enterprises. My faith in market economics compels me to argue that while the industry may be evolving, it is essential for transitions to occur at a pace that allows individuals to adapt comfortably, rather than being forced into rapid changes that could jeopardize their livelihoods. The reality is that people who have depended on a particular socio-economic structure for generations often find themselves at a crossroads during such transitions. Emotional ties to their hometowns and heritage run deep; these places are not merely geographic locations but repositories of their identities and histories. Although crafting plans for reskilling, retraining, and relocating may seem straightforward from a policy standpoint, the implementation of these initiatives poses considerable challenges.To illustrate this complex issue, I propose using the framework of the three Ps: Place, People, and Process. Each of these elements plays a vital role in understanding the broader implications of change and the importance of developing solutions that are sensitive to the realities of those affected. By considering Place, we acknowledge the significance of geographical roots; with People, we recognize the emotional and social fabric that binds communities together; and through Process, we delve into the practical steps needed to facilitate smooth transitions while preserving the dignity and agency of individuals involved. While discussions among government officials and corporate leaders often center on the Place and Process, the critical aspect of people is frequently neglected. Having lived approximately 100 miles from Washington, D.C., I find myself in close proximity to lower-income communities that heavily rely on coal for their livelihoods. This unique position enables me to appreciate both sides of the debate surrounding the transition away from coal. It's easy for those who are disconnected from these communities to suggest solutions like, "Just move to the city," but for many individuals, this recommendation fails to recognize the complexity of their situation. Residents often grapple with profound emotional ties to their homeland. Questions arise like, "Why should I leave the place where I've lived for years? My grandparents and great-grandparents have deep roots here, having lived in this region for decades, or even centuries. What incentive do I have to uproot my life? If there is an expectation for me to shift away from coal or mining, I need a viable and realistic alternative before considering such a significant change." The truth is most individuals would be more willing to embrace change if they were presented with a compelling reason and practical options that align with their needs. The realities of life for many coal miners are stark. Many feel grateful to reach their sixties, as the grueling nature of their work often leads to a reduced life expectancy, often into their fifties. Given this backdrop, why would they gamble with their financial security when stable and sustainable alternatives are lacking? The challenge of leaving a place where they have been born and raised is not just a logistical issue; it is deeply emotional. Human beings are inherently creatures of habit, forming strong attachments to their environment. Historically, humans were nomadic, but in modern society, many people have established roots that bind them to a specific locale. When your heart is intertwined with the land, leaving that place can feel akin to abandoning a piece of your identity and history. This reality underscores the urgent need to prioritize addressing the people's aspect first. Without understanding and meeting the needs of local communities, any efforts to facilitate change in other areas are unlikely to succeed. Individuals are deeply connected to the land they call home, and while some may leave in pursuit of educational and economic opportunities, it's crucial to acknowledge that not everyone has the capacity or desire to do so. The most effective solution is to cultivate opportunities that enable people to thrive in the very places where they have culturally and emotionally invested—where their families have established roots for generations. Regrettably, many experts often misinterpret this delicate relationship. They mistakenly presume that everyone is eager to chase new opportunities or readily acclimate to technological innovations. I frequently hear discussions about reclaiming land for techno parks, which could be established in the heart of coal mining areas. Yet, many of these high-tech initiatives do not align well with the local economy or the skills of the residents. While some tech projects may achieve success, essential questions arise: Will these initiatives genuinely benefit local residents? What motivates someone to engage in tech work if it doesn't resonate with their interests or if they feel ill-equipped for such jobs? The concept of re-skilling holds potential and could form an integral part of a broader solution. However, it is imperative that such initiatives are implemented gradually and with sensitivity to the unique circumstances of each community over generations. The first wave of individuals may not immediately transition into high-tech fields, particularly if they lack the interest or aptitude for digital work. The fundamental question remains: Why should they? For many, the pull to stay within the familiar landscape of their lives and history is often stronger than the allure of uncertain opportunities in unfamiliar territories. Thus, any approach to transition must be rooted in understanding and compassion for the people who are directly impacted. Many individuals are comfortable living with a median income, as this is how their parents and grandparents led their lives. They tend to believe that such a lifestyle leads to happiness. Rather than seeking vast wealth or extravagant opportunities, they simply aim to protect their current income from being diminished by inflation or economic changes. This concern sheds light on a significant issue. In 2004, I delved into Adam Smith's "Wealth of Nations" and the Division of Labor. From this study, combined with my own experiences and insights, I adopted the motto, "Jobs are like energy. They can either be created or destroyed." Jobs don't disappear; they transform from one form to another. The Division of Labor makes it clear that the economic prosperity of a region hinges on the jobs generated locally. Although it's possible to create jobs based on remote economic activities in today's digital age, not every model from Western economies will thrive in local contexts. If these strategies fail to adapt to the local environment, it essentially turns local labor into mere fodder for foreign economic gain. Economies are vulnerable; history shows that the American economy has weathered multiple downturns. There's no guarantee that external economies will remain stable, making it risky to bet on their fortunes. While trade can bring benefits, relying on an employment model from another context to create service-sector jobs isn't the best approach. Ultimately, people are the core component in this equation. Now, let's turn our attention to another crucial factor: place. Reclamation, particularly regarding land, is a hot topic, especially how land acquisition processes unfold after transformations. That said, reclamation can be a tough challenge, often burdened by various regulations, such as those in Poland. Current laws mandate that mining operations occur within a five-year period to allow for new models to emerge. Although some of these regulations may work to an extent, what's the purpose of imposing such frameworks if they don't result in increased economic activity? This is where many initiatives fall flat. Two types of places come into play: the original location from which you're transitioning and the new economic settlement you are moving toward. When crafting transitional programs, they must cover two key areas: one that focuses on land repurpose, and another that drives the economic revitalization of the surrounding region. Similarly, while discussing shifts to new work economies propelled by digitalization, it's essential to implement a strong transformational framework, like mayaNomics. Several key factors are vital - substantial investments, the repurposing of land and infrastructure, and ensuring that the target state aligns with both initial and intermediate states—a concept known as state transition in the business and technology realm. For mayaNomics to work effectively, extensive modeling, transformational design blueprints, socio-economic architecture, business architecture templates, deep learning networks, algorithms, intelligence, tools, and methodologies are required. With the talent pool available globally, thanks to advances in business, technology, capital markets, and innovative thinkers and economists, we can successfully implement mayaNomics for the greater good, steering everyone smoothly into a digitally transformed world.

All the best!
Sincerely,
Maya Suresh Kannan

Best ways to be in touch base with Maya Kannan
www.mayakannan.com
www.mayanomics.com
www.youtube.com/@mayasureshkannan
https://mayanomics.substack.com
https://www.linkedin.com/in/mayasureshkannan
https://www.x.com/mayaskannan

References:

1. Karma Capsule Network (Reinforced CapsNet) – White Paper
2. Economic State Craft: David A. Baldwin
3. Wealth Of Nations – Adam Smith
4. The World Tamil Merchants – Kanakalatha Mukhund
5. Ocean of Trade – Pedro Mechando
6. Tolkappiyam – Sanga Tamil Age Literature
7. Pattinapaalai – Sanga Age Tamil Poem
8. GeoEconomics – Klaus Soleburg Soilen
9. The Cholas by Nilakanta Sastri
10. Rome and the Distant East – Raoul Mclaughlin
11. GeoEconomics and Power Politics in the 21st Century – The revival of Economic Statecraft - Mikael Wigell, Sören Scholvin, et al
12. Ecodynamics by Kenneth Boulding
13. Capitalism, Socialism and Democracy by Joseph Schumpeter
14. The Econometric Analysis of Recurrent Events in Macroeconomics and Finance -Don Harding, Adrian Pagan
15. Public Economics, Principles and Practice – Peter Abelson

Made in the USA
Middletown, DE
05 November 2026

36537964R10170